GOD OF THE
OPPRESSED

James H. Cone

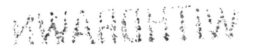

GOD
OF THE
OPPRESSED

JAMES H. CONE

WITHDRAWN

A CROSSROAD BOOK

THE SEABURY PRESS, NEW YORK

Grateful acknowledgment is made to the following for permission to reprint sections from copyrighted material:

Harold Ober Associates, Inc., for Langston Hughes, "A New Song," in *Opportunity* 1933 , © 1938 by Langston Hughes.

Mari Evans, for Mari Evans, "The Insurgent," "Speak The Truth To The People," "I Am a Black Woman," and "Who Can Be Born Black," in *I Am a Black Woman*, Wm. Morrow and Company, 1970.

Twayne Publishers, Inc., for Claude McKay, "If We Must Die," in *Selected Poems of Claude McKay*, copyright 1953 Bookman Associates, Inc.

The Seabury Press
815 Second Avenue
New York, N.Y. 10017

Copyright © 1975 by The Seabury Press, Inc.
Designed by Publishing Synthesis
Printed in the United States of America

LIBRARY OF CONGRESS CATALOGING IN PUBLICATION DATA

Cone, James H
   God of the oppressed.

   "A Crossroad book."
   Includes index.
   1. Liberation theology—Addresses, essays, lectures.
2. Negroes—Religion—Addresses, essays, lectures.
3. Theology—Addresses, essays, lectures.   I.   Title.
BT83.57.C67   261.8'34'5196073   74-31474
ISBN 0-8164-2607-4

To Macedonia A.M.E. Church
where I first heard shouts of praise
to the God of whom I speak
and
to my brothers, Charles and Cecil,
who struggled with me to figure out
what all the shouting was about

Contents

Preface

Theologians do not normally reveal the true source of their theological reflections. They often tell us about the books that are similar and not so similar to their perspectives, but seldom do they tell us about those nonintellectual factors that are decisive for the arguments advanced on a particular issue. More often than not, it is a theologian's *personal* history, in a particular sociopolitical setting, that serves as the most important factor in shaping the methodology and content of his or her theological perspective. Thus theologians ought to be a little more honest, and let the reader know something about those nonintellectual factors that are so important for the opinions they advance.

In this book, I take the risk of revealing the origin of my commitment to the Christian faith; not for its own sake, but for the sake of the theology I seek to explicate. In previous books and articles, I have discussed the intellectual foundation of Black Theology and sought to show theologically that any analysis of the gospel which did not begin and end with God's liberation of the oppressed was *ipso facto* unchristian. In this present work, I do not abandon the intellectual search but simply integrate it with the existential and social formation of my faith as it was and is being shaped in the black community. I hope that this approach will not only help to clarify my perspective on Black Theology, but more importantly will help to join the black theological enterprise more firmly with the true source of its existence—the black community.

Without the assistance and encouragement of many people, this book could not have been written. Most of the material of this book was presented as lectures at seminaries, universities, and churches in America and on the continents of Africa and Europe. Although I cannot mention everyone, I must say a word of thanks to those persons who directly influenced the outcome of my labors.

I wish to express my thanks to Michael Novak and the Rockefeller Humanities Foundation for financial assistance toward the research and writing of this book. Thanks is also due to the Faculty and Board of Directors of Union Theological Seminary for granting me a sabbatical leave, thereby enabling me to devote a year of research and writing on this book. In addition, several of my colleagues at Union read all or part of my manuscript and provided helpful criticisms. They include: Paul Lehmann, George Landes, James Martyn, Cyril Richardson, James Sanders, Bobby Joe Saucer, and Roger Shinn.

A special thanks is due to Archie Le Mone, the Youth Coordinator of the World Council of Churches. Through his efforts, I was afforded the opportunity of making several trips to Geneva and other places in Europe, thereby enabling me to appreciate more deeply the importance of the Ecumenical Movement for the Church and its theology. I am sure that my subsequent writing will reflect more directly the significance of this experience. Thanks is also due to Paulo Freire who, along with Archie Le Mone, read my manuscript and spent many hours discussing it with me.

As with my previous writings, C. Eric Lincoln and William Hordern read my manuscript and provided helpful criticisms. I will always be grateful to both for their continued encouragement. I am also grateful to Gayraud S. Wilmore who read and discussed my manuscript with me.

A word of appreciation is due to the members of the Society for the Study of Black Religion. Because of the encouragement and critique of my black colleagues, I have been motivated to probe more deeply the resources of the black experience as a primary datum for the development of a Black Theology. Of course, not everyone will agree with my major theological thrust, but I do hope that this book will help to enhance our efforts to create a form of theological speech that is consistent with black people's struggle for liberation.

It is difficult for me to express properly my appreciation to Lester B. Scherer of Eastern Michigan University, my friend and former colleague. We spent many days wrestling over the theological issues in this work. He not only read the manuscript at every stage of its development but also provided invaluable editorial assistance.

As with everything I have written, my brother, Cecil W. Cone, has been an excellent critic and a strong supporter of my theological perspective. I will always be grateful for the many years we have spent together trying to discover Jesus' relation to black people's struggle of freedom.

A special word of thanks is also due to my secretary, Ms. Babbie Mallery, who, in addition to her normal duties, typed my manuscript several times.

My family, Rose, Michael and Charles, continue to show unusual understanding when I am engaged in writing and research. I am deeply grateful.

J. H. Cone
Union Theological Seminary
New York, 1974

I.
INTRODUCTION

I was born in Fordyce, Arkansas, a small town about sixty miles southwest of Little Rock. My parents moved to Bearden, fourteen miles from Fordyce, when I was a year old. In Bearden, a small community with approximately eight hundred whites and four hundred blacks, two important realities shaped my consciousness: the black Church experience and the sociopolitical significance of white people.

The black Church introduced me to the essence of life as expressed in the rhythm and feelings of black people in Bearden, Arkansas. At Macedonia African Methodist Episcopal Church (A.M.E.), I encountered the presence of the divine Spirit, and my soul was moved and filled with an aspiration for freedom. Through prayer, song, and sermon, God made frequent visits to the black community in Bearden and reassured the people of his concern for their well-being and his will to bring them safely home. Home was often identified with heaven—that "otherworldly" reality beyond the reach of the dreadful limitations of this world. It was that place on the "other side of Jordan," "down by the riverside," where the streets are gold and the gates are pearl. Home was that eschatological reality where the oppressed would "lay down that heavy load," singing and shouting because "there would be nobody there to turn [them] out." Every Sunday the black brothers and sisters of Macedonia experienced a foretaste of their "home in glory" when God's Spirit visited their worship, and they responded with thankfulness and humility, singing joyfully:

1

> Sooner-a-will be done with the trouble of this world,
> Sooner-a-will be done with the trouble of this world,
> Going home to live with God.

I responded to the black Church experience by offering myself for membership at Macedonia when I was only ten and by entering the ministry at the early age of sixteen. It was a natural response, a response consistent with the beauty and joy of black life and an expression of my deep yearning for human definitions not bound by this earthly sphere. The black Church taught me how to deal with the contradictions of life and provided a way to create meaning in a society not of my own making. In the larger "secular" black community, this perspective on life is often called the "art of survival"; but in the black Church, we call it the "grace of God." It is called *survival* because it is a way of remaining physically alive in a situation of oppression without losing one's dignity. We call it *grace* because we know it to be an unearned gift from him who is the giver of "every good and perfect gift." This is what black people mean when they sing: "We've come this far by faith, leaning on the Lord, trusting in his holy Word."

Unfortunately the black Church experience was not my *only* experience in Bearden, Arkansas. The presence of eight hundred whites made me realize, at an early age, that black existence cannot, indeed *must* not, be taken for granted. White people did everything within their power to define black reality, to tell us who we were—and their definition, of course, extended no further than their social, political, and economic interests. They tried to make us believe that God created black people to be white people's servants. We blacks, therefore, were *expected* to enjoy plowing their fields, cleaning their houses, mowing their lawns, and working in their sawmills. And when we showed signs of displeasure with our so-called elected and inferior status, they called us "uppity niggers" and quickly attempted to put us in our "place."

To be put in one's place, as defined by white society, was a terrible reality for blacks in Bearden. It meant being beaten by the town cop and spending an inordinate length of time in a stinking jail. It meant attending "separate but equal" schools, going to the balcony when attending a movie, and drinking water from a "colored" fountain. It meant refusing to retaliate when called a nigger—unless you were prepared to leave town at the precise moment of your rebellion. You had no name except your first name or "boy"; and if you were past the age of sixty-five, you might attain the dubious honor of being called "uncle" or "auntie."

The white people of Bearden, of course, thought of themselves as "nice" white folks. They did not lynch and rape niggers, and many attended church every Sunday. They honestly believed that they were *Christian* people, faithful servants of God. Their affirmation of faith in Jesus Christ was a source of puzzlement to me, because they excluded blacks not only socially but also from their church services. My brother and I (aspiring young theologues at the time) often discussed the need to confront the white "Christians" of Bearden with the demands of the gospel by invading their Sunday worship service with our presence, making them declare publicly that *all* are not welcome in "God's" house. But the fear of bodily harm prevented us from carrying out that wish.

If Richard Wright is correct in his contention that "expression springs out of an environment,"[1] then I must conclude that my theological reflections are inseparable from the Bearden experience. I say with Claude McKay that "what I write is urged out of my blood" and out of the blood of blacks in Bearden and elsewhere who see what I see, feel what I feel, and love what I love. This is why Black Theology differs in perspective, content, and style from the western theological tradition transmitted from Augustine to Barth. My theology will not be the same as that of my white colleagues at Union Theological Seminary, because our experience is different. They were not born black in Bearden. They did not know about Macedonia A.M.E. Church, and the Black Spirit of God who descended upon that community when folks there gathered for worship and praise to him who had brought them a "mighty long way." They could not know the significance of black prayer, because they had not heard nor felt the invested meaning of those familiar words as Brother Elbert Thrower invited the congregation to pray with him a little while:

Once more and again, O Lawd, we come to thee, with bowed heads and humble hearts, thankin' thee for watchin' over us last night as we slept and slumbered, and gave us the strength to get up and come to church this mornin'. I thank thee that my last night's sleepin' couch was not my coolin' board and my cover was not my windin' sheet. I thank thee, Lawd, because you have been with me from the earliest rockin' of my cradle up to this present moment. You know my heart, and you know the range of our deceitful minds. And if you find anything that shouldn't be, I ask you to pluck it out and cast it into the sea of forgetfulness where it will never rise to harm us in this world.

As familiar as the words of that prayer were the words of "Amazing Grace." When Sister Ora Wallace raised her melodious voice and filled Macedonia with its rich and resonant tones, the entire congregation joined with her, because "Amazing Grace" spoke to their condition.

> Amazing grace! how sweet the sound,
> That saved a wretch like me!
> I once was lost, but now am found,
> Was blind, but now I see.
>
> Thro' many dangers, toils, and snares,
> I have already come;
> 'Tis grace hath bro't me safe thus far,
> And grace will lead me home.

Ironically, this song was written by an ex-slave trader; but when the sons and daughters of black slaves sang it, "Amazing Grace" was infused with black power and meaning. For blacks in Bearden, the "dangers, toils, and snares" referred to their daily struggle to survive, the ups and downs of black existence, and the attempt to seize a measure of freedom in an extreme situation of oppression. "Amazing Grace" was the miracle of survival, because it is difficult to explain how we made it through slavery, Reconstruction, and the struggle against oppression in the twentieth century. Blacks in Bearden said: "It must have been the grace of God!"

Because I have lived the Bearden experience, I cannot separate it from my theological perspective. I am a *black* theologian! I therefore must approach the subject of theology in the light of the black Church and what that means in a society dominated by white people. I did not recognize the methodological implication of that assumption until the summer of 1966 when Willie Ricks sounded the cry of "black power" and Stokely Carmichael joined him as the philosophical spokesman. Yet long before that, I knew in the depths of my being that European and American approaches to theology did not deal with the questions arising out of my experience.

Like most college and seminary students of my generation, I faithfully studied philosophy and theology—from the pre-Socratics to modern existentialism and linguistic analysis, from Justin Martyr, Irenaeus, and Origen to Karl Barth, Bultmann, and Tillich. I was an expert on Karl Barth and knew well the theological issues that shaped his theology. I wrote papers in seminary on the Barth and Brunner debates, the knowledge of God in contemporary theology, Bultmann's program of demythologization, the Tillichian doctrine of God as being-itself, and concluded my formal education with a Ph.D. dissertation on Barth's anthropology. But when I left Garrett Theological Seminary and Northwestern University (1963) and began to teach at Philander Smith College in Little Rock, Arkansas, I encountered head-on the *contradictions* of my seminary education as I attempted to inform black students about the significance of theological discourse. What could Karl Barth possibly mean for black students who had come from the cotton fields of Arkansas, Louisiana and Mississippi, seeking to change the structure of their lives in a society that had defined *black* as nonbeing? What is the significance of Nicea and Chalcedon for those who knew Jesus *not* as a thought in their heads to be analyzed in relation to a similar thought called God; they knew Jesus as a Savior and a friend, as the "lily of the valley and the bright and morning star"?

Those black students drove me back to the primary art forms of the black religious experience by refusing to accept a prefabricated theology from the lips of James Cone. I began once more to listen to the heartbeat of black life as reflected in the song and speech of black people. As I did so, I asked myself, What is theology? What is the substance of this "reasoning about God" that the Church has undertaken for nearly twenty centuries? And I knew that Calvin and Bultmann could not answer the question for me. Indeed the heart of the problem was the relation of the black religious experience to my knowledge of classical theology.

My concern was intensified during the black insurrection in Detroit in the summer of 1967. I had moved the year before to teach in Adrian, Michigan, just seventy miles from Detroit. I remember the feeling of dread and absurdity as I asked myself, "What has all this to do with Jesus Christ—his birth in Bethlehem, his baptism with and life among the poor, and his death and resurrection?" I intuitively knew that the responses of white preachers and theologians were not correct. The most sensitive whites merely said: "We deplore the riots but sympathize with the reason for the riots." This was tantamount to saying: "Of course we raped your women, lynched your men, and ghettoized the minds of your children and you have a right to be upset; but that is no reason for you to burn our buildings. If you people keep acting like that, we will never give you your freedom."

I knew that that response was not only humiliating and insulting but wrong. It revealed not only an insensitivity to black pain and suffering but also, and more importantly for my vocation as a theologian, a *theological bankruptcy*. The education of white theologians did not prepare them to deal with Watts, Detroit, and Newark. What was needed was a new way of looking at theology that must emerge out of the dialectic of black history and culture.

Instinctively, I went to the Scriptures as the primary source for this new approach and asked, "What has the biblical message to do with the black power revolution?" My answer is found in my first book, *Black Theology and Black Power* (Seabury, 1969). My second book, *A Black Theology of Liberation* (Lippincott, 1970), is a continued probing of that question in the light of the classical structures of theology. Although I do not think that those books represent the only possible *answers*, I do think that it is impossible to do Christian theology with integrity in America without asking the *question*, What has the gospel to do with the black struggle for liberation?

Reflecting on those books I realized that something important was missing. They did not show clearly enough the significance of Macedonia A.M.E. Church and the imprint of that community upon my theological consciousness. After all, I was insisting that theology has to arise out of an oppressed community as they seek to understand their place in the history of salvation. Therefore I had to inquire about the theological significance of the black experience as reflected in sermon, song, and story.

> O I been rebuked, and I been scorned,
> Done had a hard time sho's you born.

> I don't know what my mother wants to stay here fuh,
> Dis ole worl' ain't been no friend to huh.

> If de blues was whiskey,
> I'd stay drunk all de time.

> I wrote these blues, gonna sing 'em as I please,
> I wrote these blues, gonna sing 'em as I please,
> I'm the only one like the way I'm singing' 'em,
> I'll swear to goodness ain't no one else to please.

Some of the results of this inquiry were published as *The Spirituals and the Blues* (Seabury, 1972).

The present work deals with the social basis of theology and is concerned with, among other related matters, the problem of the particular and the universal in theological discourse. The book is prompted by three considerations. One is that my previous work obliged me to raise certain important problems but did not provide the context for dealing fully with them. Second, I have been overwhelmed in recent years with the seemingly endless theological fertility of the black experience, not merely as a slogan but in all its rich, concrete detail. Finally, there is the need to respond to a certain kind of critical dismissal of Black Theology, typified by the statement of one distinguished theologian that blacks "are not free to violate the canon of exact reflection, careful weighing of evidence, and apt argument, if they want to make a case for other intellectually responsible listeners."[2] Because theological discourse is *universal*, I am constrained to reply to this comment, serious despite its patronizing mood, by a fellow theologian. But because theology is also *particular*, my reply is (in brief) that he is wrong, and that he is wrong because his theological perspective is determined by his whiteness. He is saying nothing other than, "Unless you black people learn to think like us white folks, using our rules, then we will not listen to you." And that is bad theology.

For these reasons then—a feeling of unfinished business, a desire to explore further the theological riches of the black experience, and a hope of bridging a gap in the theological community—it seems important to talk about theology and its social sources, beginning with some reflection on the task of the theologian.

Like most theologians, I believe that Christian theology is language about God. But it's more than that, and it is the "more" that makes theology *Christian*. Christian theology is language about the *liberating* character of God's presence in Jesus Christ as he calls his people into being for freedom in the world. The task of the theologian, as a member of the people of God, is to clarify what the Church believes and does in relation to its participation in God's liberating work in the world. In doing this work, the theologian acts in the roles of exegete, prophet, teacher, preacher, and philosopher.

The theologian is *before all else* an exegete, simultaneously of Scripture and of existence. To be an exegete of Scripture means that the theologian recognizes the Bible, the witness to God's Word, as the primary source of theological discourse. To be an exegete of existence means that Scripture is not an abstract word, not merely a rational idea. It is God's Word to those who are oppressed and humiliated in this world. The task of the theologian is to probe the depths of Scripture exegetically for the purpose of relating that message to human existence.

Because the theologian is an exegete, he is also a prophet. As prophet he must make clear that the gospel of God stands in judgment upon the existing order of injustice. This task involves, as Abraham Heschel said, the "exegesis of existence from a divine perspective,"[3] disclosing that God is not indifferent to suffering and not patient with cruelty and falsehood. But God's power and judgment will create justice and order out of chaos.

As teacher, the theologian is an instructor in the faith, clarifying its meaning and significance for human life. He investigates the past and relates the struggles of the apostles and the Fathers to our present struggles. Thus he becomes the defender of the faith, showing its reasonableness, its "fittingness" for the oppressed community now.

As preacher, the theologian is a proclaimer of the Word, the truth of Jesus Christ as the Liberator of the poor and the wretched of the land. Here the theologian recognizes the *passionate* character of theological language. It is a language of celebration and joy that the freedom promised is already present in the community's struggle for liberation.

As philosopher, the theologian is a keen observer of the alternative interpretations of the meaning of life. He knows that the gospel cannot be taken for granted, cannot be accepted without the continued test of life in struggle. The philosophic side of the theological task keeps one intellectually honest and open to other perspectives. It guards against dogmatism and provides the groundwork for dialogue with other faiths.

In all roles the theologian is committed to that form of existence arising from Jesus' life, death, and resurrection. He knows that the death of the man on the tree has radical implications for those who are enslaved, lynched, and ghettoized in the name of God and country. In order to do theology from that standpoint, he must ask the right questions and then go to the right sources for the answers. The right questions are always related to the basic question: What has the gospel to do with the oppressed of the land and their struggle for liberation? Any theologian who fails to place that question at the center of his work has ignored the essence of the gospel.

Identifying the right source is more complicated. Of course, the sources include Scripture and tradition as they bear witness to the higher source of revelation as particularized and universalized in Jesus Christ. But also with equal and sometimes greater weight, the sources must include the history and culture of oppressed peoples. In the United States and its cultural dependencies that must mean people of color—black, yellow, red, and brown. Here the theologian asks: How have black people understood their history and culture, and how is that understanding related to their faith in Jesus Christ? The place to go for answers is the black sermon, prayer, song, and story. These sources must not be evaluated with the same methods used in analyzing the classical tradition. The methods one employs for analysis must arise from the sources themselves. Only then can one do justice to the complexity of black thought forms and the depth of theological expression found in black life.

It is of course possible to assume that black religion and white religion are essentially the same, since white people introduced "Christianity" to black people. However, that assumption will deprive the theologian of vital insights into black religious thought forms, because it fails to recognize the significant connection between thought and social existence. If Ludwig Feuerbach is correct in his contention that "Thought is preceded by suffering,"[4] and if Karl Marx is at least partly correct in his observation that "it is not consciousness that determines life but life that determines consciousness,"[5] then it is appropriate to ask, What is the connection between life and theology? The answer cannot be the same for blacks and whites, because blacks and whites do not share the same life. The life of a black slave and white slaveholder were radically different. It follows that their thoughts about things divine would also be different, even though they might sometimes use the same words about God. The life of the slaveholder and others of that culture was that of extending white inhumanity to excruciating limits, involving the enslavement of Africans and the annihilation of Indians. The life of the slave was the slave ship, the auction block, and the plantation regime. It involved the attempt to define himself without the ordinary historical possibilities of self-affirmation. Therefore when the master and slave spoke of God, they could not possibly be referring to the same reality. When the slave spoke of Jesus Christ, he spoke out of the depths of suffering and despair and the pain of "rolling through an unfriendly world."

In order for the theologian to recognize the particularity of black religion, he must imagine his way into the environment and the ethos of black slaves, probing the language and rhythm of a people who had to "feel their way along the course of American slavery," enduring the stress of human servitude, while still affirming their humanity. How could this be? How was it possible for black people to keep their humanity together in the midst of servitude, affirming that the God of Jesus is at work in the world, liberating them from bondage? The record shows clearly that black slaves believed that just as God had delivered Moses and the Israelites from Egyptian bondage, he also will deliver black people from American slavery. And they expressed that theological truth in song.

> Oh Mary, don't you weep, don't you moan,
> Oh Mary, don't you weep, don't you moan,
> Pharaoh's army got drownded,
> Oh Mary, don't you weep.

That truth did not come from white preachers; it came from a liberating encounter with the One who is the Author of black faith and existence. As theologians, we must ask: What is the source and meaning of freedom expressed in this spiritual?

> Oh Freedom! Oh Freedom!
> Oh Freedom, I love thee!
> And before I'll be a slave,
> I'll be buried in my grave
> And go home to my Lord and be free.

Here freedom is obviously a structure of, and a movement in, historical existence. It is black slaves accepting the risk and burden of self-affirmation, of liberation in history. That is the meaning of the phrase, "And before I'll be a slave, I'll be buried in my grave." But without negating history, the last line of this spiritual places freedom beyond the historical context. "And go home to my Lord and be free." In this context, freedom is eschatological. It is the anticipation of freedom, a vision of a new heaven and a new earth. Black slaves recognized that human freedom is transcendent—that is, a constituent of the future—

which made it impossible to identify humanity exclusively with meager attainment in history.

If theologians could penetrate the depths of that affirmation, then they could understand the significance of John Cassandra's bold affirmation: "You treat me like a mule and I came out like a man."[6] And they might be able to comprehend the theological significance of my mother's melodious rendition of her favorite song:

> This little light of mine,
> I'm goin' to let it shine;
> This little light of mine,
> I'm goin' to let it shine,
> Let it shine, let it shine.
>
> Everywhere I go,
> I'm goin' to let it shine;
> Everywhere I go,
> I'm goin' to let it shine
> Let it shine, let it shine.
>
> God give it to me,
> I'm goin' to let it shine;
> My God give it to me,
> I'm goin' to let it shine,
> Let it shine, let it shine.

Here *thought* is connected with the substance of black life, the rhythm and feelings of a people who intuitively recognized that they were more than what had been defined for them in white society. They were human beings—though whites treated them as nonpersons. They were *somebody* despite the humiliating limits placed on their existence.

The same ethos flourished appropriately in the northern ghettos and the Jim Crow south after the end of institutional slavery. After being told six days of the week that they were nothings by the rulers of white society, on the Sabbath, the first day of the week, black people went to church in order to experience another definition of their humanity. Like Mary Magdalene at the tomb, looking for the body of Jesus, folks in Bearden went to Macedonia looking for the One who said, "I am the way, and the truth, and the life" (John 14:6 RSV). And like Mary, they were overjoyed to find him alive and present at Macedonia. That is why they shouted and prayed and why Reverend Hunter preached such fervent sermons, proclaiming Jesus' presence among them. Those six days of wheeling and dealing with white people always raised the anxious question of whether life was worth living. But when blacks went to church and experienced the presence of Jesus' Spirit among them, they realized that he bestowed a meaning upon their lives that could not be taken away by white folks. That's why folks at Macedonia sang: "A little talk with Jesus makes it right": not that "white is right," but that God had affirmed the rightness of their existence, the righteousness of their being in the world. That affirmation enabled black people to meet "the Man" on Monday morning and to deal with his dehumanizing presence the remainder of the week, knowing that white folks could not destroy their humanity.

The power of that insight came to me at an early age, although I did not know what it meant. I only knew that when my mother sang her favorite song, "This little light of mine," she was affirming much more than what was apparent in the lines. And the emotional response of the congregation reinforced my intuitions. The "light" was what illumined her existence, an alternative view of life, different from the current estimations of her being in the world. It was her attempt to make a statement about her life and to say to the world that she is who she is because and only because of the presence of God in her world.

As a child I could not really understand the meaning and depths of my parent's faith. It was only recently that the profundity of their religious affirmation broke through to me. I realized that they and the others of Macedonia possessed something essential to the very survival of black humanity, and it ought not be dismissed or belittled. They were in fact providing me with my only possible theological point of departure.

In this book, I am not writing simply a personal account of my religious faith, though that is partly involved. I am writing about my parents, Lucy and Charlie Cone, and other black people in

Bearden and elsewhere who gave me what it takes to deal with life's contradictions and negations. For it was they who introduced me to the man called Jesus, the One whom they said could "lift your feet out of the muck and miry clay and place them on the solid rock of salvation." They sometimes called him that "wheel in the middle of the wheel," the "Rose of Sharon and the Lord of life." He was their "ever present help in time of trouble."

I respect what happened at Nicea and Chalcedon and the theological input of the Church Fathers on Christology; but that source alone is inadequate for finding out the meaning of black folks' Jesus. It is all right to say as did Athanasius that the Son is *homoousia* (one substance with the Father), especially if one has a taste for Greek philosophy and a feel for the importance of intellectual distinctions. And I do not want to minimize or detract from the significance of Athanasius' assertion for faith one iota. But the *homoousia* question is not a black question. Blacks do not ask whether Jesus is one with the Father or divine and human, though the orthodox formulations are implied in their language. They ask whether Jesus is walking with them, whether they can call him up on the "telephone of prayer" and tell him all about their troubles. To be sure Athanasius' assertion about the status of the *Logos* in the Godhead is important for the church's continued christological investigations. But we must not forget that Athanasius' question about the Son's status in relation to the Father did not arise in the historical context of the slave codes and the slave drivers. And if he had been a black slave in America, I am sure he would have asked a different set of questions. He might have asked about the status of the Son in relation to slaveholders. Perhaps the same is true of Martin Luther and his concern about the ubiquitous presence of Jesus Christ at the Lord's Table. While not diminishing the importance of Luther's theological concern, I am sure that if he had been born a black slave his first question would not have been whether Jesus was at the Lord's Table but whether he was really present at the slave's cabin, whether the slave could expect Jesus to be with him as he tried to survive the cotton field, the whip, and the pistol.

Unfortunately not only white seminary professors but some

blacks as well have convinced themselves that only the white experience provides the appropriate context for questions and answers concerning things divine. They do not recognize the narrowness of their experience and the particularity of their theological expressions. They like to think of themselves as *universal* people. That is why most seminaries emphasize the need for appropriate *tools* in doing theology, which always means *white* tools, i.e., knowledge of the language and thought of white people. They fail to recognize that other people also have thought about God and have something significant to say about Jesus' presence in the world.

My point is that one's social and historical context decides not only the questions we address to God but also the mode or form of the answers given to the questions. That is the central thesis of this book. And I intend to illustrate it through selected theological themes, with particular reference to the contrasting ways that black and white people think about God.

II.
SPEAKING
THE TRUTH

Speak the truth to the people
Talk sense to the people
Free them with reason
Free them with honesty
Free the people with Love and Courage and Care for their
    being. . . .[1]

Black theologians are living in a period in which we must investigate anew "the problem of the color-line," as that problem is reflected in the social existence of African peoples. We cannot afford to do theology unrelated to human existence. We cannot be "objective," but must recognize, with Imamu Baraka, that "there is no objective anything"[2]—least of all theology. Our theology must emerge consciously from an investigation of the socioreligious experience of black people, as that experience is reflected in *black* stories of God's dealings with black people in the struggle of freedom. Tertullian's question, "What . . . has Athens to do with Jerusalem?"[3] is not our central question. His concern was to state the primacy of faith in relation to reason on matters of theological discourse. We have another concern and thus must rephrase that question in the light of our cultural history, asking: "What has *Africa* to do with Jerusalem, and what difference does Jesus make for African people oppressed in North America?" As Gerard Bissainthe puts it:

From the despair of our cry,
The heart's intensity,

Out of death and dereliction
In the land of our uprootedness,
We shall one day give birth to our Christ,
A Christ made flesh of our flesh,
Our dark flesh of the black people.[4]

If our theological vocation emerges out of the matrix of that vision, then we will not be limited to Euro-American definitions of theology. The ecstasy of the poet's vision and the concreteness of the historical reality from which the vision is created bestow upon us a new perspective, a *black* perspective that grants free thinking in relation to our cultural history and thus enables us to hear the urgent call to speak the truth. In this context, truth is not an intellectual datum that is entrusted to academic guilds. Truth cannot be separated from the people's struggle and the hopes and dreams that arise from that struggle. Truth is that transcendent reality, disclosed in the people's historical struggle for liberation, which enables them to know that their fight for freedom is not futile. The affirmation of truth means that the freedom hoped for will be realized. Indeed, the freedom hoped for is already partly realized in our present history, because the realization of hope is the very ground of our present struggle. We do not struggle in despair but in hope, not from doubt but from faith, not out of hatred but out of love for ourselves and for humanity. And as black theologians, who have been grasped by the truth, we are accountable to black people.

What does it mean to speak the truth from a black theological perspective, that is, what are the sources and the content of theology? To explore this question we must begin by exploring the theological function of the black experience.

The Black Experience as a Source of Theology

There is no truth for and about black people that does not emerge out of the context of their experience. Truth in this sense is black truth, a truth disclosed in the history and culture of black people. This means that there can be no Black Theology which does not take the black experience as a source for its starting point. Black Theology is a theology of and for black people, an examination of their stories, tales, and sayings. It is an investigation of the mind into the raw materials of our pilgrimage, telling the story of "how we got over." For theology to be black, it must reflect upon what it means to be black. Black Theology must uncover the structures and forms of the black experience, because the categories of interpretation must arise out of the thought forms of the black experience itself.

What are we to make of the moan and the shout and the call to get on board the gospel train? What must we say about the song, the sermon, the prayer, and the feeling of the Spirit when the people gather for worship and praise to the One they say is "a rock in the weary land, a shelter in a mighty storm, and a stronghold in the day of trouble"?[5]

When dealing with the sermon, we must listen to the proclamation of the gospel as disclosed in the black Word. Sometimes the Word is expressed with apocalyptic imagination:

> And now I leave dis thought wid you,
> Standing out on de eaves of ether
> Breathing clouds from out of his nostrils,
> Blowing storms from 'tween his lips
> I can see!!
> Him seize de mighty axe of his proving power
> And smite the stubborn-standing space,
> And laid it wide open a mighty gash—
> Making a place to hold the world
> I can see him—
> Molding de world out of thought and power
> And whirling it out on its eternal track,
> Ah hah, my strong armded God![6]

This sermon makes clear that the Word and its proclamation in the black Church is more than the conceptualization of theological doctrine. The Word is more than *words* about God. God's Word is a poetic happening, an evocation of an indescribable reality in the lives of the people. This is the meaning behind the occasion when a black preacher "who after reading a rather cryptic passage took off his spectacles, closed the Bible with a bang and by way of preface said, 'Brothers and sisters, this morning—I intend to explain the unexplainable—find out the undefinable—ponder over the imponderable—and unscrew the inscrutable.' "[7] Here the preacher is affirming not only his freedom in relation to the text; he is also making a sharp distinction between the *words* of the text and the *Word* disclosed in the text. The black theologian must also make similar distinctions in his use of the sermon as a source of theology. He must not be bound to white, academic conceptualizations of the Christian gospel. If the gospel means freedom, then the freedom disclosed in that gospel must also be revealed in the event of proclamation. The preaching of the Word must itself be the embodiment of freedom. When freedom is a constituent of the language itself, then that language refuses to be bound to the limitations of categories not indigenous to its being. Possibilities are thus given for the communication of the Word that transcends intellectual concepts. In black preaching, the Word becomes embodied in the rhythm and the emotions of language as the people respond bodily to the Spirit in their midst. The black sermon arises out of the totality of the people's existence—their pain and joy, trouble and ecstasy.[8]

When the Word is spoken as truth and the people feel the presence of truth in the midst of their troublesome situation, they respond to the preached word by ratifying it with resounding "Amens." The "Amen" is the congregation's witness to, and participation in, the proclamation. It is their Yes to the preacher in order to let him know that he is on the "right track," affirming that they know the truth about which he speaks. At this point the Word of truth transcends conceptual analysis and becomes a liberating event wherein the people are moved to another level of existence, and they are permitted to experience a foretaste of the New Jerusalem. Because the participation of the congregation is so crucial for black preaching, the preacher often asks, "Can I get a witness?" or rhetorically says, "I don't believe you are praying with me!" These expressions are the preacher's appeal to the people to let him know whether divine truth is being mediated through the proclamation-event. If the people say "Amen," it is an affirmation that what they hear is a certification of the reality and truthfulness of the proclaimed word. It is the equivalent of "That's right!"

What was said about the freedom inherent in the sermon can also be said about the prayers of black people. Black prayers are not the same as white prayers. In the black perspective white folks prayed like this:

> O Lahd, the first thing I want you to understand, is that it is a white man talking to you. This ain't no nigger whooping and hollering for something and then don't know what to do with it after he gets it. This is a white man talking to you, and I want you to pay some attention. Now, in the first place, Lahd, we would like a little rain. It's been powerful dry around here, and we needs rain mighty bad. But don't come in no storm like you did last year. Come ca'm and gentle and water our crops.
>
> And now another thing, Lahd—don't let these niggers be as sassy this coming year as they have been in the past. That's all, Lahd. Amen.[9]

When the black man prayed, he did not accept the religious outlook of the white master. To be sure, the historical situation of slavery may have forced the black person to worship with and "like" the white master, but in many subtle ways the slave transcended the limitations of servitude and affirmed a religious value system that differed from his master's. In response to a white minister, conducting a revival at a black church, "the brother in black" offered this prayer for "his brother in white."

> Oh Lawd, gib him de eye ob de eagle, dat he may spy out sin afar off, weave his hands to the gospel plow, tie his tongue to de limbs ob truth, nail his ear to de South Pole. Bow his head away down between his knees, and his knees way down in some lonesome dark and narrow valley where prayer is much wanted to be made. 'Noint him wid de kerosene oil of salvation and set him on fire.[10]

Sometimes black people in their praying were more direct in their rejection of white people's value system. On one occasion, the white preacher, in his sermon to a black congregation, suggested that "in heaven there must be some Jim Crow partition, with the white saints on one side and the black saints on the other. And after the sermon, when one of the black deacons was called on to pray, he got his chance to reply to this white preacher; for like many praying people, the old black man knew how to talk *to* the Lord and talk *at* other people, in the same phrases. . . ." This is what he said:

> And, O Lord, we thank thee fer the brother preacher who has spoke to us,—we thank thee for heaven,—we thank thee that we kin all go to heaven,—but as to that partition, O Lord, we thank thee that we'se a shoutin' people—we thank thee that we kin shout so hard in heaven that we will break down that partition an' spread all over heaven,—an' we thank thee that if the white fokes can't stand it, they can git on out of heaven an' go to elsewhere![11]

Here the black theologian should reflect not only upon humor as an artistic expression of black survival but also upon the Word of prayer as disclosed in the affirmation of black identity. God is the Spirit of Jesus that guides and moves the people in their struggle to be what they were created to be. He is their "Captain who never lost a battle." In prayer, sometimes, he is called the "mighty good leader," the "dying-bed maker" and the "soul's emancipator." All these phrases point to God as the living and ever present One who grants freedom for the humiliated and stands in judgment upon oppressors who attempt to destroy black dignity.

In black prayer the soul is laid bare before the Lord. All pretensions of goodness are rejected before what the people call "the throne of grace." It was a form of self-criticism not derived from the value system of white people.

> You heard me when I laid at hell's dark door
> With no weapon in my hand
> And no God in my heart,
> And I cried for three long days and nights.
> You heard me, Lawd,
> And stooped so low
> And snatched me from the hell
> Of eternal death and damnation.
> You cut loose my stammerin' tongue;

> You established my feet on the rock of Salvation
> And yo' voice was heard in rumblin' judgment.[12]

Here is the affirmation of the gift of divine freedom and dignity in the context of religious worship.

A similar emphasis is found in the song—the spirituals, gospels and other melodious expressions of the people's struggle for freedom.[13] The function of the song is to sing the truth as it is lived by the people.

> Who found me when I was lost?
> Who helped me to bear my heavy cross?
> Who fixed me up, turned me 'round,
> Left my feet on solid ground?
> I know it was Jesus!
> I know it was the Lord!
>
> Who do you think gave sight to the blind?
> Made the lame to walk
> And dead men rise?
> Who took the fishes and the loaves of bread
> And made five hundred so all could be fed?
> Oh, Jesus, Oh Lord, Jesus! My Lord!
> I know it was Jesus! I know it was the Lord!

As with the sermon and prayer, the spirituals and gospel songs reveal that the truth of black religion is not limited to the literal meaning of the words. Truth is also disclosed in the movement of the language and the passion created when a song is sung in the right pitch and tonal quality. Truth is found in shout, hum, and moan as these expressions move the people closer to the source of their being. The moan, the shout, and the rhythmic bodily responses to prayer, song, and sermon are artistic projections of the pain and joy experienced in the struggle of freedom. It is the ability of black people to express the tragic side of social existence but also their refusal to be imprisoned by its limitations.

In these "churchly expressions," among others, the divine One informs and discloses himself in black reality and is best defined in terms of black people's response in body and spirit to that divine source believed to be greater than themselves. If asked the theological question, "Who is God?" one black person might say: "I don't know much about him. All I know is that I was weak and he gave me strength. I was lost and he found me. I was crying and he wiped away the tears from my eyes." Another might proclaim her testimony in this manner: "God is a heart-fixer and a mind-regulator. He is the One who binds the broken heart and eases the pain of the afflicted. He rescued me from the gates of hell and restored my soul to his bosom." The key to the theological affirmation here is not only the verbal assent to the power of God to grant identity and liberation to an oppressed and humiliated people. Equally important is the verbal passion with which these affirmations are asserted and the physical responses they elicit in the community in which the testimony is given. Some will shout, moan, and cry; others will walk, run, and clap their hands. Then there are those who will keep still, using silence as a sign of the presence of God in their midst. This is part of the matrix of Black Theology and the source out of which truth is given.

However, the black experience as a source of theology is more than the so-called "church experience," more than singing, praying, and preaching about Jesus, God, and the Holy Spirit. The other side of the black experience should not be rigidly defined as "secular," if by that term one means the classical Western distinction between secular and sacred, for it is not antireligious or even nonreligious. This side of the black experience is secular only to the extent that it is earthy and seldom uses God or Christianity as the chief symbols of its hopes and dreams. It is sacred because it is created out of the same historical community as the church experience and thus represents the people's attempt to shape life and to live it according to their dreams and aspirations. Included in these black expressions are animal tales, tales of folk figures, slave seculars, blues, and accounts of personal experiences.

In the animal and folk figure tales, the emphasis is often on the wit and cleverness of the weak in triumph over the strong. The hero of many animal tales is Br'er Rabbit, whose significance is described by J. Mason Brewer.

The role of the rabbit in the tales of the American Negro is similar to that of the hare in African folk narratives—that of the trickster who shrewdly outwits and gains a victory over some physically stronger or more powerful adversary. The animal tales told by Negro slaves with Brer Rabbit as the hero had a meaning far deeper than mere entertainment. The rabbit actually symbolized the slave himself. Whenever the rabbit succeeded in proving himself smarter than another animal the slave rejoiced secretly, imagining himself smarter than his master.[14]

With this perspective on rabbit lore, it is understandable why folktales have been described as "hitting a straight lick with a crooked stick."[15] The slave was "putting one over on the white man, in a subtle, and partially disguised way,"[16] often singing to himself

> Got one mind for white folks to see
> 'Nother for what I know is me;
> He don't know, he don't know my mind,
> When he see me laughing
> Just laughing to keep from crying.

The wry humor of the animal tales is also found in many other stories and sayings, both religious and secular. Humor is an important element in black survival, and it is often related to the theme of freedom. Through humor, black slaves transcended their servitude and affirmed their right to freedom without the risks of revolutionary violence against slave masters. Consider the tale entitled "A Laugh That Meant Freedom," in which Nehemiah's wit and humor was a means of liberating himself from slavery. The day of freedom came when David Wharton, known as the most cruel slave master in southwest Texas, concluded: "I bet I can make the rascal work."

> The morning of the first day after his purchase David Wharton walked over to where Nehemiah was standing and said, "Now you are going to work, you understand. You are going to pick four hundred pounds of cotton today."

"Wal Massa, dat's aw right," answered Nehemiah, "but ef Ah meks you laff, won' you lemme off fo' terday?"

"Well," said David Wharton, who had never been known to laugh, "if you make me laugh, I won't only let you off for today, but I'll give you your freedom."

"Ah decla', Boss," said Nehemiah, "yuh sho' is uh goodlookin' man."

"I am sorry I can't say the same thing about you," retorted David Wharton.

"Oh, yes, Boss, yuh could," Nehemiah laughed out, "yuh could, if yuh tole ez big uh lie ez Ah did."

David Wharton could not help laughing at this; he laughed before he thought. Nehemiah got his freedom.[17]

A similar theme of freedom is found in tales about the folk hero, High John the Conqueror.[18] He was the "hopebringer," an expression of the slave's desire to transcend the historical limitations of servitude and the attempt to affirm the "otherness" of existence not defined by the auction block and slave codes. High John, though not identical with Jesus Christ in the spirituals, serves a similar function. He symbolizes the slaves' desire for freedom and the recognition that they are not alone in the world. That was why High John was described as "a whisper, a will to hope, a wish to find something worthy of laughter and song." But the "whisper was put into flesh" and was "sure to be heard when and where the work was the hardest and the lot the most cruel."[19] High John was the slaves' incarnation of hope, that unbeatable reality deep in the souls of the slaves, enabling them to endure the harsh realities of servitude without losing their dignity. "So they pulled the covers up over their souls and kept them from all hurt, harm and danger. . . ."[20]

Unlike Jesus who came from Nazareth and taught in Galilee, High John the Conquerer came from Africa, "walking on the waves of sound,"[21] and took flesh in America. Just as Jesus' birth in Bethlehem took place without the Romans and Jewish religious leaders recognizing his significance, so John came without slave masters knowing the meaning of his appearance. The "Messianic secret" so dominant in Mark's portrayal of Jesus is also present in the tales about John. While the slaves knew who he was, the white masters did not perceive that they were not dealing with an ordinary slave. And perhaps the significance of John was best described by Aunt Sutton when she said John meant power,[22] the power of the slaves to hold themselves together in struggle.

In the slave seculars and blues are revealed another black expression in song.[23] In contrast to the spirituals and gospels, God is not the subject of these songs. The seculars and blues deal with the concreteness of life's contradictions without reference to a divine reality as a source of strength. What are we to make of this expression of truth?

> I'll eat when I'm hungry
> An' I' drink when I'se dry;
> An' if de whitefolks don't kill me,
> I'll live till I die.

The seculars deal with the absurdity of existence without using Jesus Christ as their central focal point. There is hope and transcendence but only as the vision is created from life itself.

The same this-worldly emphasis is found in the blues. "The blues ain't nothin' but a poor man's heart disease." With that affirmation the singer establishes an existential contact with his audience and blows the blues to the rhythm of life as lived by those who had so little to show for living—nothing except themselves. It is not that they denied God; they simply did not use God as a symbol of victory over suffering and pain. Their theme is endurance and transcendence in the face of despair.

> House catch on fire
> And ain't no water around,
> If your house catch on fire,
> Ain't no water around,
> Throw yourself out the window,
> Let it burn on down.

The blues deal with areas of bodily expression and desire that were only indirectly touched in church music. They deal openly with sex, love, and agony when a man loses his woman.

How long, baby, how long
Has that even' train been gone?
How long? How long? I say, How long?
Standin' at the station watchin' my baby leave town,
Sure am disgusted—for where could she be gone—
For how long? How long? I say, how long?

And when a woman cannot find her man,

> The man I'll marry ain't born yet,
> An' his mammy's dead.

In the blues, black people sing about the tragic side of life and use the artistic expression of tragedy as the means for transcending it.

> Ef you ever been down, you know jes how I feel—
> Lak a broken-down engine got no drivin' wheel,
> Lak a po' sojer boy lef' on de battle-fiel.

Another important theological source of the black experience is the narratives of slaves and ex-slaves, the personal accounts of black people's triumph and defeats.[24] Here are found many dimensions of the black experience as told by those who lived it in the midst of servitude and oppression. There are slaves who might be described as "religious," and others who are indifferent toward "religion." There are slaves who praise their masters for "kind" treatment; and those who say: "I had much rather starve in England, a free woman than be a slave for the best man that ever breathed upon the American continent."[25] This is the stuff of the black experience which makes Black Theology possible and necessary.

More recent black literature is another expression of the black experience. Particularly notable are the poets of the Harlem Renaissance (1920s and 1930s) and their successors. In the midst of the destruction of black dignity, Claude McKay articulated a poetic vision of black people's strivings for freedom.

> If we must die, let it not be like hogs,
> Hunted and penned in an inglorious spot,
> While all around us bark the mad and hungry dogs,
> Making their mock at our accursed lot.[26]

Like many black artists of that period, he recognized that art is never for its own sake but for people's sake. Black art is black people creating values based on their own experience and affirming the willingness to invent new definitions and life-styles commensurate with their struggle to be free. That was why Claude McKay said: "If we must die, O let us nobly die."[27]

The affirmation of *blackness* as an essential ingredient in the definition of humanity has never been easy in *white* America. But to believe in the *divine* in the context of black suffering can often place a curious burden upon a poet. As Countee Cullen put it:

> Yet do I marvel at this curious thing:
> To make a poet black and bid him sing![28]

What shall a black poet sing? What is the role of the black thinker in a society where black people sing

> I wish I knew how it would feel to be free
> I wish I could break all the chains holdin' me?[29]

The artists of the Harlem Renaissance did not exhaust the fullest depths of that question. The black artists of the 1960s and 70s, who are influenced by the new black consciousness as defined in the context of the black power revolution, usually take their cue from Imamu Amiri Baraka:

> The Black Artist's role in America is to aid in the destruction of America as he knows it. His role is to report and reflect so precisely the nature of the society, and of himself in that society, that other men will be moved by the exactness of his rendering and, if they are black men, grow strong through this moving, having seen their own strength, and weakness; and if they are white men, tremble, curse, and go mad, because they will be drenched with the filth of their evil.[30]

To summarize: the folklore of black people centers on the ability of the weak to survive through cunning, trickery, and sheer deception in an environment of the strong and powerful. Br'er Rabbit tricked Br'er Fox into throwing him into the brier-patch and hollered out: "Bred en bawn in a brier-patch, Br'er Fox —bred en bawn in a brier-patch!"[31] High John the Conquerer outwits the master and another slave survives. This same theme of survival and liberation is found in sermon, prayer, and song— including seculars, spirituals, and blues. On the one hand, there is the theological emphasis that God will liberate the weak from the injustice of the strong:

> When Israel was in Egypt's land,
> Let my people go;
> Oppressed so hard they could not stand,
> Let my people go;
> Go down Moses, 'way down in Egypt's land.
> Tell ole Pharaoh
> Let my people go.

On the other hand, transcendence over historical negations was affirmed through the recognition that

> De big bee flies high
> De little bee makes the honey
> De black man raised the cotton,
> An' de white man gets de money.

But in both cases, black people expressed the contradictions of existence while affirming the need to live in history without being conquered by it. The whole of black expression, Christian and non-Christian, preacher and poet, deals with the theme of liberation and the transcendence that happens in struggle.

It is the encounter of the truth of black experience that enables black theologians to know that they must speak the truth to the people. To speak the truth to black people is to relate the story of our mothers' and fathers' struggles to our present struggles and thereby create a humane future for our children. We must take the speeches and tales, the blues and the spirituals, the prayers and the sermons of black people and incorporate them into our present existence, relating our parents' strivings to our daily fight to survive in a land defined by George Washington, Thomas Jefferson, and Richard Nixon. Indeed our survival and liberation depend upon our recognition of the truth when it is spoken and lived by the people. If we cannot recognize the truth, then it cannot liberate us from untruth. To know the truth is to appropriate it, for it is not mainly reflection and theory. Truth is divine action entering into our lives and creating the human action of liberation. Truth enables us to dance and live to the rhythm of freedom in our lives as we struggle to be who we are. Therefore, to *speak* the truth we black theologians must set forth the authentic experience of blackness. We must respond to the urgent call of sister Desirée Barnwell:

> Will the real black people please stand:
> Those fearless in the unconventional,
> Moved towards their own blackness,
> Prone to influence and set trends,
> Schooled in *their* times and folkways,
> Dedicated to worthwhile endeavors,
> Attentive to meaningful expressions.[32]

Black Experience, Scripture, and Jesus Christ

The question inevitably arises, What is the relation of the black experience as a source of Black Theology to the Bible, which is traditionally identified as the source of Christian theology? The connection is this. When black people sing, preach, and tell stories about their struggle, one fact is clear: they are not dealing simply with themselves. They are talking about another reality, "so high you can't get over him, so low you can't get under him, so wide you can't get around him." It is this affirmation of transcendence that prevents Black Theology from being reduced merely to the cultural history of black people. For black people the transcendent reality is none other than Jesus Christ, of whom Scripture speaks. The Bible is the witness to God's self-disclosure in Jesus Christ. Thus the black experience requires that Scripture be a source of Black Theology. For it was Scripture that enabled slaves to affirm a view of God that differed radically from that of the slave masters. The slave masters' intention was to present a "Jesus" who would make the slave obedient and docile. Jesus was supposed to make black people better slaves, that is, faithful servants of white masters. But many blacks rejected that view of Jesus not only because it contradicted their African heritage, but because it contradicted the witness of Scripture. That was why Richard Allen and his companions walked out of St. George Methodist Episcopal Church in 1787 as a prophetic protest against segregated worship.[33] The same was true for Henry Highland Garnet. Through the reading of Scripture he concluded that liberty was a gift from God, and therefore black slaves ought to use any available means that promises success in the attainment of freedom.[34] Throughout black history Scripture was used for a definition of God and Jesus that was consistent with the black struggle for liberation. Further examples are found in Henry M. Turner's affirmation that "God is a Negro," Howard Thurman's association of Jesus with the disinherited, and Martin Luther King's view that political struggle was consistent with the gospel of Jesus.[35] Scripture established limits to white people's use of Jesus Christ as a confirmation of black oppression.

The importance of Scripture as the witness to Jesus Christ does not mean that Black Theology can therefore ignore the tradition and history of Western Christianity. It only means that our study of that tradition must be done in the light of the Word disclosed in Scripture as interpreted by black people. Although we recognize the interrelationship of Scripture and tradition, especially in the early centuries of the Church, yet the full meaning of Scripture is not limited to the interpretation of it as given in that particular tradition. Indeed Scripture and tradition often contradict each other. As the meaning of Jesus Christ is not to be identified with the *words* of Scripture, so the meaning of Scripture as the witness to the Word is not defined exclusively by Cyprian, Anselm, and Thomas. As theologians, we must interpret the latter in the light of the former.

On the one hand, we must evaluate a given interpreter of Scripture in the light of the *particularity* of his history, refusing to use the relativity of our present as the norm for the investigation of the past. We cannot criticize the early Church Fathers for their failure to address the critical questions of our contemporary situation. They are accountable only for dealing with the historical issues in their time as they relate to Jesus' presence among them. On the other hand, there are common elements in human experience that enable us to evaluate past interpreters of the faith. Since oppression of the weak by the powerful is one of those elements, we can put the critical question to Athanasius, Augustine, or Luther: What has the gospel of Jesus, as witnessed in Scripture, to do with the humiliated and the abused? If they failed to ask that question or only made it secondary in their interpretation of the gospel, then it is our task to make clear how their approach to the gospel differs from Scripture. This creates the possibility of distinguishing valid theology from heresy, a matter to be discussed later in this chapter.

Having described the two sources of Black Theology (black experience and Scripture), it is now important to distinguish both sources from their subject or essence, which is Jesus Christ. The subject of theology is that which creates the precise character of theological language, thereby distinguishing it from other ways of speaking. By contrast, the sources of theology are the materials that make possible a valid articulation of theology's subject.

Jesus Christ is the subject of Black Theology because he is the content of the hopes and dreams of black people. He was chosen by our grandparents, who saw in his liberating presence that he had chosen them and thus became the foundation of their struggle for freedom.[36] He was their Truth, enabling them to know that white definitions of black humanity were lies. When their way became twisted and senseless, they told Jesus about it. He lifted their burdens and eased their pain, thereby bestowing upon them a vision of freedom that transcended historical limitations. That was why they sang:

Sometimes I hangs my head an' cries,
But Jesus goin' to wipe my weepin' eyes.

Of course, for some people who live in this modern, scientific age with its emphasis on unlimited human possibilities, such a faith sounds simplistic and childish. But that is because their consciousness is defined by masters and rulers who really believe that they know what is best for everybody. However, the victims of such attitudes have only two alternatives: (1) to accept the oppressor's value system and thus be contented with the place set for them by others, or (2) to find a completely new way of looking at reality that enables them to fight against oppression. Many black slaves chose the latter, using Jesus Christ as the basis of their struggle. Through Jesus Christ they could know that they were *people*, even though they were bought and sold like cattle. Jesus Christ was that reality who invaded their history from beyond and bestowed upon them a definition of humanity that could not be destroyed by the whip and the pistol.

The emphasis on Jesus Christ and the Scripture as the subject and source of the presence of transcendence in black experience raises the question of the precise relationship between them. Some of my critics have stated the issue in this manner. "On page 32 of *Black Theology and Black Power*, quoting Ron Karenga, you said that 'The fact that I am Black is my ultimate reality.' But then on page 34 of the same book, you wrote that 'Christianity begins and ends with the man Jesus—his life, death and resurrection.' Which do you *really* mean? Blackness or Jesus Christ? You cannot have it both ways."

This is an important matter, and perhaps the place to begin for clarification is to state emphatically that, like Scripture, the black experience is a *source* of the Truth but not the Truth itself. Jesus Christ is the Truth and thus stands in judgment over all statements about truth. But having said that, we must immediately balance it with another statement, without which the first statement falsifies what it intends to affirm. We must state the other side of the paradox emphatically: There is no truth in Jesus Christ independent of the oppressed of the land—their history and culture. And in America, the oppressed are the people of color—

black, yellow, red, and brown. Indeed it can be said that to know Jesus is to know him as revealed in the struggle of the oppressed for freedom. Their struggle is Jesus' struggle, and he is thus revealed in the particularity of their cultural history—their hopes and dreams of freedom.

The difficulty some people have in understanding the relation between Jesus and the black experience in Black Theology is due partly to their inability to appreciate the dialectical character of theological speech, especially when related to the black struggle for liberation. They use a dialectical model when dealing with such things as divinity and humanity in Jesus Christ or justification and sanctification in St. Paul or John Wesley. But there is a failure of nerve when their abstractions about Jesus are applied to the historical present. Jesus Christ is not a proposition, not a theological concept which exists merely in our heads. He is an event of liberation, a happening in the lives of oppressed people struggling for political freedom. Therefore, to know him is to encounter him in the history of the weak and the helpless. That is why it can be rightly said that there can be no knowledge of Jesus independent of the history and culture of the oppressed. It is impossible to interpret the Scripture correctly and thus understand Jesus aright unless the interpretation is done in the light of the consciousness of the oppressed in their struggle for liberation.

A similar convergence occurs when it is asked whether the black experience exists independently of Jesus Christ. If by Jesus Christ is meant the formal preaching and teaching of white missionaries, at a particular point in time, then the answer is an unqualified Yes. As we must say that Jesus' existence in himself is not a product of culture, so the black experience began before black people were introduced to Christianity. However, that is such an obvious historical fact that we need not debate it further. But if by Jesus Christ is meant "the image of the invisible God, the first-born of all creation, for in him all things were created in heaven and on earth, visible and invisible" (Col. 1:15-16 RSV), then the answer is an unqualified No. In this context, Jesus is not simply a doctrine or even a particular event limited by time. He is the eternal event of liberation in the divine person who makes freedom a constituent of human existence. There is no existence apart from him because he is the ground of existence without whom nothing is. Therefore, where human beings struggle for freedom and refuse to be defined by unauthorized earthly authorities, there Jesus Christ is present among them. His presence is the sustaining and liberating event in the lives of the oppressed that makes possible the continued struggle for freedom.

From the context of the eternal presence of Christ, the Liberator, emerges the interdependence of Jesus and the black experience as expressed in the lives of many black people. This interdependence is expressed so forcefully and concretely that *truly* to speak of the black experience is to speak of Jesus. He is the Word in their lives, and thus to speak of their experience as it is manifested in the joys and sorrows of black life is to speak of the One they say is the Comforter in time of trouble, "the lily of the valley," and "the bright and morning star."

> He's King of King's, and Lord of Lords,
> Jesus Christ, the first and the last
> No man works like him.

Others have testified that he is a "bridge over troubled waters," the "One who has been better to us than we have been to ourselves." In *God Struck Me Dead,* a collection of conversion experiences and autobiographies of ex-slaves, one called him a "time-God"! "He don't come before time; he don't come after time. He comes just on time."[37] And he comes as the preserver of the weak in time of trouble and as the sustaining Spirit of freedom in wretched places. This encounter of Jesus as the Christ of God makes his reality an eternal presence of liberation before and after the slave ships and Middle Passage.

The convergence of Jesus Christ and the black experience is the meaning of the Incarnation. Because God became man in Jesus Christ, he disclosed the divine will to be with humanity in our wretchedness. And because we blacks accept his presence in Jesus as the true definition of our humanity, blackness and divinity are dialectically bound together as one reality. This is the theological meaning of the paradoxical assertion about the primacy of the black experience and Jesus Christ as witnessed in Scripture.[38]

This brings us to the issue of heresy, which is an important matter if the Church intends to be clear about its message and its vocation in the world. Heresy here refers to any activity or teaching that contradicts the liberating truth of Jesus Christ. It is an action that denies the Lordship of Christ or a word that refuses to acknowledge his liberating presence in the struggle for freedom. Heresy is the refusal to speak the truth or to live the truth in the light of the One who is the Truth.

The early Church was correct in identifying problems of heresy as a critical theological issue, although it was often itself the heretic. But every community that is serious about the gospel of Jesus Christ must ask, When does the Church cease to be the Church of Jesus Christ? When do the Church's actions deny the faith that it verbalizes? These questions must be answered for every given situation, if the people of God are to remain relatively clearheaded about the relation between their existence as God's people and Jesus' existence as their Lord. Not every church that claims to be the Church is the Church, because being the Church requires concrete commitments to the One who is the essence of the Church. Not every theology that claims to be Christian is Christian, because the doing of Christian theology requires specific commitments to the One who is the content of that reality to which the word "Christian" points.

The question of heresy must be reopened in our time, *not* for the purpose of witch-hunting, but for the sake of the Church's life. We need to be clear about the subject to which our proclamation points and the relation of our words about that Subject to our *actions* in the world. Here it must be emphasized that we are not simply concerned with our theological conceptualizations of Jesus Christ, although that is included. Theological concepts have meaning only as they are translated into theological praxis, that is, the Church living in the world on the basis of what it proclaims. This means that theology and ethics, though not identical, are closely interrelated: the mission of the Church is defined by its proclamation, and the proclamation is authenticated by the mission. For the sake of the mission of the Church in the world, we must continually ask, What actions deny the Truth disclosed in Jesus Christ? Where should the line be drawn? Can the Church of Jesus Christ be racist and Christian at the same time? Can the Church of Jesus Christ be politically, socially, and economically identified with the structures of oppression and also be a servant of Christ? Can the Church of Jesus Christ fail to make the liberation of the poor the center of its message and work, and still remain faithful to its Lord?

On the level of theory these questions are easy to answer. Yet they are very difficult to answer in the day-to-day life of the Church. This difficulty is increased because we live in a society of many denominations under an ethos of the "freedom" of religion. But difficulties do not make the questions less important. Indeed their importance is grounded in the integrity of our faith and the obedience that is inherent in the reality of Jesus Christ. The answer to the question of heresy as it relates both to our past and to our present situation begins and ends with the centrality of Jesus Christ as the Liberator of the oppressed. Any interpretation of the gospel in any historical period that fails to see Jesus as the Liberator of the oppressed is heretical. Any view of the gospel that fails to understand the Church as that community whose work and consciousness are defined by the community of the oppressed is not Christian and is thus heretical. Within this context the issue of heresy must be debated.

It is true that identifying the liberation of the oppressed as crucial to the authenticity of the gospel could be interpreted as accidental to my historical situation. I admit readily that the social context of my existence plays an important role in my understanding of the gospel message. However, it would be ridiculous to claim that there is some secret language by which Africans could be persuaded by what I say while non-Africans could never understand it. Clearly there is a basis for speaking across cultural lines, namely, the Bible. Looking at the message of Scripture exegetically, we ask: Does the Bible in fact center upon the proclamation of the liberation of the oppressed? I have shown on other occasions that the message of Scripture is the proclamation and record of God's liberation, and I will speak of this again in later chapters. Indeed it is the encounter of this truth of Scripture that enables us black theologians to know that we must

> Speak the Truth to the people
> To identify the enemy is to free the mind
> Free the mind of the people
> Speak to the mind of the people
> Speak Truth.[39]

III.
THE SOCIAL
CONTEXT OF THEOLOGY

The dialectic of theology and its sources pushes us to examine more closely the social context of theological language. Because Christian theology is *human* speech about God, it is always related to historical situations, and thus all of its assertions are culturally limited. H. Richard Niebuhr makes this point forcefully: "Whatever be the case in other human inquiries there is no such thing as disinterestedness in theology, since no one can speak of God or gods at all save as valued beings or as values which cannot be apprehended save by a willing, feeling, responding self."[1] Here Niebuhr rightly connects theology with social existence. Although God, the subject of theology, is eternal, theology itself is, like those who articulate it, limited by history and time. "Though we direct our thought to eternal and transcendent beings, it is not eternal and transcendent; though we regard the universal, the image of the universal in our mind is not a universal image."[2] It is a finite image, limited by the temporality and particularity of our existence. Theology is not universal language; it is *interested* language and thus is always a reflection of the goals and aspirations of a particular people in a definite social setting.

Feuerbach, Marx, and the Sociology of Knowledge

The anthropological character of theological speech was asserted with rare philosophical clarity by Ludwig Feuerbach.

Reacting against Hegelian idealism, which equated the rational with the real and the real with the rational, Feuerbach proclaimed the concreteness of reality in its social and political manifestations. The clue to the meaning of the real, he insisted, is not found in philosophical abstractions but in concrete life, its feelings, wants, and needs. The uncovering of truth, therefore, is not identical with the rational investigation of the unfolding of the Absolute Idea, said Feuerbach, but with the analysis of the common experience of humanity. Theology is not what theologians claim it to be, i.e., a reflection upon an eternal being; "theology is anthropology."[3] What theologians mistake for God is nothing but man's "latent nature." Such is the case because

> Man cannot get beyond his true nature. He may indeed by means of the imagination conceive individuals of a so-called higher kind, but he can never get loose from his species, his nature. . . . A being's understanding is its sphere of vision. As far as thou seest, so far extends thy nature.[4]

By limiting humanity to its nature, Feuerbach asserted the social and psychological limitations of all human knowledge. Thus the idea of God is humanity itself projected to infinity. Divinity is humanity transcending itself while remaining enclosed within itself.

> That which is to man the self-existent, the highest being, to which he can conceive nothing higher—that is to him the Divine Being. How then should he inquire concerning this being, what he is in himself? If God were an object to a bird, he would be a winged being: the bird knows nothing higher, nothing more blissful, than the winged condition. . . . Such as are a man's thought and disposition, such is his God; so much worth as a man has, so much and no more has his God. Consciousness of God is self-consciousness, knowledge of God is self-knowledge.[5]

Whatever may be the theological and philosophical weaknesses of Feuerbach's view of religion,[6] he nonetheless challenges theologians to take seriously the anthropological undergirdings of their statements. It is difficult to ignore the cogency of Feuerbach's logic in view of the obvious sociological context of human speech. What people think about God cannot be divorced from their place and time in a definite history and culture. While God may exist in some heavenly city beyond time and space, human beings cannot transcend history. They are limited to the specificity of their finite nature. And even when theologians claim to point beyond history because of the possibility given by the Creator of history, the divine image disclosed in their language is shaped by their place in time. Theology is *subjective* speech about God, a speech that tell us far more about the hopes and dreams of certain God-talkers than about the Maker and Creator of heaven and earth.

The political and economic implications of Feuerbachian materialism were pressed to radical consequences by Karl Marx. While praising Feuerbach for his critique of Hegelian idealism, Marx contended that Feuerbach failed to pursue his line of criticism to its logical conclusion. Marx agreed with Feuerbach: thinking begins with sense data; perception not conception is the clue to reality. But Marx rejected Feuerbach's stopping at the stage of "contemplative sensuousness," that is, with merely thinking correctly about the world instead of changing it. While Feuerbach remained satisfied with the description of a "correct consciousness about an *existing* fact," Marx insisted that it is necessary to overthrow the "existing state of things."[7]

One of Marx's chief contributions was his disclosure of the ideological character of bourgeois thought, indicating the connection between the "ruling *material* force of society" and the "ruling *intellectual* force." Ideas do not have an independent existence but are from beginning to end a social product. "The ruling ideas," writes Marx, "are nothing more than the ideal expression of the dominant material relationships grasped as ideas."[8] Here he affirms not only the connection between sensory data and the pursuit of truth, but also the role of economics and politics in the definition of truth. Contrary to Feuerbach, truth is not simply the contemplation of sensuous nature; such a procedure leads to a philosophical abstraction and thus a distortion of the true nature of reality as sensuous *activity*, i.e., as praxis. The task of philosophy is not merely to interpret the world but to change it.[9] Truth is a question not only of what is but of what ought to be. What *is*, is determined by the existing societal relations of material production, with the ruling class controlling the means of production as well as the intellectual forces which justify the present political arrangements. What *ought to be* is defined by what can be through the revolutionary praxis of the proletarian class, overthrowing unjust societal conditions. Thus the future is introduced into the historical process, wherein thought is shaped by open human possibilities. Truth is not "a question of theory but is a practical question. In practice man must prove the truth,"[10] by destroying the existing relations of untruth. Feuerbach's mistake was that "he direct[ed] too much attention to nature and too little to politics."[11] For if he had recognized the significance of politics as the real clue to the correct understanding of nature, he then would have realized the real import of religious self-alienation. Self-alienation as revealed in religious self-projections is nothing but a reflection of the contradictions in the material world. The ruling class promotes religion because it justifies the present material relations and also because it serves as a sedative for the oppressed, making them remain content with humiliation and suffering. As long as the oppressed believe that their future is found in a heavenly world, they will not focus on the needed revolutionary praxis to change this world. While Feuerbach pointed out the unreality of the heavenly world, he did not show its revolutionary connection with this world. For "once the earthly family is discovered to be the secret of the holy family, the former must then itself be criticized in theory and revolutionized in practice."[12]

The importance of Marx for our purposes is his insistence that thought has no independence from social existence. In view of his convincing assertion that "consciousness can never be anything else than conscious existence,"[13] theologians must ask, "What is the connection between dominant material relations and the ruling theological ideas in a given society?" And even if they do not accept the rigid causality of so-called orthodox Marxists, theologians will find it hard to avoid the truth that their thinking about things divine is closely intertwined with the "manifestations of actual life."[14] A serious encounter with Marx will make theologians confess their limitations, their inability to say anything about God which is not at the same time a statement about the social context of their own existence. Nor will an appeal to the objectivity of revelation solve the theological dilemma. Although the revelation of God may be universal and eternal, theological talk about that revelation is filtered through human experience, which is limited by social realities. Therefore, not only the questions which theologians ask but the answers given in their discourse about the gospel are limited by their social perceptions and thus largely a reflection of the material conditions of a given society. Theology arises out of life and thus reflects a people's struggle to create meaning in life.

Marx's critique of bourgeois thought influenced the proponents of the sociology of knowledge, of which Karl Mannheim, Werner Stark, Peter Berger, and Thomas Luckmann are prominent representatives. While most advocates of this recent sociological discipline[15] move beyond Marx in their insistence that there is a distinction between the "social element in thinking" (sociology of knowledge) and the "political element in thought"[16] (ideology), yet they all agree with Marx's contention that "consciousness . . . is a social product."[17] This does not mean that consciousness is a mechanical duplication of social reality. Marx himself is emphatic in his concern to retain the freedom and spontaneity of thought and the point that ideas influence social structures. As his Thesis 3 puts it: "It is men that change circumstances, and [thus] the educator himself needs educating."[18] The sociologists of knowledge clarify Marx's point by emphasizing the *reciprocity* between ideas and social reality (that is, between subject and object or superstructure and substructure), so that an investigation of the latter cannot fail to provide essential clues into the conceptual universe of the former. This is what Stark means by such phrases as "social a priori," "social determination," and "axiological system." Berger and Luckmann have a similar point in mind with the phrase "the social construction of reality." Ideas do not have an existence separate from life but arise out of a framework of reality constructed by people.

Marx's chief concern was to uncover the ideological distortion of bourgeois thought which he believed could be overcome through the revolutionary praxis of the proletariat. While the proponents of the sociology of knowledge are greatly motivated by Marx's critique of the ideology of the ruling class; yet, unlike Marx, their analysis is primarily *sociological*, not political. Their concern is not only to locate the false thinking of rulers but to show that *all* thinking (including Marxism) is open to error and that *all* thinking is necessarily dependent upon a social a priori, which may or may not lead to false thinking. As Werner Stark says: "We see the broad and deep acres of history through a mental grid . . . through a system of values which is established in our minds *before* we look out on to it—and it is this grid which decides . . . what will fall into our field of perception." Stark illustrates this point by showing how the differences in British and German philosophies are partly traceable to "the great difference of socio-political development in the two countries." While "British philosophy has been predominantly realistic, sober and down-to-earth," "German philosophy has been predominantly . . . metaphysical and divorced from reality." One important reason for these contrasting approaches is traceable to the appearance of a working democracy early in Britain's history and Germany's tendency to remain "a country of authoritarianism."[19] Of course, Stark points out that such an observation is not all that needs to be said for a comprehensive understanding of the factors responsible for the distinctive characteristics of German and British philosophies; but a careful scrutiny of their sociopolitical histories does illuminate the function of a mental grid as the prerequisite for thinking.

Despite the important differences between their respective disciplines, theologians can learn much from the sociologists of knowledge. The latter, in addition to freshening up Feuerbach's contention that religion is a human projection and going deeper than Marx on the problem of ideology, also demonstrates convincingly the function of a social a priori in all thinking and thus refutes decisively the naïve assumption of many theologians who claim that God-ideas are objective and universal. Theologians must face the relativity of their thought processes: their ideas about God are the reflections of social conditioning; their dreams and visions are derived from this world. For those who are accustomed to speaking *ex cathedra* on matters of faith, this will be a difficult pill to swallow. Nor do I have the Pope primarily in mind, though he is certainly included. The domestic academic scene affords scores of cases. After Mannheim, Stark, and Berger, whatever may be their differences among themselves or our differences with them, the assumption that theological thinking is objective or universal is ridiculous.

Of course black theologians do not escape the truth of the sociology of knowledge. The difference between Black Theology and white theology does not lie in the absence of a social a priori in the former. Like white theologians, black theologians do theology out of the social matrix of their existence. The dissimilarity between Black Theology and white theology lies at the point of each having different mental grids which account for their different approaches to the gospel. While I believe that the social a priori of Black Theology is closer to the axiological perspective of biblical revelation,[20] for the moment the point is simply the inescapable interplay between theology and society—whether white or Black Theology. This means that theology is political language. What people think about God, Jesus Christ, and the Church cannot be separated from their own social and political status in a given society.

White American Theology

The dialectic of theology and social existence is particularly obvious in its white American branch when that theology is related to the people of African descent on the American continent. While some white theologians in the twentieth century have emphasized the relativity of faith in history, they have seldom applied this insight to the problem of the color line.[21] Because the conceptual framework of their consciousness has been shaped already by white sociopolitical interests, their exposition of the problem of faith and history is limited to defending the intellectual status of religious assertions against erosion by historical criticism. Even a casual look at the contemporary discussion of the problem of faith in the context of the historical-critical method reveals that such problems are unique to oppressors as they seek to reconcile traditional theology with modern scientific thinking about history.

It is not that the problem of faith and history is unimportant. Rather, its importance, as defined by white theologians, is limited to their social interests. Although oppressed blacks are interested in faith as they struggle in history, the shape of the faith-history problem in contemporary American theology did not arise from the social existence of black people. On the contrary, its character was shaped by those who, sharing the consciousness of the Enlightenment, failed to question the consequences of the so-called enlightened view as reflected in the colonization and slavery of that period.

Perhaps it is true to say, as does Van Harvey, that the Enlightenment created a "revolution in the consciousness of Western man";[22] but not all people are Western and not all people in the West experienced the Enlightenment in the same way. For black and red peoples in North America, the spirit of the Enlightenment was socially and politically demonic, becoming a pseudo-intellectual basis for their enslavement or extermination.

Through an examination of the contemporary white theological scene, it is clear that the children of the Enlightenment have simply accepted the issues passed on by their grandparents. Although the historical events of the twentieth century have virtually destroyed the nineteenth-century confidence in the goodness of humanity and the inevitable progress of history, twentieth-century white theologians are still secure in their assumption that important theological issues emerge, primarily if not exclusively, out of the white experience. Despite the sit-ins and pray-ins, the civil rights movement and black power, Martin Luther King and Stokely Carmichael, white theologians still continue their business as usual. These theologians fail to realize that such a procedure is just as racist and oppressive against black people as Billy Graham's White House sermons. This is so because the black judgment on this matter is that those who are not for us must be against us.

In this connection, one is reminded of an observation by Karl

Marx: "Philosophy [and we could add theology] and the study of the actual world have the same relation to one another as masturbation and sexual love."[23] Since most professional theologians are the descendants of the advantaged class and thus often represent the consciousness of the class, it is difficult not to conclude that their theologies are in fact a bourgeois exercise in intellectual masturbation. Certainly, if one takes seriously the exploitation and suffering of black people in America and Jesus' proclamation that he came "to set at liberty those who are oppressed" (Luke 4:18 RSV), then the absence of the urgency of the gospel of black liberation in modern and contemporary American theology can only confirm Marx's contention that "your very ideas are but the outgrowth of the conditions of your bourgeois production and bourgeois property. . . . [For] the ruling ideas of each age have ever been the ideas of its ruling class."[24]

Unfortunately, American theology from Cotton Mather and Jonathan Edwards to Reinhold Niebuhr and Schubert Ogden, including radicals and conservatives, have interpreted the gospel according to the cultural and political interests of white people. They have rarely attempted to transcend the social interests of their group by seeking an analysis of the gospel in the light of the consciousness of black people struggling for liberation. White theologians, because of their identity with the dominant power structure, are largely boxed within their own cultural history.

During slavery the social limitation of white theology was expressed in three main forms: (1) some white theologians ignored slavery as a theological issue; (2) others justified it; and (3) only a few spoke out against it.

First, it was not uncommon for Anglicans, Presbyterians, Congregationalists, Baptists, Methodists, and other assorted denominational theologians to do theology as if slavery did not exist. For example, Jonathan Edwards, often called America's most outstanding theologian, could preach and write theological treatises on total depravity, unconditional election, limited atonement, irresistible grace, and the perseverance of the saints without the slightest hint of how these issues related to human bondage. He simply defined the gospel in the light of his Calvinistic heritage; and with unusual conceptual skills derived from the

Enlightenment, he defended the Reformed faith. If pressed, he perhaps would have expressed his sentiments for the cause of freedom. But what is crucial is that his understanding of the theological task did not consciously or directly involve the political issue of slavery. Many of his contemporaries followed his example.

The second group of theologians represent those who defended the slave institution on theological grounds. Cotton Mather was one of its early spokesmen. He urged white people to teach their slaves "that it is GOD who has caused them to be *Servants,* and that they serve JESUS CHRIST, while they are at Work for their *Masters.*" Since Mather owned slaves, it is obvious that that fact alone would influence his theological observations. But he was not unique. Other highly visible spokesman for "God" defended slavery, including George Whitefield and Thomas Bacon.[25]

The influence of social realities on theological reflections was particularly obvious in the Methodist and Baptist churches' reaction to the issue of slavery during the late eighteenth and early nineteenth centuries. Immediately following the Revolutionary War, both churches, responding to the ethos of freedom, took radical positions against slavery. In 1780 at the Baltimore Conference, the Methodists condemned slavery as "contrary to the laws of God, man, and nature, and hurtful to society."[26] And four years later, at the Christmas Conference of 1784, they strengthened their position. They "voted to expel all slaveholding members of Methodist societies . . . who would not, within twelve months after due notification, perfect a legal document to manumit all their slaves when they reached certain specific ages. The conference also voted to expel immediately all Methodists who bought (except for the purpose of liberation) or sold slaves."[27] Many Baptists took similar action throughout the south.

But by the beginning of the nineteenth century, when cotton became king, the churches allowed the change in social reality to influence a change in their religious views. The Methodists not only suspended their 1784 rules within six months but in 1816 a General Conference committee reported:

> The committee . . . are of opinion that, under the present
> existing circumstances in relation to slavery, little can be done to
> abolish a practice so contrary to the principles of moral justice.
> They are sorry to say that the evil appears to be past remedy. . . .
> Your committee find that in the South and West the civil authori-
> ties render emancipation impracticable, and . . . they are con-
> strained to admit that to bring about such a change in the civil
> code as would favour the cause of liberty is not in the power of
> the General Conference.[28]

Other churches made similar compromising statements, creating
not only a place for slaveholders in the churches but providing
a context for the adamant defenders of the peculiar institution.
Indeed, as late as 1900, Charles Carroll wrote a book entitled *The
Negro a Beast*. Although many clergymen condemned it, the
attitude of the churches on slavery in particular and black people
generally prepared the way for its appearance.

The third group of theologians were those who openly condemned slavery. Persons in this group included John Woolman,
Leonard Bacon, William Ellery Channing, and Theodore Weld.
The latter achieved national prominence for his fight against
slavery. He published his views in two works, *The Bible against
Slavery* (1837) and *American Slavery as It Is: Testimony of a
Thousand Witnesses* (1839). Weld and other white abolitionists
should be commended for their courage in taking a stand against
the cultural and theological ethos of their time. They are concrete examples that social existence is not mechanical and deter-
ministic. The gospel grants people the freedom to transcend
their cultural history and to affirm a dimension of universality
common to all peoples.

However, even Weld and most white abolitionists were partly
limited by their cultural history still viewing humanity from a
white perspective, usually as defined by the Enlightenment.[29]
They almost never used the resources of black culture as an
approach to the problem of slavery but simply assumed that black
freedom would result from the end of legal servitude. This may
explain why "the constitution of the American Anti-Slavery Society failed to mention social equality as an objective" and why

its members considered its work completed after the Civil War.[30]

The attitudes of these three groups are still with us today. The second group is primarily represented in conservative churches and seminaries of the South. It is most dramatically symbolized in Billy Graham and Norman Vincent Peale. Of course, their view of the gospel is not arrived at through an open encounter with the biblical message, but is exclusively determined by the continued social and political dominance of whites over blacks. They are the best examples that religious conservatism and white racism are often two sides of the same reality.

Theological representatives in the third group are quite rare in contemporary theology. To my knowledge, only one white theologian, Frederick Herzog in *Liberation Theology*, has attempted to reorder theological priorities in the light of the oppression of black people. Others like Paul Lehmann, Richard Schaull, and Carl Braaten have been defining the theological task according to "the politics of God," relating theology to the struggle of liberation throughout the world.[31] The difference between Herzog's way of doing theology and the persons just named is the manner in which the former calls into question typical theological options. He not only makes the oppressed and their liberation as his theological point of departure, but he also rejects the process theologies of John Cobb and Schubert Ogden because he does not see how abstract arguments about God relate to the marginal people or the land.[32] What difference does it make if one should "prove" a philosophical point, if that point has nothing to do with spreading of freedom throughout the land? Whatever else may be said about Herzog's *Liberation Theology*, it is concrete evidence that white theologians do not have to remain enclosed in their little white boxes.

Nevertheless most white theologians who attend learned societies and write books and articles on theology fall in the first group. These theologians believe in rigorous scholarship and disciplined scientific thinking, but this process invariably fails to grapple with the problem of color. They conveniently play down the fact that their very definition of theology is culturally bound and thus belies their claims about universality. Indeed, if we take seriously H. Richard Niebuhr's observation that "theological opinions have their roots in the relationship of the religious life to the cultural and political conditions prevailing in any group of Christians,"[33] then it is perhaps correct to conclude that the various white theological perspectives which ignore color are nothing but white cultural projections.

Consider the definitions of theology by Harold DeWolf and Paul Tillich. The former says: "Systematic Theology is the critical discipline devoted to discovering, expounding and defending the more important truths implied in the experience of the Christian community."[34] The latter says: "Theology, as a function of the Christian Church, must serve the needs of the Church. A theological system is supposed to satisfy two basic needs: the statement of the truth of the Christian message and the interpretation of this truth for every new generation."[35] Despite my affinity with the existential orientation of Tillich against DeWolf's rationalism, there is a conspicuous cultural similarity in them. Neither one defines theology as a discipline which speaks for and about the liberation of the oppressed from *political* bondage. May we conclude that this is just a careless oversight and that, like Jonathan Edwards, they would take their stand with the oppressed? Certainly, this is the case, as Tillich's early theological treatises demonstrate and so does DeWolf's stand on civil rights. It is not my intention to question the integrity of their personal ethics. My concern is with the essence of Christian theology and the influence of culture on a theologian's understanding of the theological task. Because DeWolf and Tillich were not politically threatened in America, they did not include politics in their theological point of departure. In accepting the axiological system of American culture, they were prevented from regarding the political suffering of black people as critical evidence for the shaping of their theological perspectives. I would also contend that they missed the decisive ingredient of the gospel message. For if the essence of the gospel *is* the liberation of the oppressed from sociopolitical humiliation for a new freedom in Christ Jesus (and I do not see how anyone can read the Scriptures and conclude otherwise), and if Christian theology is an explication of the meaning of that gospel for our time, must not theology itself have liberation as its starting point or run the risk of being at best idle talk and at worst blasphemy?

The same conclusion can be drawn from most other contemporary theologians. Because white theologians live in a society that is racist, the oppression of black people does not occupy an important item on their theological agenda. Again as Karl Marx put it: "It is not consciousness that determines life, but life that determines consciousness."[36] Because white theologians are well fed and speak for a people who control the means of production, the problem of hunger is not a theological issue for them. That is why they spend more time debating the relation between the Jesus of history and the Christ of faith than probing the depths of Jesus' command to feed the poor. It is theologically much more comfortable to write essays and books about the authenticity or non-authenticity of this or that word of Jesus than it is to hear his Word of liberation, calling the humiliated into existence for freedom. To hear Jesus' Word of liberation requires a radical decision, not just about my self-understanding (although that is definitely included, as Rudolf Bultmann clearly demonstrated) but about *practice*, a decision that defines theology as a weapon in the struggle of the little ones for liberation.

The history of white American theology illustrates the concept of the *social a priori* asserted by Werner Stark and the other sociologists of knowledge whom we discussed earlier. The social environment functions as a "mental grid," deciding what will be considered as relevant data in a given inquiry. For example, because white theologians are not the sons and daughters of black slaves but the descendants of white slave masters, their theological grid automatically excludes from the field of perception the data of Richard Allen, Henry H. Garnet, and Nathaniel Paul, David Walker, and Henry M. Turner. This same axiological grid accounts for the absence of the apocalyptic expectations of the spirituals among the so-called "hope theologians"; and the same explanation can be given why the white existentialists do not say anything about absurdity in the blues. Why would we even expect them to say something, since their value system is the reason why so many blacks had to sing

Sometimes I feel like nothin', somethin' th'owed away,
Then I get my guitar and play the blues all day.

Great gawamighty, folks feelin' bad,
Lost everything they ever had.

The mental grid influences not only what books theologians read when doing their research, but also which aspects of personal experience will shape theological style and methodology. Again it is obvious that because white theologians were not enslaved and lynched and are not ghettoized because of color, they do not think that color is an important point of departure for theological discourse. Color is not *universal* they say, moving on to what they regard as the more important problems of theological scholarship. Universalism is a social product and it remains such even (especially!) when it is legitimated in pious or scholarly language. The only way people can enhance their vision of the universal is to break out of their cultural and political boxes and encounter another reality. They must be challenged to take seriously another value system. That is, instead of studying only Jonathan Edwards, they must also examine the reality of David Walker. Here truth is expanded beyond the limitations of white culture.

Black Religious Thought

Like white American theology, black thought on Christianity has been influenced by its social context. But unlike white theologians, who spoke to and for the culture of the ruling class, black people's religious ideas were shaped by the cultural and political existence of the victims in North America. Unlike Europeans who immigrated to this land to escape from tyranny, Africans came in chains to serve a nation of tyrants. It was the slave experience that shaped our idea of this land. And this difference in social existence between Europeans and Africans must be recognized, if we are to understand correctly the contrast in the form and content of black and white theology.

What then is the form and content of black religious thought when viewed in the light of their social situation? Briefly, *the form of black religious thought is expressed in the style of story and its content is liberation.* Black Theology, then, is the story of black people's struggle for liberation in an extreme situation of oppression. Consequently there is no sharp distinction between thought and practice, worship and theology, because black theological reflections about God occurred in the black struggle of freedom.

White theologians built logical systems; black folks told tales. Whites debated the validity of infant baptism or the issue of predestination and free will; blacks recited biblical stories about God leading the Israelites from Egyptian bondage, Joshua and the battle of Jericho, and the Hebrew children in the fiery furnace. White theologians argued about the general status of religious assertions in view of the development of science generally and Darwin's *Origin of Species* in particular; blacks were more concerned about their status in American society and its relation to the biblical claim that Jesus came to set the captives free. White thought on the Christian view of salvation was largely "spiritual" and sometimes "rational," but usually separated from the concrete struggle of freedom in this world. Black thought was largely eschatological and never abstract, but usually related to their struggle against earthly oppression.

The difference in the form of black and white religious thought is, on the one hand, *sociological.* Since blacks were slaves and had to work from sun-up to nightfall, they did not have time for the art of philosophical and theological discourse. They, therefore, did not know about the systems of Augustine, Calvin, or Edwards. And if Ernst Bloch is correct in his contention that "need is the mother of thought,"[37] then it can be said that black slaves did not *need* to know about Anselm's ontological argument, Descartes's *Cogito, ergo sum,* and Kant's *Ding an sich.* Such were not their philosophical and theological problems as defined by their social reality. Blacks did not ask whether God existed or whether divine existence can be rationally demonstrated. Divine existence was taken for granted, because God was the point of departure of their faith. The divine question which they addressed was whether or not God was with them in their struggle for liberation. Neither did blacks ask about the general status of their personal existence or that of the physical world. The brutal presence of white people did not allow that sort of philosophical skepticism to enter their consciousness. Therefore the classical philosophical debate about the priority of concepts versus things, which motivated Kant and his predecessors' reflective endeavors, did not interest black people. What was "real" was the presence of oppression and the historical need to strive against it. They intuitively perceived that the problem of the auction block and slave drivers would not be solved through philosophical debate. The problem had to be handled at the level of concrete history as that history was defined by the presence of the slave masters. Slaves therefore had to devise a language commensurate with their social situation. That was why they told stories. Through the medium of stories, black slaves created concrete and vivid pictures of their past and present existence, using the historical images of God's dealings with his people and thus breaking open a future for the oppressed not known to ordinary historical observation.

The difference between black and white thought is also *theological*. Black people did not devise various philosophical arguments for God's existence, because the God of black experience was not a metaphysical idea. He was the God of history, the Liberator of the oppressed from bondage. Jesus was not an abstract Word of God, but God's Word made flesh who came to set the prisoner free. He was the "Lamb of God" that was born in Bethlehem and was slain on Golgotha's hill. He was also "the Risen Lord" and "the King of Kings." He was their Alpha and Omega, the One who had come to make the first last and the last first.

While white preachers and theologians often defined Jesus Christ as a spiritual Savior, the deliverer of people from sin and guilt, black preachers were unquestionably historical. They viewed God as the Liberator in history. That was why the black Church was involved in the abolitionist movement in the nineteenth century and the civil rights movement in the twentieth. Black preachers reasoned that if God delivered Israel from

Pharaoh's army and Daniel from the lion's den, then he will deliver black people from American slavery and oppression. So the content of their thought was liberation and they communicated that message through preaching, singing, and praying, telling their story of how "we shall overcome."

Consider the song about that "Old Ship of Zion" and how "she had landed many a thousand, . . . and will land as many a more. O glory, Hallelu!" They say "she is loaded down with angels," . . . and "King Jesus is the Captain." The presence of Jesus as the Captain was black people's assurance that the ship would "carry [them] all home." The "Old Ship of Zion" was a symbol that their life had meaning despite the condition of servitude. It was their guarantee that their future was in the hands of the One who died on Calvary. That was why they proclaimed: "Glory hallelujah!" It was an affirmation of faith that black slaves would triumph over life's contradictions, because they had met the Captain of that "Old Ship of Zion" and were already on board.

At other times, the salvation story was described as "the gospel train." Blacks described this reality with eschatological and future expectation: "The gospel train is coming." And they also saw it as already realized in their present: "I hear it just at hand" and "the car wheels moving and rumbling thro' the land." One can "hear the bell and the whistle" and its "coming round the curve." Of course, this is not a normal train, not one created by white society. This is an eschatological train, the train of salvation and it will carry the oppressed to glory. If you miss this train "you're left behind." That partly accounts for the urgency of the call to

Get on board, Children,
Get on board, Children,
Get on board, Children,
There's room for many a more.

There is no excuse for not making the existential decision to "Get on board" because

The fare is cheap and all can go,
The rich and the poor are there

No second-class on board the train,
No difference in the fare.

Salvation was not only a train and a ship but also a sweet
chariot, swinging low, "coming for to carry me home." It was that
"Old time religion" that brought the slaves out of bondage, and
"good when you're in trouble." It's that "rock in a weary land"
and the "shelter in the time of storm. It was the divine presence
in their situation that held their humanity together in the midst
of the brokenness of black existence. It was the power to endure
in struggle and the patience to remain calm when surrounded by
inexplicable evil. That was why black people sang, "Been down
in the valley so long, and I ain't got weary yet." They did not give
up in despair during slavery and subsequent oppression, because
of the presence of the One who controls life and who can
overcome its contradictions. This is the theme of black religion,
and it was expressed in concrete images derived from their social
situation.

The relation between the form and the content of black
thought was dialectical. The story was both the medium through
which truth was communicated and also a constituent of truth
itself. In the telling of a truthful story, the reality of liberation
to which the story pointed was also revealed in the actual *telling*
of the story itself. That was why an equal, and often greater,
emphasis was placed on the storyteller.

In black churches, the one who preaches the Word is primarily a storyteller. And thus when the black church community
invites a minister as pastor, their chief question is: "Can the
Reverend tell the story?" This question refers both to the theme
of black religion and also to the act of storytelling itself. It refers
to a person's ability to recite God's historical dealings with his
people from Abraham to Jesus, from St. Paul to John on the
island of Patmos, and to the preacher's ability to relate these
biblical stories to contemporary black stories. The past and present are joined dialectically, creating a black vision of the future.

Black churches usually do not emphasize academic degrees as
a criterion for preaching, because they do not associate a learned
discourse with storytelling. Indeed many blacks are suspicious of

"intellectuals" in the pulpit, because of their identity of that term with white people. Black church people contend that one needs more than "book-learning" in order to tell God's story. One needs to be *converted* to the faith and *called* to the ministry of Jesus Christ. When these two events happen, then one is ready to be used by God as the instrument of his story, of his dealings with his people.

In the black Church, little emphasis is placed on the modern distinction between liberals and fundamentalists as found in white churches. Blacks show little concern about the abstract status of the Bible, whether fallible or infallible. Their concern is with the Scripture as a living reality in the concreteness of their existence. Since the biblical story of God's dealings with people can be told in various ways, the chief concern of the people is not the information the preacher includes in his message but, rather, *how* he arranges that information into a story and how he relates it all to the daily lives of the people. The preacher may begin with Adam and Eve in the Garden of Eden or with John on the island of Patmos. The concern is not *where* he begins because the people already know the various scenes in God's drama with his people. They are concerned with how the preacher takes the bare facts of God's story and weaves them into the structure of their lives, giving his unique touch as a storyteller.

Consider the sermon "Behold the Rib!" The preacher begins by emphasizing the power of God. He is "High-riding and strong armed God" who "walk[s] acrost his globe creation . . . wid de blue elements for a helmet, . . . and a wall of fire round his feet." "He wakes the sun every morning from its fiery bed wid de breath of his smile and commands de moon wid his eyes." Then the preacher moves to the essence of the story as suggested by his subject:

> So God put Adam into a deep sleep
> And took out a bone, ah hah!
> And it is said that it was a rib.
> Behold de rib!
> A bone out of man's side.

He put de man to sleep and made wo-man,
And men and women been sleeping together ever since.
Behold the rib!
Brothers, if God
Had taken dat bone out of man's head
He would have meant for woman to rule, hah
If he had taken a bone out of his foot,
He would have meant for us to dominize and rule.
He could have made her out of back-bone
And then she would have been behind us.
But, no, God Almighty, he took de bone out of his side
So dat places de woman beside us;
Hah! God knowed his own mind.
Behold the rib![38]

This sermon stresses not only the power of God but the equality of man and woman in God's creation. The rib rather than symbolizing the woman's inferiority actually stands for equal status, the right to be fully human. That is why the preacher placed so much emphasis on the phrase "Behold de rib!" The rib is not a "foot-bone" or a "back-bone," both of which represent inferiority. It is a "side-bone," thereby making woman equal to man.

Sometimes it was difficult to understand the exact verbal point the black preacher was making. But because the power of the story was embedded in the *act* of telling itself, it did not always matter. One could hear the message in the passion and mood which was created by the rising and falling of the voice as the preacher moved in bodily rhythm across the pulpit and in the aisle, describing rapidly the different scenes of God's salvation drama. The message was in the feeling of the Spirit that moved "from heart to heart and from breast to breast" throughout the congregation as the preacher hummed and moaned the story. The truth of the story was dependent upon whether the people received that extra strength to go one more mile in their struggle to survive and whether they received the courage to strive one more time to right the wrongs in this world. The message was the passion for affirming the truth of their lives, a truth not recognized in the white world. And this "knowledge" was received every time the biblical story was preached as it was meant to be. That was why the people inquired of every minister: "Can the Reverend tell the story?

The theme of liberation expressed in story form is the essence of black religion. Both content and form were essentially determined by black people's social existence. Because black people were oppressed but not destroyed by it, they intuitively knew that servitude was a denial of their essential worth. They therefore looked for religious and secular themes in their social existence that promised release from the pain of slavery and oppression. It was not simply through an exegetical study of the Bible that blacks decided to center their preaching on the Exodus and not on Paul's letter to Philemon; neither was it through exegesis that they centered their spirituals on the cross and resurrection of Jesus and not on his birth in Bethlehem. In view of their social situation of oppression, black people needed liberating visions so that they would not let historical limitations determine their perception of black being. Therefore when Christianity was taught to them and they began to read the Bible, blacks simply appropriated those biblical stories that met their historical need. That was why some themes are stressed and others are overlooked. The one theme that stood out above all other themes was *liberation*, and that was because of the social conditions of slavery. Such traditional Calvinistic problems as unconditional election and limited atonement did not occur to them. They did not debate religion on an abstract theological level but lived their religion concretely in history.

Like the theme of liberation, the form of black religion in story was chosen for similar sociological reasons. The easiest way for the oppressed to defy conceptual definitions that justify their existence in servitude is to tell stories about another reality where they are accepted as human beings. Story is not only easy to understand and to remember; it is often deceptive to those who stand outside the community where it was created. This is the meaning behind the black comment:

> The white man is always trying to know into somebody else's business. All right, I'll set something outside the door of my mind

for him to play with and handle. He can read my writing but he
sho' cain't read my mind. I'll put this play toy in his hand, and
he will seize it and go away. Then I'll say my say and sing my
song.[39]

What white slave masters would have recognized that the tales
of Br'er Rabbit and his triumphs over the stronger animals
actually expressed black slaves' conscious hopes and dreams of
overcoming the slave masters themselves? Who among the white
community would have perceived that in the singing and preaching about "crossing the river Jordan and entering the New
Jerusalem" black slaves were sometimes talking about Canada,
Africa, and America north of the Mason-Dixon line? White slave
masters were no brighter than our contemporary white theologians who can only see in black religion what their axiological
presuppositions permit them to see. And that vision usually
extends no further than some notion of black "otherworldliness"
leading to passivity. But there is something much deeper than
that simplistic idea in black religion. Nat Turner's spirit is buried
beneath the shouts and the cries. And that spirit will soon rise
and claim the eschatological future promised in God's encounter
with his community.

It is difficult to express this liberating truth in rational discourse alone; it must be told in story. And when this truth is told
as it was meant to be, the oppressed are transformed, taken into
another world and given a glimpse of the promised land. And
when they leave the church, they often say to one another what
the disciples said after having experienced the Risen Lord: "Did
not our hearts burn within while he talked to us on the road,
while he opened to us the scriptures" (Luke 24:32).

IV.
BIBLICAL REVELATION
AND SOCIAL EXISTENCE

The social context of theology is not only evident in our language as human beings with certain political and social interests; it is also implied in the nature of divine revelation. Unlike the God of Greek philosophy who is removed from history, the God of the Bible is involved in history, and his revelation is inseparable from the social and political affairs of Israel. Theology therefore is interested speech not simply because theologians are creatures of time, but because Yahweh, the God of the Exodus and of Jesus Christ, is the Subject of its discourse. The God of Abraham, Isaac, and Jacob and of Peter, James, and John is not an eternal idea, and neither is the divine an absolute ethical principle to whom people ought to appeal for knowledge of the Good. Rather, Yahweh is known and worshiped as the Lord who brought Israel out of Egypt, and who raised Jesus from the dead. He is the political God, the Protector of the poor and the Establisher of the right for those who are oppressed. To know him is to experience his acts in the concrete affairs and relationship of people, liberating the weak and the helpless from pain and humiliation. For theologians to speak of this God, they too must become interested in politics and economics, recognizing that there is no truth about Yahweh unless it is the truth of freedom as that event is revealed in the oppressed people's struggle for justice in this world.

The Social Context of Divine Revelation in the Old Testament

The Old Testament is a history book. To understand it and the divine revelation to which it witnesses, we must think of the Old Testament as the drama of God's mighty acts in history. It tells the story of God's acts of grace and of judgment as he calls the people of Israel into a free, liberated existence.

Historically, the story began with the Exodus. The Exodus was the decisive event in Israel's history, because through it Yahweh revealed himself as the Savior of an oppressed people. The Israelites were slaves in Egypt; thus, their future was closed. But Yahweh "heard their groaning, and remembered his covenant with Abraham, Isaac and Jacob; he saw the plight of Israel, he took heed of it" (Exod. 2:24-25 NEB). Yahweh, therefore, took Israel's history into his own hands, and gave this people a divine future, thereby doing for Israel what she could not do for herself. "With arm outstretched and with mighty acts of judgments" (Exod. 6:6 NEB), he delivered Israel out of Egypt and across the Red Sea. And "when Israel saw the great power which the Lord had put forth against Egypt, . . . they put their faith in him," responding with a song to the Lord:

> I will sing to the Lord, for he has risen up in triumph;
> the horse and his rider he has hurled into the sea.
> Exodus 15:1 NEB

In the Exodus event, God is revealed by means of his acts on behalf of a weak and defenseless people. He is the God of power and of strength, able to destroy the enslaving power of the mighty Pharaoh.

> The Lord is my refuge and my defence,
> he has shown himself my deliverer.
> Exodus 15:2 NEB

The centrality of the Exodus for Israel's consciousness, seen first through the people's recognition of deliverance, was further developed at Sinai, as the Exodus became the basis for Israel's covenant with Yahweh.

> You have seen with your own eyes what I did to Egypt, and how I carried you on eagles' wings and brought you here to me. If only you will now listen to me and keep my covenant, then out of all peoples you shall become my special possession; for the whole earth is mine. You shall be my kingdom of priests, my holy nation.
>
> Exodus 19:4-5 NEB

This passage connects the Exodus, the revelation of Yahweh through his acts ("You have seen . . . what I did"), with the covenant, which is the foundation of Yahweh's revelation through his Word ("If only you will listen to me and keep my covenant"). The Exodus is the point of departure of Israel's existence, the foundation of her peoplehood established at Sinai. This is the meaning of the preface to the Ten Commandments in Exodus 20:2: "I am the Lord your God who brought you out of Egypt, out of the land of slavery." *Therefore,* "you shall have no other god to set against me" (20:3 NEB).

The covenant is an invitation to Israel to enter into a responsible relationship with the God of the Exodus wherein he will be her God and she his "special possession." This invitation places Israel in a situation of decision, because the covenant requires obedience to the will of Yahweh. To accept the covenant means that Israel must now live as Yahweh's liberated people, becoming the embodiment of freedom made possible through his freeing presence. The covenant not only places upon Israel the responsibility of accepting the absolute sovereignty of Yahweh as defined in the first commandment; it also requires Israel to treat the weak in her midst as Yahweh has treated her. This is the significance of the apodictic laws in the Covenant Code:

> You shall not wrong a stranger or oppress him;
> for you were strangers in the land of Egypt.
>
> Exodus 22:21; cf. 23:9 RSV

You shall not ill-treat any widow or fatherless child.
If you do, be sure that I will listen if they appeal to me;
My anger will be roused and I will kill you with the sword.

Exodus 22:23-24 NEB

In the Exodus–Sinai tradition Yahweh is disclosed as the God of history, whose revelation is identical with his power to liberate the oppressed. There is no knowledge of Yahweh except through his political activity on behalf of the weak and helpless of the land. This is the significance of Yahweh's contest with Pharaoh, the plagues against Egypt, and the "hardening" of Pharaoh's heart. The biblical writer wishes to emphasize that Israel's liberation came not from her own strength but solely from the power of Yahweh, who completely controls history. The same emphasis is found in the stories of divine guidance in the wilderness and of the defeat of the Amalekites. The Israelites were a weak and defenseless people—a fact that played a crucial role in her election, for Yahweh in his very nature stands against the so-called mighty in their oppression of the poor. Only Yahweh is the universal sovereign ruler.

God's election of oppressed Israelites has unavoidable implications for the doing of theology. If God had chosen as his "holy nation" the Egyptian slave masters instead of the Israelite slaves, then a completely different kind of God would have been revealed. Thus Israel's election cannot be separated from her servitude and liberation. Here God discloses that he is the God of history whose will is identical with the liberation of the oppressed from social and political bondage. The doing of theology, therefore, on the basis of the revelation of Yahweh, must involve the politics which takes its stand with the poor and against the rich. Indeed, theology ceases to be a theology of the Exodus–Sinai tradition when it fails to see Yahweh as unquestionably in control of history, vindicating the weak against the strong.

The Old Testament story does not end with the Exodus and the gift of the covenant. Yahweh does not withdraw from his people's history. On the contrary, the covenant means that Yahweh's liberating presence continues to sustain the people through the wilderness to the Promised Land. And when Israel failed to keep her side of the covenant by running after the gods of Canaan, Yahweh did not reject his people. His will to save and to make them free was a constituent of his being with them. God's grace could not be destroyed by Israel's disobedience.

The conflict between grace and disobedience was escalated when Israel became a monarchy, for the rulers often forgot the Exodus–Sinai experience and the function of the King in Israel, as the protector of the poor and weak. It is within this social and political context that we ought to understand the rise of prophecy. The prophets were messengers of Yahweh who gave God's Word to the people, reminding them of God's deliverance and covenant which brought the community into existence. They also proclaimed Yahweh's future activity of judgment and renewal that was about to burst into the present.

The prophets gave a large measure of their addresses to proclaiming the emptiness and tragedy of Israel's present existence. The tragedy of Israel is due to her failure to remember the Exodus–Sinai tradition. As Amos said,

> It was I who brought you up from the land of Egypt,
> I who led you in the wilderness forty years,
> > to take possession of the land of the Amorites.
> > > > Amos 2:10 NEB

Because Israel often failed to live on the basis of God's saving event of the Exodus, she also failed to understand the significance of Yahweh's imminent eschatological judgment. Amos proclaimed the connection between the past and the future as they both invaded Israel's present moment.

> For you alone have I cared
> among all the nations of the world;
> therefore I will punish you
> > for all your iniquities.
> > > Amos 3:2 NEB

What was Israel's sin that aroused the anger of their Lord? The prophets were almost unanimous in their contention that Israel disobeyed the first commandment. The people failed to recognize Yahweh's sovereignty in history, and thus began to trust their own power and the power of political alliances with other nations (Isa. 31:1). But that was not all! The disobedience of the first commandment always has consequences in the social life of the community. Israel, therefore, began to oppress the weak and the poor in their own community. That was why Amos said, "the Lord has sworn by his holiness that your time is coming," because you "grind the destitute and plunder the humble" (4:2; 8:4 NEB). Even though Yahweh "cared for you in the wilderness, in a land of burning heat, as if you were in a pasture," you "forgot [him]," becoming "an oppressor trampling on justice, doggedly pursuing what is worthless" (Hos. 13:5-6; 5:11 NEB). Because Yahweh will not permit the triumph of evil, Israelites must be punished for their wrongdoings. Therefore, Yahweh "will be like a panther to them" and "will prowl like a leopard by the wayside." He "will meet them like a she-bear robbed of her cubs and tear their ribs apart." "Like a lioness" Yahweh "will devour them on the spot" and "will rip them up like a wild beast" (Hos. 13:7-8 NEB).

According to Amos and Hosea, Israel will be punished because the people do not "practice loyalty and justice" (Hos. 12:6 NEB), but rather "have turned into venom the process of the law and justice itself into poison" (Amos 6:12 NEB). They " 'buy the poor for silver and the destitute for a pair of shoes.' The Lord has sworn by the pride of Jacob: I will never forget any of their doings."

> Shall not the earth shake for this?
>   Shall not all who live on it grieve?
> All earth shall surge and seethe like the Nile
>   and subside like the river of Egypt.
>
> Did I not bring Israel up from Egypt,
>   the Philistines from Captor, the Aramaeans from Kir?
>   Behold, I, the Lord God,
>   have my eyes on this sinful kingdom,
> and I will wipe it off the face of the earth.
>   Amos 8:6-8; 9:7-8 NEB

We may shudder at the anger of Yahweh as voiced in the prophecy of Amos and say that the latter lacks the tender mercy found in Hosea. Nevertheless God's mercy can never invalidate his will for justice. There is no divine grace in the Old Testament (or in the New Testament) that is bestowed on oppressors at the expense of the suffering of the poor. The theme of justice and Yahweh's special concern for the poor and the widows have a central place in Israelite prophecy. Thus Jeremiah:

> For among my people there are wicked men,. . .
> Their houses are full of fraud,
>   as a cage is full of birds.
> They grow rich and grand,
>   bloated and rancorous;
> their thoughts are all of evil,
>   and they refuse to do justice,
> the claims of the orphan they do not put right
> nor do they grant justice to the poor.
>
> Jeremiah 5:26-28 NEB

And Micah:

> God has told you what is good;
>   and what is it that the Lord asks of you?
>   Only to act justly, to love loyalty,
>   to walk wisely before your God
>
> Micah 6:8 NEB

The emphasis upon justice for the poor is present even in a prophet like Isaiah of Jerusalem, for whom David's reign, rather than the Exodus, is the significant act of deliverance. According to Isaiah, "Yahweh bound himself by a covenant oath to David, promising to preserve the Davidic line to spare the Davidic kingdom 'for the sake of my servant David' . . . (Isa. 37:35; see II Sam. 7)."[1] Isaiah thus represents what scholars designate as the David–Zion tradition. Yet Isaiah, in perfect solidarity with

the prophets of the Mosaic tradition, proclaimed that Yahweh is
the God of justice who sides with the weak against the strong.

> Put away the evil of your deeds, away out of my sight.
> Cease to do evil and learn to do right,
> pursue justice and champion the oppressed;
> give the orphan his rights, plead the widows' cause.
>
> Isaiah 1:16-17 NEB

In Israel, only Yahweh is King:

> For the Lord our judge, the Lord our law-giver,
> the Lord our king—he himself will save us.
>
> Isaiah 33:22 NEB

The function of the human king in Israel is to be Yahweh's
servant, executing justice in his name. "The King is God's son
. . . He is commissioned to rule by God himself, he governs with
perfect justice and wisdom, he is the great benefactor and shep-
herd of his people. . . ."[2] As Yahweh's son by adoption (ps. 2:7),
the king is enthroned to "rescue the needy from their rich oppressors, the distressed who have no protector."

> May he have pity on the needy and the poor,
>   deliver the poor from death;
> may he redeem them from oppression and violence
>   and may their blood be precious in his eyes.
>
> Ps. 72:12-14 NEB

The poor are Yahweh's own, his special possession. These are
the people the divine has called into being for freedom. Therefore as the sovereign King of Israel whose existence is dependent
upon God's saving power, Yahweh judges Israel in the light of
their treatment of the poor. The indictment is severe.

> The Lord comes forward to argue his case
> and stands to judge his people.

> The Lord opens the indictment
> against the elders of his people and their officers:
> They have ravaged the vineyard,
>   and the spoils of the poor are in your houses.
> Is it nothing to you that you crush my people
>   and grind the faces of the poor?
>
> Isaiah 3:13-15 NEB

It is a fact: in almost every scene of the Old Testament drama of salvation, the poor are defended against the rich, the weak against the strong. Yahweh is the God of the oppressed whose revelation is identical with their liberation from bondage. Even in the wisdom literature, where the sages seem to be unaware of Israel's saving history, God's concern for the poor is nonetheless emphasized.

> He who is generous to the poor lends to the Lord.
>
> Proverbs 19:17 NEB

> He who oppresses the poor insults his Maker;
> he who is generous to the needy honours him.
>
> Prov. 14:13 NEB

Like Moses and the prophets, the wise man is concerned for the orphan:

> Do not move the ancient boundary-stone
> or encroach on the land of orphans:
> they have a powerful guardian
> who will take their cause against you.
>
> Proverbs 23:10-11 NEB

If theological speech is based on the traditions of the Old Testament, then it must heed their unanimous testimony to Yahweh's commitment to justice for the poor and the weak. Accordingly it cannot avoid taking sides in politics, and the side that theology must take is disclosed in the side that Yahweh has already taken. Any other side, whether it be with the oppressors or the side of neutrality (which is nothing but a camouflaged identification with the rulers), is unbiblical. If theology does not side with the poor, then it cannot speak for Yahweh who is the God of the poor.

As the Old Testament story continues, we see that the people of Israel did not listen to the voice of prophecy. Thus they went into exile—the Northern Kingdom in 722 B.C. and the Southern Kingdom of Judah in 597 B.C. and 587 B.C. The experience of exile was a shattering event for Israel. "They believed that Yahweh had manifested his lordship in Palestine; but could he be worshipped in a strange land where other gods seemed to be in control?"[3]

> By the rivers of Babylon we sat down and wept
>   when we remembered Zion.
> There on the willow-trees
>   we hung up our harps,
> for there those who carried us off
>   demanded music and singing,
> and our captors called on us to be merry:
>   "Sing us one of the songs of Zion."
> How could we sing the Lord's song
>   in a foreign land?
>
> Psalm 137 NEB

In the midst of Israel's despair, prophecy began to strike a new note. Jeremiah began to speak of the new covenant (31:31-34) and Ezekiel of a new heart and a new spirit (36:26). And then there was the voice of the unknown prophet who began by proclaiming:

> Comfort, comfort my people;
>   —it is the voice of your God;
> speak tenderly to Jerusalem
>   and tell her this,
> that she has fulfilled her term of bondage,

> and that her penalty is paid;
> she has received at the Lord's hand
> double measure for all her sins.
>   Isaiah 40:1-2 NEB

Again Yahweh revealed himself as the deliverer of weak and defenseless Israel. This was Israel's second Exodus, and like the first it was due exclusively to the power of Yahweh overwhelming those who asserted their power against his people.

On the people's return to their homeland there was the rebuilding of the Temple and the rededication of the community to the obedience of the Law. But Israel's story logically does not end with the Old Testament. If Yahweh is to keep his promise to bring freedom, then the Old Testament cannot be the end of Yahweh's drama with Israel. The Old Testament pushes beyond itself to an expected future event which Christians say happened in Jesus Christ.

The Social Context of Divine Revelation in the New Testament

Christians believe that the Old Testament story of salvation is continued in the New Testament. Indeed, they affirm that the New Testament is the witness to the fulfillment of God's drama of salvation begun with Israel's liberation from Egypt. This view is expressed in the New Testament itself: "Do not suppose that I have come to abolish the Law and the prophets," says the Matthean Jesus. "I did not come to abolish it, but to complete" (5:17 NEB). Without exception, the New Testament writers believe that the God present in Jesus is none other than the God of Abraham, Isaac and Jacob, and that through the divine act in the man from Nazareth something radically new has happened. On the one hand, Jesus is the continuation of the Law and the prophets; but on the other, he is the inauguration of a completely new age, and his words and deeds are signs of its imminent coming.

The Gospels according to Matthew and Luke begin the Jesus story with his birth in Bethlehem. Although most New Testament scholars rightly question the historicity of the two apparently independent accounts, both sources (often designated "M" and "L") nonetheless reflect accurately the character of the early Church's memory of the historical Jesus. Continuing the Exodus –Sinai and David–Zion traditions in which there is a special connection between divine revelation and the poor, the early Church remembered Jesus' historical person as exemplifying the same character. That character, they concluded, *must* have been present in his birth. This is the significance of the birth stories in Matthew and Luke, the Son of God Christology in Mark, and the Fourth Gospel's contention that "When all things began, the Word already was" (1:1 NEB). The four Gospels intend to express divine purpose; and the content of the purpose is disclosed clearly in the Magnificat:

> His name is Holy;
> his mercy sure from generation to generation
>   toward those who fear him;
> the deeds his own right arm has done
>   disclose his might:
> the arrogant of heart and mind he has put to rout,
> he has brought down monarchs from their thrones,
>   but the humble have been lifted high.
> The hungry he has satisfied with good things,
>   the rich sent empty away.
>
> Luke 1:49-53 NEB

From the outset, the Gospels wish to convey that the Jesus story is not simply a story about a good man who met an unfortunate fate. Rather, in Jesus God is at work, telling his story and disclosing the divine plan of salvation.

The first historical reference to Jesus is his baptism by John the Baptist.[4] Whatever may be said about the messianic consciousness of Jesus at this stage in his ministry, it seems clear from the evidence of the synoptic Gospels that something happened between Jesus and God wherein the former became aware of a special calling. The clue to the meaning of his divine election is found in "the Spirit . . . descending upon him" (Mark 1:10 NEB; cf. Matt. 3:16f.; Luke 3:21f.) and the much discussed proclamation: "Thou art my Son, my Beloved; on thee my favour rests" (Mark 1:11 NEB; cf. Matt. 3:17; Luke 3:22). The saying about the descent of the Spirit suggests Jesus' awareness of the prophetic character of his vocation as well as the presence of something entirely new in his person. This new thing was Jesus' recognition that the dawn of the time of salvation, inaugurated by the return of the Spirit, was inseparable from his person and also that this new age was identical with the liberation of the poor and the afflicted. Apparently Jesus in his own eyes was not merely a prophetic messenger like John the Baptist, who, proclaiming the advent of the coming age, stood between the old age and the new.[5] Rather, through his words and deeds he became the *inaugurator* of the Kingdom, which is bound up with his person as disclosed in his identification with the poor.

The proclamation (Mark 1:11; Matt. 3:17; Luke 3:22) following the baptism supports the contention that Jesus saw a connection between his person and the dawning of the Kingdom. This proclamation is reminiscent of Psalm 2:7 and Isaiah 42:1, and it suggests Jesus' awareness of a kingship role in the context of servanthood.

> "You are my son," he said;
> "This day I become your father."
> Psalm 2:7 NEB

> Here is my servant, whom I upheld,
> my chosen one in whom I delight,
> I have bestowed my spirit upon him,
> and he will make justice shine on the nations.
> Isaiah 42:1 NEB

If we take this echo of Psalm 2:7 and Isaiah 42:1 as a clue to Jesus' self-understanding at baptism, then his subsequent words and deeds also become clearer. Psalm 2:7, a coronation hymn, emphasizes his role as King, who is God's representative to bring justice to the nation. Here the political note emerges in Jesus' consciousness. Isaiah 42:1 refers to the Servant of Yahweh, who brings justice by his own suffering. Jesus' synthesis of these two themes produced a new messianic image. Servanthood provides the context for exercising kingship or lordship. The King is a *Servant* who suffers on behalf of the people. He takes their pain and affliction upon himself, thereby redeeming them *from* oppression and *for* freedom. Here, then, we have the key to Jesus' understanding of his mission: *Lordship and Servanthood together, that is, the establishment of justice through suffering.*

This same theme is connected with the temptation story which follows (Luke 4:1f.; Matt. 4:1f.; cf. also Mark 1:12-13). The chief point in this narrative is not so much Jesus' rejection of the role of a "political," revolutionary messiahship (as defined by the Zealots), though that may be partly involved. Most New Testament interpreters are so quick to make that point that they miss the heart of the matter,[6] namely, *Jesus' rejection of any role that would separate him from the poor.* This story affirms that Jesus rejected such roles as wonder worker or political king, because they would separate him from the suffering of the poor, the very people he had come to liberate.

The theme of God's liberation of the poor is continued in the story of Jesus' reading in the Nazareth synagogue from the book of Isaiah.

> The spirit of the Lord is upon me because he has anointed me,
> he has sent me to announce good news to the poor,
> to proclaim release for prisoners and recovery of sight for the blind;
> to let the broken victims go free,
> to proclaim the year of the Lord's favour.
>
> Luke 4:18-19; Isaiah 61:1-2 NEB

After the reading, Jesus commented, "Today in your very hearing this text has come true," thus tying the promised deliverance to his own mission.

The theme appears again when John the Baptist sent his

disciples to Jesus to ask of him, "Are you the one who is to come, or shall we expect another?" And Jesus replied: "Go and tell John what you have seen and heard: how the blind recover their sight, the lame walk, the lepers are made clean, the deaf hear, the dead are raised to life, the poor are hearing the good news . . ." (Luke 7:22f. NEB; cf. Matt. 11:5f.). This reply echoes Isaiah 61:1-2 (the passage read at Nazareth) in combination with Isaiah 35:ff. and 29:18f., which depict the day of salvation.[7]

> Then shall blind men's eyes be opened,
>   and the ears of the deaf unstopped,
> Then shall the lame man leap like a deer,
>   and the tongue of the dumb shout aloud;
>   for water springs up in the wilderness,
>   and torrents flow in dry land.
>   The mirage becomes a pool,
>   ، the thirsty land bubbling springs. . . .
>   Isaiah 35:5f. NEB

On that day deaf men shall hear
    when a book is read,
    and the eyes of the blind shall see
    out of impenetrable darkness.
The lowly shall once again rejoice in the Lord,
    and the poorest of men exult in the Holy One of Israel.
The ruthless shall be no more, the arrogant shall cease to
        be;
    those who are quick to see mischief,
    those who charge others with a sin
or lay traps for him who brings the wrongdoer into court
or by falsehood deny justice to the righteous—
    all these shall be exterminated.
                                Isaiah 29:18-21 NEB

The reply to John's disciples, like the saying in the Nazareth synagogue, shows that Jesus understood his person and work as the inauguration of the new age, which is identical with freedom for the oppressed and health for the sick. Accordingly any understanding of the Kingdom in Jesus' teachings that fails to make the poor and their liberation its point of departure is a contradiction of Jesus' presence.

Jesus' conquest of Satan and the demons also carries out the theme of the liberation of the poor. "If it is by the finger of God that I drive out the devils, then be sure that the kingdom of God has already come upon you" (Luke 11:20 NEB). Jesus' power to exorcise demons is the *sine qua non* of the appearance of the Kingdom, because freedom for the oppressed can come about only by overcoming the forces of evil. Jesus saw this victory already in hand after his disciples returned from the mission of the Seventy: "I watched how Satan fell, like lightning, out of the sky" (Luke 10:18 NEB).

The reference to Satan and demons is not simply an outmoded first-century world-view. The issue is much more complex than that. Bultmann and his program of demythologization notwithstanding, the *offense* of the gospel is and ought to be located precisely at the point where our confidence in modern knowledge encounters the New Testament message, namely, in Jesus' liberating exorcisms. Unlike the fundamentalists I am not contending that the biblical cosmology ought to replace contemporary science in college classrooms. Rather, I intend to make the *theological* point that the "scandal" (*skandalon*, stumbling block) is no different for us today than for the people who encountered Jesus in the first century. It is that the exorcisms disclose that God in Jesus has brought liberation to the poor and the wretched of the land, and that liberation is none other than the overthrow of everything that is against the fulfillment of their humanity. The scandal is that the gospel means liberation, that this liberation comes to the poor, and that it gives them the strength and the courage to break the conditions of servitude. This is what the Incarnation means. God in Christ comes to the weak and the helpless, and becomes one with them, taking their condition of oppression as his own and thus transforming their slave-existence into a liberated existence.

To locate the scandal of the Jesus story at the point of God's liberation of the poor and in opposition to Rudolf Bultmann's emphasis on human self-understanding means that the gospel comes not only as a gift but that the acceptance of the gift of freedom transforms our perception of our social and political existence. The New Testament gospel of liberation turns our priority system upside down and demands that we fight for the freedom of those in captivity. This message of liberation cannot appeal to those who profit from the imprisonment of others but only to slaves who strive against unauthorized power. The gospel of liberation is *bad news* to all oppressors, because they have defined their "freedom" in terms of the slavery of others. Only the poor and the wretched who have been victims of evil and injustice can understand what Jesus meant when he said: "Come to me, all whose work is hard, whose load is heavy; and I will give you relief. Bend your neck to my yoke, and learn from me, for I am gentle and humble-hearted; and your souls will find relief. For my yoke is good to bear, my load is light" (Matt. 11:28-30 NEB).

The gospel will always be an offense to the rich and the powerful, because it is the death of their riches and power. That was why the man from the ruling class could not follow Jesus. The price was too high: "Sell everything you have and distribute it to the poor, and you will have riches in heaven; and come, follow me" (Luke 18:22 NEB). This man was incapable of separating himself from his commitment to his possessions. There were others who could not follow Jesus because they had priorities higher than the gospel of liberation for the poor. There was the person who wanted to bury his father and another who wanted to say goodbye to the people at home (Luke 9:59f.). They, like the five foolish girls in the parable of Matthew 25:1f., did not recognize the *urgency* of the hour nor the *priority* inherent in the acceptance of the coming kingdom. Jesus expressed the claim of the Kingdom in radical terms: "If anyone comes to me and does not hate his father and mother, wife and children, brothers and sisters, even his own life, he cannot be a disciple of mine" (Luke 14:26 NEB).

Because most biblical scholars are the descendants of the advantaged class, it is to be expected that they would minimize Jesus' gospel of liberation for the poor by interpreting poverty as a spiritual condition unrelated to social and political phenomena.

But a careful reading of the New Testament shows that the poor of whom Jesus spoke were not primarily (if at all) those who are spiritually poor as suggested in Matthew 5:3. Rather, as the Lucan tradition shows, these people are "those who are really poor, . . . those who are really hungry, who really weep and are persecuted."[8] The poor are the oppressed and the afflicted, those who cannot defend themselves against the powerful. They are the least and the last, the hungry and the thirsty, the unclothed and the strangers, the sick and the captives. It is for these little ones that the gospel is preached and for whom liberation has come in the words and deeds of Jesus.

It is important to point out that Jesus does not promise to include the poor in the Kingdom *along with* others who may be rich and learned. His promise is that the Kingdom belongs to the poor *alone*. This is the significance of his baptism with and life among the poor, and his contention that he "did not come to invite virtuous people, but sinners" (Mark 2:17 NEB). The first beatitude has the same emphasis: "How blest are you who are in need; the kingdom of God is yours" (Luke 6:20 NEB). Another dimension of the same theme is stressed in Luke 10:21 (cf. Matt. 11:25 NEB): "I thank thee, Father, Lord of heaven and earth, for hiding these things from the learned and wise and revealing them to the simple." In the words of Joachim Jeremias, "God does not give his revelation to learned theologians, but to the uneducated . . . ; he opens the *basileia* (kingdom) to children (Mark 10:14) and to those who can say *'Abbā* like a child (Matthew 10:3)."[9] God's kingdom is for the bad characters, the outcasts, and the weak, but not for the self-designated righteous people. "Publicans and prostitutes will enter the *basileia* of God, and not you" (Matt. 21:31).[10] Here the gospel, by the very definition of its liberating character, *excludes* those who stand outside the social existence of the poor.

The centrality of the New Testament emphasis on God's liberation of the poor is the key to its continuity and discontinuity with the Old Testament message. The continuity is obvious: just as the Mosaic and David–Zion traditions, the prophetic and the wisdom literature focus on the divine right of the poor to be free, Jesus also defines himself as the helper and the healer of the oppressed. "Never despise one of these little ones; I tell you, they have their guardian angels in heaven, who look continually on the face of my heavenly Father" (Matt. 18:10 NEB). It was Jesus' love for the poor that caused "crowds [to] flock to him, bringing with them the lame, blind, dumb, and crippled, and many other sufferers; they threw them down at his feet, and he healed them" (Matt. 15:30 NEB). Jesus' life was a historical demonstration that the God of Israel wills salvation for the weak and the helpless. God hates injustice and will not tolerate the humiliation of the outcasts.

If Jesus' life with the poor reveals that the continuity between the Old and New Testaments is found in the divine will to liberate the oppressed from sociopolitical slavery, what then is the discontinuity? Or, more appropriately, in what sense does the New Testament witness take us beyond the Old and fulfill it? The new element is this: the divine freedom revealed in Jesus, as that freedom is disclosed in the cross and resurrection, is more than the freedom made possible in history. While God's freedom for the poor is not *less than* the liberation of slaves from bondage (Exodus), yet it is *more than* that historical freedom. And it is this *more* which separates the Exodus from the Incarnation, the Old Testament view of the Savior as the Victor in battle and the New Testament view of the Savior as the One who "give[s] up his life as a ransom for many" (Mark 10:45 NEB). While both stress the historical freedom of the unfree, the latter transcends history and affirms a freedom not dependent on sociopolitical limitations.

The cross and the resurrection of Jesus stand at the center of the New Testament story, without which nothing is revealed that was not already known in the Old Testament. In the light of Jesus' death and resurrection, his earthly life achieves a radical significance not otherwise possible. The cross–resurrection events mean that we now know that Jesus' ministry with the poor and the wretched was God himself effecting his will to liberate the oppressed. The Jesus story is the poor person's story, because God in Christ becomes poor and weak in order that the oppressed might become liberated from poverty and powerlessness. God becomes the victim in their place and thus transforms the condition of slavery into the battleground for the struggle of freedom. This is what Christ's resurrection means. The oppressed are freed for struggle, for battle in the pursuit of humanity.

Jesus was not simply a nice fellow who happened to like the poor. Rather his actions have their origin in God's eternal being. They represent a new vision of divine freedom, climaxed with the cross and the resurrection, wherein God breaks into history for the liberation of slaves from societal oppression. Jesus' actions represent God's will not to let his creation be destroyed by noncreative powers. The cross and the resurrection show that the freedom promised is now fully available in Jesus Christ. This is the essence of the New Testament story without which Christian theology is impossible.

Christian Theology and the Biblical Story

If, as suggested above, Christian theology exists only as its language arises out of an encounter with the biblical story, what then is the meaning of this encounter? Since the Bible consists of many traditions woven together, how does a theologian use the Bible as a source for the expression of truth without being arbitrary in selecting some traditions while ignoring others? Some critics have accused Black Theology of just that: a decided bias toward the Mosaic tradition in contrast to the David–Zion tradition, toward the Old Testament in relation to the New, and toward the prophets with little reference to the sages of Israel. These critics have a right to ask what is the hermeneutical principle of selection involved here, and how is its validity tested. What is valid and invalid hermeneutics, and how is one distinguishable from the other?

Black Theology's answer to the question of hermeneutics can be stated briefly: *The hermeneutical principle for an exegesis of the Scriptures is the revelation of God in Christ as the Liberator of the oppressed from social oppression and to political struggle, wherein the poor recognize that their fight against poverty and injustice is not only consistent with the gospel but is the gospel of Jesus Christ.* Jesus Christ the Liberator, the helper and the healer of the wounded, is the point of departure for valid exegesis of the Scriptures from a Christian perspective. Any starting point that ignores God in Christ as the Liberator of the oppressed or that makes salvation as liberation secondary is *ipso facto* invalid and thus heretical. The test of the validity of this starting point, although dialectically related to black cultural experience, is not found in the particularity of the oppressed culture alone. It is found in the One who freely granted us freedom when we were doomed to slavery. In God's revelation in Scripture we come to the recognition that the divine liberation of the oppressed is not determined by our perceptions but by the God of the Exodus, the prophets, and Jesus Christ who calls the oppressed into a liberated existence. Divine revelation *alone* is the test of the validity of this starting point. And if it can be shown that God as witnessed in the Scriptures is not the Liberator of the oppressed, then Black Theology would have either to drop the "Christian" designation or to choose another starting point.

The biblical emphasis on the social and the political character of God's revelation in history for the weak and the helpless has important implications for the task of theology today. (1) There can be no Christian theology that is not social and political. If theology is to speak about the God of Jesus who reveals himself in the struggle of the oppressed for freedom, then theology *must* also become political, speaking for the God of the poor and the oppressed.

(2) The biblical emphasis on God's continuing act of liberation in the present and future means that theology cannot merely repeat what the Bible says or what is found in a particular theological tradition. Theology must be prophetic, recognizing the *relativity* of human speech, but also that God can use human speech at a particular time for the proclamation of his Word to the suffering poor. As theologians, therefore, we must take the risk to be prophetic by doing theology in the light of those who are helpless and voiceless in the society.

(3) Theology cannot ignore the tradition. While the tradition is not the gospel, it is the bearer of an interpretation of the gospel at a particular point in time. By studying the tradition, we not

only gain insight into a particular past time but also into our own time as the past and the present meet dialectically. For only through this dialectical encounter with the tradition are we given the freedom to move beyond it.

(4) Theology is always a word about the liberation of the oppressed and the humiliated. It is a word of judgment for the oppressors and the rulers. Whenever theologians fail to make this point unmistakably clear, they are not doing Christian theology but the theology of the Antichrist.

V.
BLACK THEOLOGY
AND IDEOLOGY

Because Christian theology is conditioned and limited by social context through our existence in a particular political setting (Chap. III), and because God reveals himself in history (Chap. IV), we are obligated to ask: How do we distinguish our words about God from God's Word, our wishes from his will, our dreams and aspirations from the work of his Spirit? This is a crucial problem for Christian theology. Unless this question is answered satisfactorily, black theologians' distinction between white theology and Black Theology is vulnerable to the white contention that the latter is merely the ideological justification of radical black politics. While some black theologians may be content with the identification of Black Theology with current black politics, I maintain that the authenticity of black theological discourse is dependent upon its pointing to the divine One whose presence is not restricted to any historical manifestation. Indeed, unless Black Theology seeks to bear witness to the divine Word who transcends the subjective musings of black theologians, then there is no difference between Black Theology and white theology when viewed from the perspective of Feuerbach's critique that religion is nothing but human talk, nothing but human projections and illusions. Black theologians must face the question of ideology head-on: To what extent is the God in Black Theology limited to the biological origin of its advocates? Unless we black theologians can make an adequate distinction between divine revelation and human aspirations, there is nothing to keep Black Theology from identifying God's will with anything black people should decide to do at any given historical moment. Moreover, valid theology is distinguishable from heresy *only* if the former is bound to the divine One who is the ground of its existence.

H. Richard Niebuhr's *Christ and Culture*

Although the distinction between God's Word and our words is important and necessary, their exact relationship is not easy to ascertain. The complexity of this theological problem is brilliantly analyzed in H. Richard Niebuhr's *Christ and Culture*. On the one hand, Niebuhr affirms the universal claims of divine revelation in Jesus Christ which transcends the limitations of history. But on the other hand, he also recognizes that human speech about divine revelation is conditioned by cultural and historical relativity. Both principles convinced Niebuhr that Christians cannot avoid the Christ–culture problem; however, the ultimate solution to the problem does not rest with human answers, but with the One who transcends the limitations of humanity. Hence Niebuhr says: "Christ's answer to the problem of human culture is one thing, Christian answers are another; yet his followers are assured that he uses their various works in accomplishing his own."[1]'

Taking seriously both the universality of divine revelation and the particularity of theological talk about that revelation, Niebuhr proceeds to describe five typical attitudes Christians have assumed toward culture. First, there are the radical Christians who set Christ in opposition to culture. Radical Christianity "uncompromisingly affirms the sole authority of Christ over the Christian and resolutely rejects culture's claims to loyalty."[2] Since everything in culture is anti-Christian, followers of Christ must withdraw from culture. Examples of this view are found in I John's contrasting the Spirit of God with the spirits of the world (4:1f.), Tertullian's contention that Athens has nothing to do with Jerusalem, and more recently in Tolstoy's definition of Christ's new law as the opposite of the empirical churches and states and other cultural institutions.

At the opposite end of the attitudinal spectrum of radical Christianity is the view that Christ is a "part of culture in the sense that he himself is part of the social heritage that must be transmitted and conserved."[3] He is "the Messiah of [the] society, the fulfiller of its hopes and aspirations, the perfector of its true faith, the source of its holiest spirit." This view experiences "no great tension between the church and the world, the social laws and the gospels, the working of divine grace and human effort, the ethics of salvation and the ethics of social conservation or progress."[4] Jesus Christ is primarily a moral teacher and leader of the dominant values in culture. Representatives of this view are found in the early Christian Gnostics, the medieval theologian Abelard, the "cultural protestantism" of Albrecht Ritschl, and among American Christians who see no distinction between the gospel of Jesus Christ and the American way of life.

Because of Niebuhr's simultaneous emphases on faith in the universal God and the human inability to escape the matrix of culture, he rejected both of these views (the sectarian and the culturalist) of the relationship of Christ and society. While the former rightly recognized that divine revelation is not identical with culture, it failed to acknowledge that Christ calls us to obedience to God *in* culture. Conversely, cultural Christianity correctly affirmed that the works of human culture cannot be separated from God's grace, but it failed to recognize that grace is not restricted to and defined by the concrete events that make up human culture. Between the extremes of sectarian and culturalist positions are three median views, belonging respectively to the synthesists, the dualists, and the conversionists. While these Christians of the center share the sectarian view that God's work in Christ and man's work in culture are radically different; yet, like the cultural Christians, they seek to hold them together in unity. These three median answers are "distinguished from each other by the manner in which they attempt to combine the two authorities."[5]

For the synthesists, of whom Aquinas is the best representative, the relation between Christ and culture is hierarchical. That is, Christ is far *above* culture, as contrasted to the culturalist model of Christ in culture. At the same time the synthesist sees Christ and culture built into a single harmonious system, contrasting with the sectarian image of Christ against culture. Although Niebuhr was attracted to this position, he concluded that it does not take seriously enough the historical relativity of thought. "The effort to bring Christ and culture, God's work and man's, the temporal and the eternal, law and grace, into one system of thought and practice tends, perhaps inevitably, to the absolutizing of what is relative, the reduction of the infinite to the finite form, and the materialization of the dynamic."[6]

Niebuhr's fourth type is dualistic Christianity, the second alternative of the median views. The dualists affirm the paradoxical relationship of Christ and culture. For them the Christ–culture problem is not an issue between Christians and pagans but between God and us, the righteousness of God and the righteousness of self. On the one hand, dualists affirm God's act of redemption through Jesus' death and resurrection. On the other hand, they contend that believers in Christ remain subject to sin despite God's gracious act. "Grace is in God, and sin is in man."[7] This is the paradox: Christians are redeemed persons but also sinners. Like radical Christians, the dualists view culture as godless and sick unto death; but unlike the radicals, they also believe that God calls Christians to obedience in culture, sustaining them in the context of its corruption. The greatest representative of this view was Martin Luther. But others included the apostle Paul, Søren Kierkegaard, and Ernst Troeltsch. Niebuhr shared many of the dualists' convictions. He was impressed by their existential understanding of the divine-human relationship and by their dynamic interpretation of the power of the atoning work of Christ and the depth and viciousness of human sin. But he rejected its tendency toward antinomianism and cultural conservatism.

Conversionist Christianity, the fifth type and the third alternative among the median views, is the attitude that best represents Niebuhr's theological position. The conversionist defines Christ as the transformer of culture and is accordingly positive and hopeful toward culture. It is mainly this feature that distinguishes conversionism from dualism, and Niebuhr believed that this difference was connected to certain theological views about creation, the fall of humanity, and history. "The dualist tends so to concentrate on redemption through Christ's cross and resurrection that creation becomes for him a kind of prologue to the one mighty deed of atonement."[8] But for the conversionist, God's act in creation is a major theme, "neither overpowered by nor overpowering the idea of atonement." Consequently, "man the creature, working in a created world, lives, as the conversionist sees it, under the rule of Christ and by the creative power and ordering of the divine Word, even though in his unredeemed mind he may believe that he lives among vain things under divine wrath."[9] Because of this conviction about the divine creative act, the conversionist refuses to equate creation with the fall, as implied in much of the dualist language. Because "he distinguishes the fall very sharply from creation, interpreting the former as humanity's good nature becoming corrupted," history becomes the arena of the "dramatic interaction between God and man."[10] In contrast, history for the dualist is "the time of struggle between faith and unbelief, a period between the giving of the promise of life and its fulfillment." But "for the conversionist, history is the story of God's mighty deeds and of man's responses to them. He lives somewhat less 'between the times' and somewhat more in the divine 'Now' than do his brother Christians."[11] He lives in an openness for the divine future breaking into the human present, transforming human culture in and to the glory of God.

Niebuhr's analysis of the five typical responses of Christians to the Christ–culture problem should not be understood rigidly but should be viewed with flexibility and openness. His discussion is especially helpful for our examination of the issue of ideology. Given the presuppositions and the context of his theological concern, Niebuhr was right in his preference for the conversionist attitude. With this attitude, Niebuhr emphasized three important ingredients of his theological perspective: (a) the universality of God in contrast with the particularity and finitude of human existence, (b) the emphasis on the relativity of human faith in the context of culture and historicity, and (c), following from the first two points, faith's involvement in, and transformation of, culture while remaining deeply aware of its own limitations. This attitude prevents faith from identifying itself with the object of its concern even while it recognizes the importance of its involvement in culture.

While we must not detract from Niebuhr's contribution to the Christ–culture problem, his analysis nonetheless is not without difficulties. If we are to remain faithful to the theological flexibility and openness which he demanded, and more importantly, to the biblical view of divine revelation and its relations to the struggle of freedom in the black community, then we must point out these difficulties, which are connected with his definition of Christ and culture and their dialectical relationship.

The Definition of Christ: Niebuhr is right in his emphasis on the difficulties in arriving at a statement of Jesus Christ's essence. Here the theologian must be careful not to absolutize linguistic concepts and propositions in relation to Jesus' person, because all theological statements are limited by the theologian's cultural standpoint. No theologian can define Jesus Christ's essence once and for all time, for Jesus is not a category but the divine event in history who is not subject to the limitations of human concepts. While Niebuhr preferred the "moral" description of Christ, he realized that it ought to be balanced with "metaphysical or historical descriptions."[12] Because I share his preference for the ethical description of Jesus' person and work, I also must point out a shortcoming in his picture of Christ. He is right in stressing the *dialectical* relations of love, hope, obedience, faith, and humility as these virtues are particularized in Jesus' person, but he does not go far enough. Indeed, it can be said that what Niebuhr says about Christ is incorrect not so much in terms of what he says but in terms of what he fails to say. This absence is so crucial to the biblical picture of Christ that without it the biblical Christ no longer exists. I am referring to Jesus' identity with the little ones and his proclamation that God wills their freedom. If we are to accept the biblical revelation as the point of departure for a picture of Christ, then we must ask whether it is possible to talk about Christ in any sense without making his identity with the oppressed the starting point? I think not. Indeed, if the analysis in Chapter IV is correct, then the biblical Christ is primarily the Liberator of the oppressed from human bondage. He is God's revelation who has come to set the captives free. Therefore, whatever is said about love, hope, obedience, faith, and humility in Christ must be interpreted in the light of his identity with the poor for the purpose of their liberation. While Niebuhr does not exclude Christ's identity with the poor, they nonetheless are not the point of departure of his christological perspective.

The Definition of Culture: Niebuhr defines culture broadly as that total process and total result of human activity that comprises "language, habits, ideas, beliefs, customs, social organization, inherited artifacts, technical processes, and values."[13] Like his description of Christ, his definition of culture is inadequate in terms of its lack of specificity in relation to the oppressors and oppressed, whites and blacks. The particularity of human existence is important when one begins to speak of Christ's relation to culture. For Christ's relation to culture is not defined in cultural generalities but in terms of the concreteness of human pain and suffering.

Although Niebuhr's five types provide important insights into the Christ–culture problem, his presentation nevertheless is seriously weakened by his failure to make the necessary distinction between the oppressors and the oppressed as their historical strivings are related to Christ's proclamation of freedom for the captives. For example, if the biblical Christ is the Liberator of the oppressed from the sociopolitical bondage inflicted by the oppressors, then can it be said that Jesus Christ relates to both cultural expressions in the same way? Of course not! The biblical Christ stands in opposition to all cultural expressions that have their point of departure in human slavery. For the culture of the oppressed, Christ is the Liberator of culture, taking the struggle of the little ones upon himself and transforming their actions for freedom into events of divine liberation.

Of course, I recognize the complexity and the danger of identifying any human action unqualifiedly with divine revelation, and I will have occasion to say more about this later in this chapter. For the moment I merely want to emphasize the dynamic and open quality of Christ's relation to culture which cannot be limited to Niebuhr's five categories. When the scriptural witness to divine revelation is examined, it cannot be said that Christ has the *same* attitude toward all cultural expressions. Indeed the message of the exodus, prophets, and Jesus' life and death is the proclamation of God's decisive partiality toward the struggles of the unfree. Therefore, if we are to understand Christ's relation to culture, we had better be clear about whose human strivings we speak of, the oppressed or the oppressors.

Ideology, Social Determination, and Biblical Revelation

The emphasis on the concreteness of the Christ–culture problem leads naturally to an examination of the relationship of ideology and the social determination of knowledge as each relates to biblical revelation. Sociologists of knowledge make an important distinction between the ideology of thought and thought's social determination. The former often refers to the *psychological* determination of ideas while the latter designates the *sociological* element in thinking. Simply put, ideology is deformed thought, meaning that a certain idea or ideas are nothing but the function of the subjective interest of an individual or group. Truth therefore becomes what an individual wishes it to be as defined in accordance with a person's subjective desires. Most sociologists of knowledge agree that ideological thinking can occur at two levels, the particular and the total. "Whereas the particular conception of ideology," writes Mannheim, "designates only a part of the opponent's assertions as ideologies—and this only in reference to their content, the total conception calls into question the opponent's total *Weltanschauung* (including his conceptual apparatus), and attempts to understand these concepts as an outgrowth of the collective life of which he partakes."[14] When warped thinking becomes total, the psychological function of ideas is connected with the social context of the thinker. Therefore ideas can be a distortion of reality not only because of the subjective or psychological wishes of the thinker, but because the social a priori, from which his thinking emerges, is blind to certain aspects of the truth.

This brings us to the social determination of thought. In contrast to ideology, social determination is not necessarily a distortion of thinking. It is the social a priori in thought, the axiological grid without which thought cannot exist. Social determination deals with the formation of thought, the base from which thought's categories emerge. This is what sociologists of knowledge mean when they contend that social reality precedes thinking.

With this brief analysis of the distinction between ideology and the social determination of knowledge, it is now possible to relate them to biblical revelation. Here we are concerned about the following questions: What is the truth of biblical revelation? How is divine truth connected with the social a priori of Scripture? What is the ideological distortion of biblical truth, both in the particular and in the total senses? What is the connection between the social a priori of oppressors and oppressed as their thought processes are related to the truth of biblical revelation?

If the previous discussion of biblical revelation is correct (Chap. IV), then it is clear that the truth of the Bible is the story of God's call of his people from slavery to freedom. There is no understanding of this truth except through the historical consciousness of an oppressed people struggling for liberation. For divine truth is not an idea but an event breaking into the brokenness of history, bestowing wholeness in wretched places. Only one who has experienced and is experiencing the truth of divine liberation can tell the story of how God's people shall overcome.

Ideology in the context of biblical revelation is interpreting Scripture from an axiological perspective that contradicts the divine will to liberate the poor and the downtrodden. It is forgetting about the Exodus, the covenant, and the prophets' proclamation of God's liberating deeds in history. Ideological distortion in its particular sense occurred many times during

Israel's history, especially during the rise of the great prophets. The rulers in Israel began to interpret God's story in the light of the rich and the powerful in the community. They conveniently forgot that they were once slaves in Egypt until Yahweh heard Israel's cry and delivered her. This Exodus event and the covenant that followed disclosed the truth of Yahweh's revelation as the liberation of the weak. The message of the prophets reminded the people of Yahweh's mighty acts of the past and proclaimed his eschatological future wherein divine justice will be realized.

Ideology in the *particular* sense is telling the biblical story in the light of the economic and social interests of a few. It is the interpretation of Scripture as if the poor and their liberation is incidental to the gospel message. Ideology, on the particular level, is especially a serious danger to oppressed people who are afraid of the political consequences of the divine Word in their midst. The risks of fighting against oppression can lead to passive resignation. That was why the people of Israel said to Moses: "Is it because there are no graves in Egypt that you have taken us away to die in the wilderness? What have you done to us, in bringing us out of Egypt? Is not this what we said to you in Egypt, 'Let us alone and let us serve the Egyptians'?" (Exod. 14:11-12 RSV). The people's fear of the approaching Egyptians distorted their perception of divine revelation. They forgot about Yahweh's promise to their fathers and the partial realization of the promise in his mighty acts in Egypt. Could not the same God protect them from the Egyptians? That was why Moses said: "Fear not, stand firm, and see the salvation of the Lord, which he will work for you today; for the Egyptians whom you see today, you shall never see again" (Exod. 14:13 RSV).

Ideology on the particular level is also a danger for persons in the oppressed community who achieve social and economic prosperity. For personal reasons, they conveniently forget the central element in the divine story. This was the problem of the ruler who asked: "Good Teacher, what shall I do to inherit eternal life?" (Luke 18:18 RSV). Of course, he knew the commandments, and had observed them from his youth. But by asking the question he also had sensed a contradiction between his life-style and the truth of Jesus' presence. "One thing you still lack," Jesus said. "Sell all that you have and distribute to the poor, and you will have treasure in heaven; and come, follow me" (Luke 18:22 RSV). But his riches prevented him from living the truth revealed in Jesus' presence.

Ideology in the *total* sense represents that form of thinking whose intellectual grid excludes a priori the truth of the biblical story. This is characteristic of people who do not think in categories intrinsic to the story of divine liberation. They think in categories that contradict the social a priori of biblical revelation and its form as story. Truth is often interpreted in legalistic and philosophical categories. Its content is usually information about God, to be known either through assent to doctrine as exegeted by scholars or through rational, philosophical discourse. During Jesus' time, certain Pharisees identified truth with abstract ritual laws as interpreted by the scribes. The content of truth was limited to the interpretation of scholars and teachers of the Law. Because Jesus did not always use their truth language but spoke of truth also in parables and through events where the sick are being healed, they were disturbed by his words and deeds. For Jesus, divine truth was not an abstract Law but God's salvation event happening in history. That was why he spoke the truth in story form. When asked, "Who is my neighbor?" (Luke 10:29f.), he did not offer an abstract ethical discourse on the limits and meaning of duty. He merely told a story about a man who was robbed and beaten. A priest and a Levite passed by on the other side. But a Samaritan had compassion, and took care of his wounds and then paid for his restoration to health. Then Jesus asked: "Which of these three, do you think, proved neighbor to the man who fell among the robbers?" (Luke 10:36 RSV). The answer was obvious to everyone who heard.

If the truth of the biblical story is God's liberation of the oppressed, then the social a priori of oppressors excludes the possibility of their hearing and seeing the truth of divine presence, because the conceptual universe of their thought contradicts the story of divine liberation. Only the poor and the weak have the axiological grid necessary for the hearing and the doing of the divine will disclosed in their midst. Of course this does not mean that all who are poor will actually hear the Word and do the will of the One who is the Word. Often the poor internalize the values of their victimizers, thereby closing their consciousness to the events of freedom in their history. It does mean, however, that the social determination necessary for faith in God's liberating presence in Jesus Christ is present in the social existence of poor people in a way that it is not present among the rich. Since the gospel is liberation from bondage, and since the poor are obvious victims of oppression because of the inordinate power of the rich, it is clear that the poor have little to lose and everything to gain from Jesus Christ's presence in history. In contrast the rich have little to gain and everything to lose, if gain and loss are defined by values of this earthly sphere. This difference in socioeconomic status between the rich and the poor affected the way in which each responded to Jesus, and Jesus to them. While there were few of the rich and powerful who responded to Jesus' message because of the demands of Jesus' proclamation of the Kingdom, the poor heard him gladly and he received them with joy. Jesus came to heal them, to restore health to their diseased bodies and broken spirits. "Those who are well have no need of a physician, but those who are sick; I came not to call the righteous, but sinners" (Mark 2:17 RSV).

In view of the distinction between ideology and social a priori and our contention that divine truth is God's liberation of the weak from oppression, the question that theologians must ask is not whether their theology is determined by social interest, but rather, *whose* social interest, the oppressed or the oppressors? From the biblical standpoint it is misleading merely to say that ideology is the identification of God's Word with the aspirations of a social group. By that definition the Bible itself is a book of religious ideologies, because the prophets and Jesus had little difficulty in equating God's revelation with the freedom of the poor. It is true, however, that God's revelation is never static and neither is his Word ever at the mercy of human subjectivity. God's Word remains *his* Word, and not that of the oppressed. But God is free to choose the words of the oppressed as the divine Word, thereby liberating them to a new existence. This he has done and is doing in his presence with the poor. Therefore, theology that does not emerge from the historical consciousness of the poor is ideology.

Black Theology and Ideology

Black Theology, denying the charge that it is a mere reduction to current black politics, asserts that Christian theology begins and ends with divine revelation. While divine revelation takes place in history, God's reality can never be reduced merely to human goals and struggles in the historical sphere. The divine is more than what we think, perceive, and dream at any moment in time, and it is this "more" or otherness in divine reality that makes it necessary for theology to recognize its conceptual limitations. Divine revelation, about which theology speaks, cannot be boxed into the linguistic formulations derived from human experience. Any theology, therefore, that fails to accept the finitude of its categories, speaking instead as if it knows the whole truth and nothing but the truth, is guilty of blasphemy, that is, of an ideological distortion of divine reality.

Naturally the mere assertion that Black Theology accepts the above strictures on ideology is not itself a sufficient reply to the charge of its critics. In order to take seriously the danger of ideology and its implications for theological discourse, Black Theology must ask and answer the question, What is Christ's relation to human culture? As we seek to deal with that question, it must be recognized that the answer varies from situation to situation, from people to people, and from time to time. For example, God's relation to black and white cultures in America is not identical. When it is considered, on the one hand, that George Washington, Thomas Jefferson, and Richard Nixon are representatives of the white way of life, and on the other hand, that the biblical God is the God whose will is disclosed in the liberation of slaves, then the divine relationship to white culture is obvious. The biblical God stands in *opposition* to the culture of slave masters, who idolatrously usurp the power to define humanity on the assumption of white superiority. Since white theology has not transcended the axiological perspective of white culture (Chap. III), we must conclude that white theology is an ideological distortion of the gospel of Jesus.

The identification of white theology with ideology is not intended as a cavalier put-down of fellow theologians not of my genetic origin. Rather, this conclusion is derived from a careful reading of white theological sources in America from Jonathan Edwards to Langdon Gilkey. Here I found, with few exceptions, that these interpreters of the gospel are so bound to the social a priori of white culture that the liberation of people of color is at best a peripheral theme. And even when the liberation of black or red people is found on the periphery of their theologies, it is a liberation theme that is usually derived from white culture rather than biblical revelation. This is due not so much to the bad intentions of particular white theologians as it is to the social context in which their thinking occurs. Indeed, because the values of white culture are antithetical to biblical revelation, it is impossible to be white (culturally speaking) and also think biblically. Biblical thinking is *liberated* thought, i.e., thinking that is not entrapped by social categories of the dominant culture. If white theologians are to understand this thought process, they must undergo a conversion wherein they are given, by the Holy Spirit, a new way of thinking and acting in the world, defined and limited by God's will to liberate the oppressed. To think biblically is to think in the light of the liberating interest of the oppressed. Any other starting point is a contradiction of the social a priori of the Scripture.

Since the biblical God stands against the culture of oppressors, must we assume that he is the God of the culture of the oppressed? This is an important but difficult question. It is important because of its ideological dangers. It is difficult because it must be answered both negatively and positively. The positive and negative character of God's relation to oppressed people's struggle is an essential ingredient of the gospel message. In this paradoxical situation wherein God's No and Yes must be spoken, the theologian must be sensitive to both sides of the paradox, realizing that the truth of one side is dependent upon the affirmation of the other. Generally the choice of one emphasis in relation to the other depends on the situation, the people, and the time. When oppressed people are feeling proud of their successes in the struggle of freedom, and thus begin to think that *any* action is justifiable, as if their ethical judgment is infallible, then theologians, preachers, and others *in* the oppressed community must remind the people of the utter distinction between their words and God's Word. But when the oppressed are passive and afraid of the struggle of freedom, then they must be reminded that the gospel is identical with their liberation from political bondage.

The Christian theologian, therefore, is one whose hermeneutical consciousness for an interpretation of the gospel is defined by the oppressed people's struggle of freedom, seeking to adhere to the delicate balance of social existence and divine revelation. In this situation, the theologian must accept the burden and the risk laid upon him by both social existence and divine revelation, realizing that they must be approached dialectically, and thus their exact relationship cannot be solved once and for all time. There can only be tentative solutions which must be revised for every generation and for different settings. When the theologian speaks about God, he must be careful that his language takes account of the ambiguity and frailty of human speech through humility and openness. He can never assume that he has spoken the last word. But the recognition of the limitation should not lead to the conclusion that there is no word to be said. Indeed the clue to our word and God's Word is found in human history when divine revelation and social existence are joined together as one reality. From God's initiative alone the divine enters our social existence and discloses what is "wholly other" and what is "like" God. If we take seriously the clue disclosed in God's Incarnation, namely, the cross and resurrection of Jesus, then we know that we have a way of cutting through the maze of political and social confusions. Because the divine has entered the human situation in Jesus and has issued his judgment against poverty, sickness, and oppression, persons who fight against these inhumanities become instruments of God's Word.

This is the dialectic of Christian thought: God enters into the social context of human existence and appropriates the ideas and actions of the oppressed as his own. When this event of liberation occurs in thought and praxis, the words and actions of the oppressed become the Word and Action of God. They no longer belong to the oppressed. Indeed, the word of the oppressed becomes God's Word insofar as the former recognize it not as their own but as given to them through divine grace. The oppressed have been elected, not because of the intrinsic value of their word or action but because of God's grace and freedom to be with the weak in troubled times.

Thus the source of the distinction between the oppressed and the oppressors, the elected and the excluded, is not a body of rational principles derived from human experience but is, rather, God, the Creator and Redeemer of human life. The identification of the story of liberation with God's story, which troubles my critics, is not derived from the human situation. Christian theology does not move from human needs to God, but from God's revelation to our needs. This is consistent with my contention that the central message of the Incarnation is the proclamation that the divine has taken the human situation upon himself so as to redeem humanity. To be sure, there is an absolutely distinctive character in divine revelation, but God has chosen not to apply the radical otherness of divine existence to the struggle of the oppressed for freedom but to the oppressors who make people unfree. God came and is present now, in order to destroy the oppressor's power to hold people in captivity.

The task of theology is to show the significance of the oppressed's struggle against inhuman powers, relating the people's struggle to God's intention to set them free. Theologians must make the gospel clear in a particular social context so that God's people will know that their struggle for freedom is his struggle too. The victory over evil is certain because God himself has taken up the cause of the oppressed, promising today what was promised to Israel while they were yet slaves in Egypt.

> I have heard the groaning of the people of Israel whom the Egyptians hold in bondage and I have remembered my covenant. Say therefore to the people of Israel, 'I am the Lord, and I will bring you out from under the burdens of the Egyptians, and I will deliver you from their bondage, and I will redeem you with an outstrethced arm and with great acts of judgment, and I will take you for my people, and I will be your God;. . .'
>
> Exodus 6:5-7a RSV

Because we know that we can trust the promise of God, we also know that the oppressed will be fully liberated. Indeed their present struggle for liberation is God himself making real his promise to set them free.

The theological assertion that "the struggle of the oppressed is God's struggle" is not religious projection and neither is it a statement which moves from the human situation to divine revelation. It could be the former only if its validity were tested merely subjectively and not weighed against the concrete realities of historical experience. Whatever may be said about the biblical faith and black faith derived from Scripture, neither was based on a feeling of inwardness separated from historical experience. Both Israel and later the black community took history seriously and continued to test the validity of their faith in the context of historical struggle. Indeed the faith of Israel and of black people was an *historical* faith, that is, a trust in the faithfulness and loyalty of God in the midst of historical troubles. It was not from introspection, nor from mystical meditation, but from the faithful reading of history that Israel and later the black community came to believe that the God of the Exodus and of Jesus was struggling to liberate broken humanity to wholeness. This is why Absalom Jones proclaimed, on the occasion of the abolition of the slave trade, that "the history of the world shows us, that the deliverance of the children of Israel from their bondage is not the only instance, in which it has pleased God to appear on behalf of oppressed and distressed nations."[15]

Because the assertion that "the struggle of the oppressed is God's struggle" is a statement about God's initiative and not ours, we are granted the freedom to share in the divine movement of liberation. Some of my critics correctly remind me of the ideological dangers when God's struggle is identified with human actions, especially in relation to revolutionary violence and reconciliation. Being God's elect people does not entitle the oppressed to usurp the place of God and interpret divine reconciliation as vengeance. "Vengeance is mine . . . says the Lord" (Rom. 12:19; cf. Deut. 32:35). But given the importance and legitimacy of God's otherness in human history, the question nevertheless remains: *Who* decides when reconciliation has issued into vengeance? Who decides when the speech of the oppressed has lost its authentic humility or proper openness? Who decides when theology is ideology? Who decides when the oppressed are truly listening and hearing the Word of God as he invades the brokenness of their situation? As a black theologian who has experienced the dehumanizing effects of white theological reflections, I do not care to rest the future of black humanity upon the judgment of white theologians here or abroad. The decision about these critical questions must rest with those who are struggling for liberation as they encounter the eventful presence of the One who is the source of their fight for freedom.

The crux of the difference between my perspective on theology and ideology and that of my sympathetic white critics cannot be reduced to semantics alone. The difference is truly semantic to the extent that our difference in language points to radically different social contexts, which can best be summed up with the terms "black" and "white." Because they do not share the "black context" as defined by slavery and colonization, our common theological background and sympathies become incidental. The shape of our different communities and the theologies that arise from' them are not determined by our common affirmation that "Jesus is Lord." These communities and theologies are formed by the will of white people to oppress others not of their genetic origin. The "others" become a community only when they collectively decide to resist humiliation and suffering. Since my white critics, despite their well-meaning concerns and sympathies with Black Theology, have developed their theologies from the tradition of whiteness which is responsible for the oppression of the black community, I must remain cautious, even though I agree *in principle* with Barth's strictures on ideology. Checks against ideological language in theology are not derived *abstractly* from the Word of God, because God's Word is not an abstract object, but is the liberating Subject in the lives of the oppressed struggling for freedom. I believe that some of my critics probably would agree with that linguistic formulation. But the real test of the referent in the formulation is found in whether we are led to be involved on the same side in the historical struggles for freedom. We will have to wait for the answer to that observation.

Ideology and the Black Story

In the final analysis we must admit that there is no way to "prove objectively" that we are telling the truth about ourselves or about the One who has called us into being. There is no place we can stand that will remove us from the limitations of history and thus enable us to tell the whole truth without the risk of ideological distortion. As long as we live and have our being in time and space, absolute truth is impossible. But this concession is not an affirmation of unrestricted relativity. We can and must say something about the world that is not reducible to our own subjectivity. That trans-subjective "something" is expressed in story, indeed is embodied in story.

Story is the history of individuals coming together in the struggle to shape life according to commonly held values. The Jewish story is found in the Hebrew Bible and the Rabbinic traditions. The early Christian story is told in the Old and New Testaments, with the emphasis on the latter as the fulfillment of the former. The white American story is found in the history of European settlements struggling against dark forests and savage people to found a new nation. The Black American story is recorded in the songs, tales, and narratives of African slaves and their descendants, as they attempted to survive with dignity in a land inimical to their existence. Every people has a story to tell, something to say to themselves, their children, and to the world about how they think and live, as they determine and affirm their reason for being. The story both expresses and participates in the miracle of moving from nothing to something, from nonbeing to being.

When people ask me, "How do you *know* that what you say is true?" my reply is: "Ultimately, I don't know and neither does anybody else." We are creatures of history, not divine beings. I cannot claim infinite knowledge. What I can do is to bear witness to my story, to tell it and live it, as the story grips my life and pulls me out of nothingness into being. However, I am not imprisoned within my story. Indeed, when I understand truth as story, I am more likely to be open to other people's truth stories. As I listen to other stories, I am invited to move out of the subjectivity of my own story into another realm of thinking and acting. The same is true for others when I tell my story.

It is only when stories are abstracted from a concrete situation and codified into Law or dogma that their life-blood is taken away and thus a people begins to think that its ways of thinking and living are the only real possibilities. When people can no longer listen to other people's stories, they become enclosed within their own social context, treating their distorted visions of reality as the whole truth. And then they feel that they must destroy other stories, which bear witness that life can be lived in another way. White people's decimation of red people and enslavement of black people in North America is an example of an attempt to deprive people of their stories, in order to establish the white story as the only truth in history. That was why slaves were not permitted to communicate in their African languages and why red people were placed on reservations. White people were saying that black and red stories were lies and superstitions that have no place in a "civilized" country. From some perspectives, the white story of black enslavement may be a "valid" story, but from the perspective of the victims it is a tale of terror and bloodshed. From the biblical view it is an epic of rebellion, the usurpation of God's rule. In other words it is ideology.

Story can serve as a check against ideological thinking, especially from the biblical perspective. If theologians wish to retain the dialectic of story as a crucial ingredient of the gospel message, then their language about that message must speak less of philosophical principles and more of concrete events in the lives of the people. We must assume that the biblical story has its own integrity and truth independent of our subjective states. We are not free to read just anything into the biblical story. Whatever may be someone's view about the Scripture from another faith standpoint, anyone who reads the Bible sympathetically can hardly overlook its central focal point: the proclamation that God in Christ has come to redeem humankind. From this assumption, we must move through human history, Christian and non-Christian, asking what is the relation between God's story in Christ to human stories, especially to our own. By assuming that the biblical story exists independently of our stories and that it lays a claim upon us in our contemporary existence, *we are forced to move out of our subjectivity and to hear the Word that we do not possess.* And if we accept the One to whom the Bible points, then we know that the validity of our stories in the world is dependent upon his affirmation of us as his own possession. His story becomes our story through the faith made possible by the grace of his presence with us.

Although the biblical story is the major check against the limitations of our vision of truth, it is not the only one. There is the Christian tradition, the historical accounts of how others, at different periods of history, understood the story of Scripture: Cyprian, Abelard, and Zwingli, as well as Nat Turner, David Walker, and Henry McNeal Turner. We take account of such people not because they are criteria for reading the biblical story, but because they were members of Christian communities who attempted to read the biblical story in the light of their struggles. By really hearing what they said, we are taken out of the subjectivity of our present. For if ideology is to be reduced or avoided, it will be through listening to others outside of our own time and situation.

Because the Christian gospel lays a claim upon us that pushes us into relation to others, we must also be open to stories not specifically of the biblical tradition, to the stories of other religions from Africa, Asia, and elsewhere. To listen to what another culture is saying about life does not mean that we have to relinquish the biblical faith. That is neither possible nor even desirable. Indeed if one's faith is true to life and is thus the defender of life, as the biblical faith most certainly is, then the faith itself forces one to remain open to life as it is lived anywhere. By listening to another who is not of my faith, I am affirming my own faith insofar as it is the defender of life. Through this process, I am permitted to learn from another and to share with him the struggles of life. Indeed it is when we refuse to listen to another story that our own story becomes ideological, that is, a closed system incapable of hearing the truth.

Because truth is inseparable from the story of my life, I must recognize that objectivity in thought is achieved through subjectivity, i.e., the dialectic encounter of self in the situation of an Other wherein we are grasped by the One who is other than self. In story, truth is objective in the sense that what we know as truth is not self or derived from human consciousness. Truth is an event that happens *to* us and often *against* our will. However, truth does not destroy consciousness; truth affirms consciousness in the struggle to be through an affirmation of its right to be. This is what I mean by the Word of God in the lives of black people.

In black religion, story is thought of in two ways. First, there is the story of the people as a whole. This story goes back to the memories of Africa and the experience of being taken into slavery in North America. It includes the strivings of the people to survive the ordeal of servitude and to retain a measure of togetherness in struggle. But even when slavery was declared illegal, our struggle did not end, for we had to deal with the Ku Klux Klan and other self-appointed protectors of white values. The crucial point here is the universality of the experience of suffering. The animal tales frequently carry this theme. For instance Sis Goose, seized by Br'er Fox, demanded a trial. Br'er Fox obligingly dragged her to the courthouse where she found that "de sheriff, he wus er fox, an de judge, he was er fox, en der tourneys, dey was fox, en all de jurymen, dey wus foxes, too" It followed as the night the day that "dey 'victed her and dey 'scuted her, and dey picked her bones."[16] But despite, or because of, the futility of seeking justice in white people's courts, black people created structures of value through story that enabled them to survive. The victories of Stagolee and of High John the Conqueror embodied their struggle for dignity. Above all there was Jesus, the "Captain who has never lost a battle." And they responded with shouts of joy and praise, asking God to "throw round us your strong arms of protection" and to "bind us together in love and union." They pleaded to God: "Build us up where we are torn down and strengthen us where we are weak."[17]

At this point the black story moves to the second level, that of *personal* story. Personal story is accounts of individual triumphs in struggle. They are recorded in the slave narratives and personal testimonies. They include the narratives and speeches of Frederick Douglass, Harriet Tubman, and Sojourner Truth. In personal testimony a witness is made in the community of how a particular person survived through trials and tribulations, as in the case of Harriet Tubman's daring escape and repeated successes in freeing other slaves. But the content of personal story is not limited to the past and present struggles of freedom. Because black stories were dialectically related to the biblical story, the former, like the latter, moved into the future, "the time when there would be no time." Here story is a personal hope that one day this life of suffering will be over. This hope is expressed in a song by Mahalia Jackson:

> One of these mornings,
> One of these mornings
> I'm gonna lay down my cross
> And get my crown.
>
> Just as soon as my feet strike Zion,
> Lay down my heavy burden,
> Put on my robe in glory, Lord,
> Sing, Lord, and tell my story.
>
> Up over hills and mountains, Lord,
> To the Christian fountain,
> All of God's sons and daughters, Lord,
> Drinking that old healing water.[18]

Whether we speak of the story of the whole people or that of the individual, one thing is certain: we are speaking of the struggle to survive and the belief that there is meaning in life that extends beyond the structures created by oppressors. If someone asks me, "Jim, how can *you* believe that? What is the *evidence* of its truth?" my reply is quite similar to the testimonies of the Fathers and Mothers of the Black Church: let me tell you a story about a man called Jesus who was born in a stable in Bethlehem and raised in an obscure village called Nazareth. When the time had come, he was baptized by John the Baptist. After John's death, he went throughout the region of Galilee preaching that the Kingdom is coming, repent and believe the gospel. The

Kingdom is the new creation where the hungry are fed, the sick healed, and the oppressed liberated. It is the restoration of humanity to its wholeness. This man Jesus was killed because of his threat to the order of injustice. But he was resurrected as Lord, thereby making good God's promise to bring freedom to all who are weak and helpless. This resurrection is the guarantee that Jesus is the Christ who is with us now in our present and will be with us forever and ever.

I was told this story by my mother and father, and it was recited again and again at Macedonia A. M. E. Church in Bearden, Arkansas. They told this story as the truth of their lives, the foundation of their struggle. I came to know this story as the truth in my own struggle in stituations of trouble. Jesus is now my story, which sustains and holds me together in struggle. I cannot and have no desire to "prove" my story. All I can hope or wish to do is to bear witness to it, as this story leads me to an openness to other stories. Through this process, I hope to avoid imprisonment in my own subjectivity and perhaps to learn how to hear the truth when spoken by others and to speak the truth when called to give an account of the hope that is in me. (I Pet. 3:15).

VI.
WHO IS
JESUS CHRIST
FOR US TODAY?

To say that Jesus Christ is the truth of the Christian story calls for further examination. It is one thing to assert that the New Testament describes Jesus as the Oppressed One who came to liberate the poor and the weak (Chap. IV); but it is quite another to ask, Who is Jesus Christ for us today? If twentieth-century Christians are to speak the truth for their sociohistorical situation, they cannot merely repeat the story of what Jesus did and said in Palestine, as if it were self-interpreting for us today. Truth is more than the retelling of the biblical story. Truth is the divine happening that invades our contemporary situation, revealing the meaning of the past for the present so that we are made new creatures for the future. It is therefore our commitment to the divine truth, as witnessed to in the biblical story, that requires us to investigate the connection between Jesus' words and deeds in first-century Palestine and our existence today. This is the crux of the christological issue that no Christian theology can avoid.

Social Context,
Scripture, and Tradition

The interplay of social context with Scripture and tradition is the starting point for an investigation of Jesus Christ's meaning for today. The focus on social context means that we cannot separate our questions about Jesus from the concreteness of everyday life. We ask, "Who is Jesus Christ for us today?" because we believe that the story of his life and death is the answer to the human story of oppression and suffering. If our existence were not at stake, if we did not experience the pain and the contradictions of life, then the christological question would be no more than an intellectual exercise for professional theologians. But for Christians who have experienced the extreme absurdities of life, the christological question is not primarily theoretical but practical. It arises from the encounter of Christ in the struggle of freedom.

The question, "Who is Christ?" is not prior to faith, as if the answer to the christological question is the precondition of faith. Rather, our question about Christ is derived from Christ himself as he breaks into our social existence, establishing the truth of freedom in our midst. This divine event of liberation places us in a new sociopolitical context wherein we are given the gift of faith for the creation of a new future for ourselves and for humanity. It is because we have encountered Christ in our historical situation and have been given the faith to struggle for truth that we are forced to inquire about the meaning of this truth for the totality of human existence. The people of Macedonia A. M. E. Church bore witness with songs of praise and joy to Jesus' power to make the crooked straight and the rough places plain. With Jesus' coming, they contended, Isaiah's prophecy was being fulfilled. "Every valley shall be exalted, and every mountain and hill shall be made low. And the glory of the Lord shall be revealed, and all flesh shall see it together: for the mouth of the Lord hath spoken it" (Isa. 40:4-5 KJV). Because the people believed that Jesus could conquer sorrow and wipe away the tears of pain and suffering, they expressed their faith in song:

> When my way grows drear,
> Precious Lord, linger near.
> When my life is almost gone,
> Hear my cry, hear my call,
> Hold my hand lest I fall.
> Take my hand, Precious Lord,
> Lead me home.

It is therefore the people's experience of the freedom of Christ in the context of injustice and oppression that makes them want to know more about him. Who is this Christ who lightens our burdens and eases our pain? It is our faith in him, born of our deliverance by him here and now, that leads us to the christological question.

On the other hand, the truth of Jesus Christ, whom we meet in our social existence, is not exhausted by the questions we ask. The meaning of Christ is not derived from nor dependent upon our social context. There is an otherness which we experience in the encounter with Christ that forces us to look beyond our immediate experience to other witnesses. One such witness is Scripture. The Bible, it is important to note, does not consist of units of infallible truth about God or Jesus. Rather, it tells the story of God's will to redeem humankind from sin, death, and Satan. According to the New Testament witnesses, God's decisive act against these powers happened in Jesus' life, death, and resurrection. According to Luke's account in Acts, Peter told the story in this manner:

> You know about Jesus of Nazareth, how God anointed him with the Holy Spirit and with power. He went about doing good and healing all who were oppressed by the devil, for God was with him. And we can bear witness to all that he did in the Jewish country-side and in Jerusalem. He was put to death by hanging on a gibbet; but God raised him to life on the third day, and allowed him to appear, not to the whole people, but to witnesses whom God had chosen in advance—to us, who ate and drank with him after he rose from the dead. He commanded us to proclaim him to the people, and affirm that he is the one who has been designated by God as judge of the living and the dead. It is to him that all prophets testify, declaring that everyone who trusts in him receives forgiveness of sins through his name.
>
> Acts 10:38-43 NEB

This passage is one of several succinct accounts of the early apostles' witness to the revelatory significance of Jesus of Nazareth. The variety of these testimonies enriches our perception of Christ while reminding us that words cannot capture him. The Gospel of Mark speaks of him as the Son of God, while John's

Gospel says that he is "the offspring of God himself," "the Word [that] became flesh to dwell among us" (1:13-14 NEB). For the writer of I Timothy, Jesus was

> He who was manifested in the body,
>   vindicated in the spirit,
>   seen by angels;
> who was proclaimed among the nations,
>   believed in throughout the world,
>   glorified in high heaven.
>
> I Timothy 3:16 NEB

In contrast to I Timothy's emphasis on Jesus as a manifestation of the divine glory (with no stress on his pre-existence), the apostle Paul declared that the divine glory is not revealed, but hidden in the form of a slave. "For the divine nature was his from the first; yet he did not think to snatch at equality with God, but made himself nothing, assuming the nature of a slave, . . . and in obedience accepted even death—death on a cross" (Phil. 2:6,8 NEB).

The New Testament is the early Church's response to the history of Jesus Christ. That response is important for our christological reflections, because the Bible is our primary source of information about the Jesus we encounter in our social existence. Black people in America had great confidence in the holy Book. This confidence has not been shaken by the rise of historical criticism and its impact on the Bible as reflected in theological writings from Rudolf Bultmann's "New Testament and Mythology"[1] to James Barr's *The Bible in the Modern World.*[2] This does not mean that black people are fundamentalists in the strict sense of the term. They have not been preoccupied with definitions of inspiration and infallibility. Accordingly, their confidence in the Book has not been so brittle or contentious as that of white conservatives. It is as if blacks have intuitively drawn the all-important distinction between infallibility and reliability. They have not contended for a fully explicit infallibility, feeling perhaps that there is mystery in the Book, as there is in the Christ. What they have testified to is the Book's reliability: how it is the true and basic source for discovering the truth of Jesus Christ.

For this reason there has been no crisis of biblical authority in the black community. The Jesus of black experience is the Christ of Scripture, the One who was born in Bethlehem, grew up in Nazareth, taught in Galilee, and died and was resurrected in Jerusalem.

The authority of the Bible for Christology, therefore, does not lie in its objective status as the literal Word of God. Rather, it is found in its power to point to the One whom the people have met in the historical struggle of freedom. Through the reading of Scripture, the people not only hear other stories about Jesus that enable them to move beyond the privateness of their own story; but through faith because of divine grace, they are taken from the present to the past and then thrust back into their contemporary history with divine power to transform the sociopolitical context. This event of transcendence enables the people to break the barriers of time and space as they walk and talk with Jesus in Palestine along with Peter, James, and John. They can hear his cry of pain and experience the suffering as he is nailed on the cross and pierced in the side.

> They nail my Jesus down
> They put him on the crown of thorns,
> O see my Jesus hangin' high!
> He look so pale an' bleed so free:
> O don't you think it was a shame,
> He hung three hours in dreadful pain?

They also can experience the divine victory of Jesus' resurrection.

> Weep no more, Marta,
> Weep no more, Mary,
> Jesus rise from the dead,
> Happy Morning.

When the people are thrown back into their present social context, they bring with them this sense of having been a witness to Jesus' life, death, and resurrection. Through the experience of moving back and forth between the first and the twentieth centuries, the Bible is transformed from just a report of what the disciples believed about Jesus to black people's personal story of God's will to liberate the oppressed in their contemporary context. They can now testify with the apostle Paul: "For I am not ashamed of the Gospel. It is the saving power of God for everyone who has faith . . . because here is revealed God's way of righting wrong, a way that starts from faith and ends in faith" (Rom. 1:16-17 NEB).

Who Jesus is for us today is not decided by focusing our attention exclusively on either the social context alone or the Bible alone but by seeing them in dialectical relation. The true interpretation of one is dependent upon viewing it in the light of the other. We must say unequivocally that who Jesus Christ is for black people today is found through an encounter with him in the social context of black existence. But as soon as that point is made, the other side of this paradox must be affirmed; otherwise the truth of the black experience is distorted. The Jesus of the black experience is the Jesus of Scripture. The dialectic relationship of the black experience and Scripture is the point of departure of Black Theology's Christology.

Serving as an authority, in addition to Scripture, is the tradition of the Church. Tradition is important because it is the bridge that connects Scripture with our contemporary situation. While tradition does not carry the same weight of authority as Scripture, our understanding of the meaning of Jesus Christ in the latter is mediated through the former. Tradition then represents the Church's affirmation of faith in Jesus Christ at different periods of its history. By looking at the meaning of Jesus Christ in the latter, he is mediated through the former. By looking at the meaning of Jesus Christ in different church traditions, we are given clues to ways of understanding him today. Tradition, like Scripture, opens our story of Christ to other stories in the past and thus forces us to move outside of the subjectivity of our present. Tradition requires that we ask, What has my experience of Christ today to do with the Christ of Nestorius of Constantinople and Cyril of Alexandria?

However we must not forget that what is usually called "tradition" represents the Church's theological justification of its existence on the basis of its support of the state in the oppression of the poor. What are we to make of a tradition that investigated the meaning of Christ's relation to God and the divine and human natures in his person, but failed to relate these christological issues to the liberation of the slave and the poor in the society? We must not only ask about the social context of the tradition that made it possible for the Church to treat Christ's relations to the slave as peripheral to its proclamation of the gospel, but must press the question to its logical conclusion: In the absence of the theme of freedom or the liberation of the slave, did the Church lose the very essence of the gospel of Jesus Christ?

Whether we answer the foregoing question negatively or positively, it is no less true that American black people have a tradition of their own that stretches back to Africa and its traditional religions. We are an *African* people, at least to the degree that our grandparents came from Africa and not from Europe. They brought with them their stories and combined them with the Christian story, thereby creating a black religious tradition unique to North America. African culture informed black people's perspective on Christianity and made it impossible for many slaves to accept an interpretation of the Jesus story that violated their will for freedom. The passive Christ of white Christianity when combined with African culture became the Liberator of the oppressed from sociopolitical oppression. Under the influence of this Christ, Richard Allen and James Varick led black people to separate themselves from the white Methodist Church. At another time, Nat Turner saw Jesus as the spirit of violent revolution against the structures of slavery. Again this Christ takes the black believer out of history entirely and places him in a new heaven where the streets are gold and the gates are pearl. But in every case, Christ is the *otherness* in the black experience that makes possible the affirmation of black humanity in an inhumane situation. We must turn to this tradition of black Christology for a perspective on Jesus Christ that will enable us to address the right questions to the "classical" tradition and also locate the Christ of Scripture in our contemporary situation.

By focusing on the black tradition, we not only receive a check against the inordinate influence of the "classical" tradition but also gain a fresh perspective for interpreting Scripture in the light of Christ. The black tradition breaks down the false distinctions between the sacred and the secular and invites us to look for Christ's meaning in the spirituals and the blues, folklore and sermon. Christ's meaning is not only expressed in formal church doctrine but also in the rhythm, the beat, and the swing of life, as the people respond to the vision that stamps dignity upon their personhood. It does not matter whether the vision is received on Saturday night or Sunday morning or whether the interpreter of the vision is bluesman B. B. King or the Rev. C. L. Franklin. Some people will be able to participate in both expressions without experiencing any contradiction. Others will feel at home with only one, whether blues or spiritual. But the crucial point is that both expressions represent the people's attempt to transcend, to "step over,"[3] the limitations placed on them by white society. This is the context for a black analysis of Christ's meaning for today.

To summarize: the dialectic between the social situation of the believer and Scripture and the traditions of the Church is the place to begin the investigation of the question, Who is Jesus Christ for us today? Social context, Scripture, and tradition operate together to enable the people of God to move actively and reflectively with Christ in the struggle of freedom.

Jesus Is Who He was

The dialectic of Scripture and tradition in relation to our contemporary social context forces us to affirm that there is no knowledge of Jesus Christ today that contradicts who he was yesterday, i.e., his historical appearance in first-century Palestine. Jesus' past is the clue to his present activity in the sense that his past is the medium through which he is made accessible to us today. The historical Jesus is indispensable for a knowledge of the Risen Christ. If it can be shown that the New Testament contains no reliable historical information about Jesus of Nazareth or that the kerygma (early Christian preaching) bears no relation to the historical Jesus, then Christian theology is an impossible enterprise.

In this sense Wolfhart Pannenberg is correct in his insistence that Christology must begin "from below" with the historical

Jesus and not "from above" with the divine Logos separated from the Jesus of history. "Jesus possesses significance 'for us,'" writes Pannenberg, "only to the extent that this significance is inherent in himself, in his history, and in his person constituted by this history. Only when this can be shown may we be sure that we are not merely attaching our questions, wishes, and thoughts to his figure."[4] If we do not take the historical Jesus seriously as the key to locating the meaning of Christ's presence today, there is no way to avoid the charge of subjectivism, the identification of Christ today with a momentary political persuasion. Although it cannot "prove," by historical study alone, that Jesus is the Christ, the historical record provides the essential datum without which faith in Christ is impossible.[5]

The error of separating the historical Jesus from the Christ of faith has a long history. The Church Fathers, including the great theologian Athanasius, tended to make Jesus' divinity the point of departure for an understanding of his humanity. Therefore, whatever else may be said about the limitations of Harnack's perspective on the *History of Dogma*, he was not too far wrong in his contention that "no single outstanding church teacher really accepted the humanity [of Jesus] in a perfectly unqualified way."[6] For example, Athanasius stressed the humanity of Jesus because without becoming human, Christ could not have divinized us. "For he was made man," writes Athanasius, "that we might be made God".[7] Here, as with other church teachers, soteriology determined Christology. Who Christ is was controlled by the Greek view of what God had to do to save man. Few, if any, of the early Church Fathers grounded their christological arguments in the concrete history of Jesus of Nazareth. Consequently, little is said about the significance of his ministry to the poor as a definition of his person. The Nicene Fathers showed little interest in the christological significance of Jesus' deeds for the humiliated, because most of the discussion took place in the social context of the Church's position as the favored religion of the Roman State. It therefore became easy to define Jesus as the divinizer (the modern counterpart is "spiritualizer") of humanity. When this happens Christology is removed from history, and salvation becomes only peripherally related to this world.

This tendency continued through the Middle Ages and, as Schweitzer demonstrated, into the modern German tradition.[8] The historical Jesus was separated from the Christ of faith, and the result was docetism. The historical component of the New Testament witness was subordinated or discredited, leaving Christ's humanity without support. This was the danger of Kierkegaard's contention that "from history one can learn nothing about Christ"[9] and of Bultmann's program of demythologization. If the historical Jesus is unimportant, then the true humanity of Christ is relegated to the periphery of christological analysis. At best Christ's humanity is merely verbalized for the purpose of focusing on his divinity.

This error was evident in the early developments of "dialectical theology" as represented in Emil Brunner's *The Mediator*[10] and in Karl Barth's emphasis on Christ as the Revealed Word. Barth's stress on Christ as the Word of God who stands in judgment on man's word led him to subordinate the historical Jesus in his analysis of the Christian gospel. For example, he admitted in the "Preface to the Second Edition" of *The Epistle to the Romans* (1921) that his system is "limited to a recognition of what Kierkegaard called the 'infinite qualitative distinction' between time and eternity."[11] And since the historical Jesus lived in time, Barth's avowed concern to hear God's eternal Word caused him to play down the human side of Christ's presence. To be sure, the 1920s and the 1930s needed that emphasis, and later Barth corrected much of this one-sided view in *The Humanity of God* (1956).[12] But he never really recovered from the early theme of God's absolute transcendence and thus did not achieve the proper dialectical relationship between the historical Jesus and the Christ of faith.

Recently contemporary theologians have attempted to correct the one-sidedness of the early Church and the implied docetism of dialectical theologians. Pannenberg is a case in point: "Where the statement that Jesus is God would contradict his real humanity, one would probably rather surrender the confession of his divinity than to doubt that he was really a man."[13] In my perspective, this means that Christology must begin with an affirmation of who Jesus was in his true humanity in history, using that point as the clue to who Jesus is for us today.

The docetic error crossed the Atlantic to North America in the seventeenth century. Particularly during the nineteenth century, it displayed special "made in U.S.A" features, as white theologians and preachers contended that slavery was consistent with the gospel of Jesus. Like their German contemporaries whom Schweitzer criticized for allowing subjective interests to determine their analyses of the historical Jesus, the white American Church's analysis of Christ was defined by white people's political and economic interests, and not by the biblical witness.

Black slaves, on the other hand, contended that slavery contradicts the New Testament Christ. They claimed to know about a Christ who came to give freedom and dignity to the oppressed and humiliated. Through sermon, prayer, and song, black slaves bore witness to the little baby that was born of "Sister Mary" in Bethlehem and "everytime the baby cried, she'd a-rocked Him in the weary land." He is the One who lived with the poor and died on the cross so that they might have a new life. The white minister preached to black people about the joys of heaven from a white viewpoint, saying: "Now you darkies need not worry, for God has some mighty good asphalt streets and cement streets for you to walk on." But Uncle Jim's prayerful response to the white minister put the situation quite differently: "Lawd, I knows dat I's your child and when I gets to heaven I's gonna walk any damn where I please."[14] Now if there is no real basis for Uncle Jim's faith in the historical Jesus, then the distinction between the white minister's and Uncle Jim's claims about God are limited to a difference in their social contexts. The same is true of contemporary white theology and Black Theology. Unless the latter takes seriously who Jesus was as the key to who he is today, then black theologians have no reason to complain about white people using Jesus Christ for the advancement of the present system of oppression.

My assertion that "Jesus is who he was" affirms not only the importance of Scripture as the basis of Christology. It also stresses the biblical emphasis on Jesus' humanity in history as the starting point of christological analysis. For without the historical Jesus, theology is left with a docetic Christ who is said to be human but is actually nothing but an idea-principle in a theological system. We cannot have a human Christ unless we have a historical Christ, that is, unless we *know* his history. That is why the writers of the four Gospels tell the good news in the form of the story of Jesus' life. The events described are not intended as fiction but as God's way of changing the course of history in a human person.

The historical Jesus emphasizes the social context of Christology and thereby establishes the importance of Jesus' racial identity. *Jesus was a Jew!* The particularity of Jesus' person as disclosed in his Jewishness is indispensable for christological analysis. On the one hand, Jesus' Jewishness pinpoints the importance of his humanity for faith, and on the other, connects God's salvation drama in Jesus with the Exodus–Sinai event. Through the divine election of Jesus the Jew as the means of human salvation, Yahweh makes real the divine promise that through Abraham "all the families of the earth shall bless themselves" (Gen. 12:3 RSV). In order to keep the divine promise to make Israel "a kingdom of priests and a holy nation" (Exod. 19:6 RSV), Yahweh became a Jew in Jesus of Nazareth, thereby making possible the reconciliation of the world to himself (I Cor. 5:19). Jesus' Jewishness therefore was essential to his person. He was not a "universal" man but a particular Jew who came to fulfill God's will to liberate the oppressed. His Jewishness establishes the concreteness of his existence in history, without which Christology inevitably moves in the direction of docetism.

The humanity of Jesus was the emphasis of black slaves when they sang about his suffering and pain during the crucifixion.

Were you there when they crucified my Lord?
  were you there when they crucified my Lord?
Oh! sometimes it causes me to tremble, tremble, tremble;
  were you there when they crucified my Lord?

With deep passion and a transcendent leap back into first-century Jerusalem, black people described the details of Jesus suffering on the cross: "Dey whupped him up de hill," "dey crowned him wid a thorny crown," "dey nailed him to de cross," "dey pierced him in de side," "de blood came twinklin' down, an' he never said a mumbalin' word, he jes hung his head an' he died." Unless the biblical story is historically right in its picture of the humanity of Jesus, then there is no reason to believe that he shared our suffering and pain.

The authenticity of the New Testament Jesus guarantees the integrity of his human presence with the poor and the wretched in the struggle of freedom. In Jesus' presence with the poor in Palestine, he disclosed who they were and what they were created to be (Heb. 2: 17-18). Likewise, we today can lay claim on the same humanity that was liberated through Jesus' cross and resurrection. Because Jesus lived, we now know that servitude is inhuman, and that Christ has set us free to live as liberated sons and daughters of God. Unless Jesus was truly like us, then we have no reason to believe that our true humanity is disclosed in his person. Without Jesus' humanity constituted in real history, we have no basis to contend that his coming bestows upon us the courage and the wisdom to struggle against injustice and oppression.

Jesus Is Who He Is

To declare that God raised Jesus from the dead is to say that our knowledge of Jesus is not limited to his life in Palestine. Jesus is not merely a historical person who once identified with the poor people of his land and subsequently was executed by the Roman authorities for disturbing the social and political status quo. The Crucified One is also the Risen Lord. Faith in the resurrection means that the historical Jesus, in his liberating words and deeds for the poor, was God's way of breaking into human history, redeeming humanity from injustice and violence, and bestowing power upon little ones in their struggle for freedom.

While the *wasness* of Jesus is Christology's point of departure, thereby establishing Christ's inseparable relationship with the historical Jesus, the *isness* of Jesus relates his past history to his present involvement in our struggle. Unless his past existence is the clue to his present presence with us in our fight for justice, then what Jesus did in first-century Palestine is of little consequence to human existence. Against Pannenberg who uses the historical Jesus as the sole criterion for Christology, I contend that our interest in Jesus' past cannot be separated from one's encounter with his presence in our contemporary existence. To be sure, Pannenberg is correct in his insistence that soteriology should not determine Christology. Our subjectivity must not be the starting point for the definition of Jesus' person. But unlike Pannenberg, I contend that Jesus' historicity alone is insufficient christologically. In his effort to correct the soteriologically determined Christologies of the existentialists school, especially Rudolf Bultmann, Pannenberg overreacted in the opposite direction. We do not have to choose between a Christology either "from below" or "from above." Instead we should keep both in dialectical relation, recognizing that Christ's meaning for us today is found in our encounter with the historical Jesus as the Crucified and Risen Lord who is present with us in the struggle of freedom. Indeed, it is Jesus' soteriological value as revealed in his past, experienced in our present, and promised in God's future that makes us know that it is worthwhile, indeed necessary, to inquire about his person. It is because the people have encountered the power of his presence in their social existence that they are motivated to ask, "What manner of man is this?" One person might answer the question this way: "He is my helper in time of distress. He is the One that's been so good to me, he gave me victory, the Son of the Almighty God we serve." Another might testify to Jesus' presence by claiming that "he is the One who makes things right, and that's why I have to 'steal away' to him in prayer, for 'I ain't got long to stay here.' He is the One who 'calls me by the thunder,' and 'he calls me by the lightning,' 'the trumpet sounds within my soul'; and then I know that 'I ain't got long to stay here.'"

If Pannenberg is right when he says that "no one now has an experience of [Christ] as risen and exalted, at least not an experience that could be distinguished with certainty from illusion" because "the *experience* of the presence of Christ is promised for the end of time,"[15] then black religion is nothing but an account of black people's subjective fancies. I reject Pannenberg's conclusions about the absence of Christ in our present not only because of the Scripture's testimony about the promise and presence of Christ's Holy Spirit (Acts 1:8; 2:1f.), but also because of the witness of the black Church tradition and the contemporary testimonies of black people, all of whom proclaim Christ's present power to "make a way out of no way." As a black theologian whose consciousness was shaped in a black community moving from slavery to freedom, I must take my stand against Pannenberg and with my people who say that Jesus has not left us alone but is with us in the struggle of freedom. According to the black religious story, black people could survive the slave ships and auction blocks because Jesus was present with them. Jesus gave them dignity in the midst of humiliation. He gave them freedom as whites attempted to define blacks as slaves. Now I realize that not all blacks survived the brutalities of slavery, and that fact alone raises some crucial questions about the justice and righteousness of God, an issue that I will discuss in Chapter VIII. Here I merely want to argue that Jesus' identity for us today cannot be separated from his presence with us in our present existence. Without the certainty that Christ is with us as the historical Jesus was present with the humiliated and weak in Palestine, how can black people account for the power and courage to struggle against slave masters and overseers in the nineteenth century and the Ku Klux Klan and policeman in the twentieth? What is it that keeps the community together when there are so many scares and hurts? What is it that gives them the will and the courage to struggle in hope when so much in their environment says that fighting is a waste of time? I think that the only "reasonable" and "objective" explanation is to say that the people are right when they proclaim the presence of the divine power, wholly different from themselves. I can remember, at an early age, the people of Bearden bearing witness to the power and meaning of Jesus in their lives. There were times when the burden and the agony of life became very difficult, and the people felt powerless to do anything to change sorrow into joy. These occasions happened when somebody's house was destroyed by fire, leaving a family shelterless with winter approaching. Then there was death, an ever present enemy, who came like a "train blowin' at the station," leaving somebody a "motherless child." The most visible symbol of death's power was found in the everyday presence of white people who violated black dignity at every level of black existence. Black people had to deal with the reality of whites on the job, in the stores, and at other significant areas of human affirmation. Sometimes the people were passive and speechless, not knowing how to respond to the extreme contradictions of life. But on Sunday morning, after spending six days of struggling to create meaning out of life, the people of Bearden would go to church, because they believed that Jesus was going to be there with an answer for their troubling minds. At Macedonia A. M. E. Church, Sister Ora Wallace would line a familiar hymn, investing a depth of passion and meaning far greater then Isaac Watts ever intended.

> O God, our help in ages past
> Our hope for years to come,
> Our shelter from the stormy blast,
> And our eternal home.
>
> Beneath the shadow of Thy throne,
> Thy saints have dwelt secure;
> Sufficient is Thine arm alone,
> And our defence is sure.

Immediately, the entire congregation would join her in the singing of this hymn, because they felt the presence of Jesus in their midst, "guidin' their feet" and "holdin' their hands," "while they run this race." When the pastor would say, "I know the Lord is in this place! Can I get a witness?" the people responded with shouts of praise saying "Amen" and "Hallelujah." Through song, prayer, and sermon the community affirmed Jesus' presence and their willingness to try to make it through their troubled situation. Some would smile and others would cry. Another person, depending upon the Spirit's effect on him, would clap his hands and tap his feet. Then again another person would get down on her knees, waving her hands and moaning the melody of a song whose rhythm and words spoke to what she felt in her heart. All of these expressions were nothing but black people bearing witness to Jesus' presence among them. He was the divine power in their lives who gave them an "imagination to think of a good reason to keep on keepin' on" in order that black people might "make the best of a bad situation."

Of course, in the light of Feuerbach and Marx, Freud and

Durkheim, Mannheim and the sociologists of knowledge, one could interpret black people's jumping and shouting about Jesus in their midst as wishful thinking related to their political powerlessness and social and psychological maladjustment. But I contend that we cannot test the truth of the black story by using intellectual categories that were not created from black experience itself. Instead we must immerse ourselves in the existence of the people, feeling their hurts and pain, and listening to their testimony that Jesus is present with them, taking black suffering upon himself so that the people can survive with dignity the oppression and violence committed against them. Only by listening to their story and viewing it in the light of the biblical story in relation to other stories in human history are we in a position to make a judgment about the "reasonableness" of black religion. Unless the interpreter of black religion is willing to suspend his a priori definitions of reality, and open himself to another reality found in the social existence of black people, then his comments about the truth or untruth of black religion become merely an academic exercise which tell us far more about his subjective interests than about the religious life of black people. If the interpreter is willing to hear what the people have to say about their struggle and the reality of Jesus in the fight for freedom, and proceed to develop his tools of critical analysis in the light of his identification with the goals and aspirations of the people, then and only then is he prepared to ask the right questions and to hear the right answers. For in the Christian story, truth is not an object but is the project of freedom made possible by the presence of God in the midst of his people. Only stories that invite an openness to other human stories are true. In black religion, the people tell the story of their lives as they walked and talked with Jesus, telling the story of how Jesus ministered to their broken hearts and weak bodies. Because of the power of his presence with them, he has given to them not only the strength to struggle but also an openness to fight together with all victims regardless of their genetic origin.

Christologically, therefore, who Jesus is today is found by relating Jesus' past with his present activity. Black people affirm them both simultaneously and thus dialectically. On the one hand, through faith black people transcended spatial and tem-

poral existence and affirmed Jesus' past as disclosed in the
historicity of his life and death on the cross.

> Those cruel people!
> Those cruel people!
> Those cruel people!
> Those cruel people!
>
> They crucified my Lord,
> They crucified my Lord,
> They crucified my Lord,
> They crucified my Lord.

In this spiritual, the repetition of the lines enhances the reality
of Jesus' suffering and emphasizes his humanity as he struggles
against the pain of the cross.

But on the other hand, black people's faith that Jesus was
raised from the dead meant that his historicity and humanity are
not the only relevant factors about his person. He is also the
divine One who transcends the limitations of history by making
himself present in our contemporary existence. This is the meaning of Jesus' resurrection. When God raised Jesus from the dead,
he affirmed that Jesus' historical identity with the freedom of the
poor was in fact divinity taking on humanity for the purpose of
liberating human beings from sin and death.

It is within this context that the resurrection is a *political*
event. The politics of the resurrection is found in its gift of
freedom to the poor and the helpless. Being granted freedom
while they are still poor, they can know that their poverty is a
contrived phenomenon, traceable to the rich and the powerful
in this world. This new knowledge about themselves and the
world, as disclosed in and through the resurrection, requires
that the poor practice political activity against the social and
economic structure that makes them poor. Not to fight is to deny
the freedom of the resurrection. It is to deny the reality of
Christ's presence with us in the struggle to liberate the slaves
from bondage. This is the political side of the resurrection of
Jesus.

The affirmation "Jesus is Lord," like the cry "Christ is risen!"
has political overtones. The Lordship of Christ emphasizes his

present rule in the lives of the people, helping them to struggle for the maintenance of humanity in a situation of oppression. "Jesus is Lord" is an affirmation of his reigning presence, moving the people toward the future realization of their humanity. Lordship is Christ's presence with power from on high to be with the little ones in trouble. As John Knox puts it: "The phrase 'Jesus Christ is our Lord' designates, not primarily an historical individual but a *present* reality actually experienced within the common life."[16]

Jesus Is Who He Will Be

The meaning of Jesus Christ for us today is not limited to his past and present existence. Jesus Christ is who he will be. He is not only the Crucified and Risen One but also the Lord of the future who is coming again to fully consummate the liberation already happening in our present.

Since the publication of Albert Schweitzer's *The Quest of the Historical Jesus* in 1906,[17] in which he emphasized "consistent" eschatology, European and American scholars have generally recognized the importance of the future in Jesus' consciousness about his ministry. More recently, advocates of a so-called "hope theology," taking their cue from Ernst Käsemann's contention that "apocalyptic . . . was the mother of all Christian theology,"[18] have related eschatology to politics and the struggle of the oppressed to liberate themselves from bondage. Although eschatology is the study of "last things" (particularly the "end of the age"), the "hope" theologians contend that eschatology should be the beginning for theological exploration. "Christianity," according to Jürgen Moltmann, "is eschatology, is hope, forward looking and forward moving, and therefore also revolutionizing and transforming the present. The eschatological is not one element of Christianity, but it is the medium of Christian faith as such, the key in which everything in it is set. . . ."[19] Eschatology for these writers is more than longing for the next world; it is the grounding of hope in God's liberating work in this world, which thus becomes the foundation of the divine promise to liberate the oppressed from human captivity.

It is important to point out that black people in their sermons, prayers, and songs of the nineteenth and twentieth centuries were talking about the politics of hope long before the appearance of hope theology in Germany. The rise of hope theology is related to the increasing disenchantment of contemporary European theologians with the alternatives posed by Barth's kerygmatic theology and Bultmann's existentialist approach. Unlike Barth who ignored Marx and in contrast to Bultmann who seemed to depolitize the gospel, the hope theologians made political praxis a decisive ingredient in theology itself, thereby laying the groundwork for dialogue with Marxism.[20] By contrast, black people's talk about hope, though contemporary with Marx, did not arise out of a dialogue with Marxism. Black religion and its emphasis on hope came into being through black people's encounter with the Crucified and Risen Lord in the context of American slavery. In their encounter with Jesus Christ, black slaves received a "vision from on high" wherein they were given a new knowledge of their personhood, which enabled them to fight for the creation of a world defined by black affirmations. Their hope sprang from the actual presence of Jesus, breaking into their broken existence, and bestowing upon them a foretaste of God's promised freedom. They could fight against slavery and not give up in despair, because they believed that their earthly struggle was a preparation for the time when they would "cross over Jordan" and "walk in Jerusalem just like John." They were willing to "bear heavy burdens," "climb high mountains," and "stand hard trials," because they were "trying to get home." Home was the "not yet," the other world that was not like this one. Jesus was the divine coming One who would take them to the "bright mansions above."

Unfortunately, American white "hope" theologians have been influenced too much by German and American philosophical discourse on hope and too little by the actual bearers of hope in our social existence. And if they continue their talk about hope primarily in relation to Pierre Teilhard de Chardin, Alfred North Whitehead, Moltmann, and Pannenberg, while ignoring the hope disclosed in the songs and tales of black slaves, then we can only conclude that white theology's hope is a reason for despair on the part of the oppressed and thus alien to the gospel of Jesus.

How can Christian theology truly speak of the hope of Jesus Christ, unless that hope begins and ends with the liberation of the poor in the social existence in which theology takes shape? In America this means that there can be no talk about hope in the Christian sense unless it is talk about the freedom of black, red, and brown people.

I am baffled that many American white theologians still continue to do theology independently of the oppressed of the land. That a public conference on Hope and the Future of Man[21] could be held in New York (1971) featuring Moltmann, Pannenberg, and Metz but including no one from Africa, Latin America, or even black America is completely beyond my comprehension. I contend that when theological discourse overlooks the oppressed and the hope given by Jesus Christ in their struggle, it inevitably becomes "abstract" talk, geared to the ideological justification of the status quo.

Jürgen Moltmann raised this issue in the New York conference on hope in his public response to the American theologians of hope.

> The future which does not begin in this transformation of the present is for me no genuine future. A hope which is not the hope of the oppressed today is no hope for which I could give a theological account. A resurrection symbol which is not the symbolizing resurrection of the crucified one does not touch me. If theologians and philosophers of the future do not plant their feet on the ground and turn to a theology of the cross and the dialectic of the negative, they will disappear in a cloud of liberal optimism and appear a mockery of the present misery of the suffering. If we cannot justify the theme of the conference, "Hope and the Future of Man," before the present reality of the frustration and oppression of man, we are batting the breeze and talking merely for our own self-satisfaction.[22]

The public reaction was intense but mixed. Some thought the comment was in bad taste and others said that Moltmann rightly exposed the navel-gazing of academic theologians. This issue was taken up again in a small working group of about forty theologians. I was the only black person present, which seemed to be due to my faculty status at Union Theological Seminary. (All Union Theological Seminary faculty were invited.) In the first workshop meeting (there were three in all), theologians discussed hope's relation to politics as defined by Moltmann. Most seemed uncomfortable with the discussion, because they had come to discuss the philosophical structure of hope as defined by Whitehead, Teilhard, and Bloch and not the political status of poor people. In the other two workshops, discussion returned to its expected status.

Because Black Theology's Christology is based on the biblical portrayal of Jesus Christ and Jesus' past and present involvement in the struggle of oppressed peoples, it affirms that who Jesus Christ is for us today is connected with the divine future as disclosed in the liberation fight of the poor. When connected with the person of Jesus, hope is not an intellectual idea; rather, it is the praxis of freedom in the oppressed community. To hope in Jesus is to see the vision of his coming presence, and thus one is required by hope itself to live as if the vision is already realized in the present. Black slaves combined the vision of the new Jerusalem with the struggle of freedom in this world. They talked about Jesus not only as the One who was born in Bethlehem and died on Calvary, and as the Risen One present with them, but also as the One who would come again and take them home to glory. That is why they sang:

> I'm going back with Jesus when He comes,
> I'm going back with Jesus when He comes,
> O He may not come today,
> But He's coming anyway
> I'm going back with Jesus when He comes.
>
> And we won't die anymore when He comes,
> And we won't die anymore when He comes,
> O He may not come today,
> But He's coming anyway
> And we won't die anymore when He comes.

This spiritual connects hope in Jesus with human suffering, wherein Jesus becomes the Expected One who is coming to liberate the oppressed from slavery.

The vision of the future and of Jesus as the Coming Lord is the central theme of black religion. This theme is expressed with the idea of heaven, a concept that has been grossly misunderstood in black religion. For many people the idea of heaven, in the songs and sermons of black people, is proof of Marx's contention that religion is the opiate of the people. Unfortunately, many uninformed young blacks, hearing this Marxian analysis in college, have accepted this criticism as true without probing deeper into the thought forms of black people. To be sure, white missionaries and preachers used Jesus Christ and heaven to make black slaves obedient and docile. But in reality, the opposite happened more often than not. For many black slaves, Jesus became the decisive Other in their lives who provided for them a knowledge of themselves, not derived from the value system of slave masters. How could black slaves know that they were human beings when they were treated like cattle? How could they know that they were somebody when everything in their environment said that they were nobody? How could they know that they had a value that could not be defined by dollars and cents, when the symbol of the auction block was an ever present reality? Only because they knew that Christ was present with them and that his presence included the divine promise to come again and to take them to the "New Jerusalem." Heaven, therefore, in black religion was inseparably connected with Jesus' promise to liberate the oppressed from slavery. It was black people's vision of a new identity for themselves which was in sharp contradiction to their present status as slaves. This vision of Jesus as the Coming One who will take them back to heaven held black people together mentally as they struggled physically to make real the future in their present.

Christologically, we are required to affirm Jesus Christ in terms of his past, present, and future. This means that we do not have to choose between a Christology "from below" (Pannenberg) or "from above" (Barth), or even "from before" (Moltmann).[23] These three aspects of his history and person must be approached dialectically, recognizing that each is a valid experience of Jesus Christ when viewed in relation to the others. We can truly know Jesus' past and its soteriological significance only if his past is seen in dialectical relation to his present presence and his future coming. Unlike Pannenberg who postpones the validity of Jesus' truth disclosed in the resurrection experience until the end of time, black theologians claim, on the basis of the biblical witness and the past and contemporary testimonies of black people, that Jesus is who he is as his *isness* is known in his present activity with the oppressed in the struggle of freedom. In our analysis of the past history of Jesus, we cannot ignore his present soteriological value as the Lord of our present struggle. The same is true for his future coming. The past and present history of Jesus are incomplete without affirmation of the "not yet" that "will be." The power of Christ's future coming and the vision that it bestows upon the people is the key to why the oppressed can "keep on keepin' on" even when their fight seems fruitless. The vision of Christ's future that breaks into their slave existence radically changes their perspective on life; and to others who stand outside the community where the vision is celebrated, black people's talk about "long white robes" and "golden slippers" in heaven seem to be proof that black religion is an opium of the people. But in reality it is a radical judgment which black people are making upon the society that enslaved them. Black religion, therefore, becomes a revolutionary alternative to white religion. Jesus Christ becomes the One who stands at the center of their view of reality, enabling slaves to look beyond the present to the future, the time when black suffering will be ended. The future reality of Jesus means that what is contradicts what ought to be.

When Jesus is understood as the Coming One who will establish divine justice among people, then we will be able to understand why black slaves' religion emphasized the *other* world. They truly believed the story of Jesus' past existence with the poor as told in the Bible. Indeed, their own power to struggle to be human was due to the presence of Jesus with them. From his past history with the weak and his present existence with them, black people received a vision of his coming presence to fully heal the misery of human suffering. That is why they sang with unique passion and meaning:

> If I walk in the pathway of duty,
> If I work to the close of the day,
> I shall see the great King in his beauty,
> When I've gone the last mile of the way.

When I've gone the last mile of the way,
I shall rest at the close of the day,
And I know there are joys that await me,
When I've gone the last mile of the way.

Black people knew that they could not trust the power of their
own strength to break the chains of slavery. People get tired of
fighting for justice and the political power of oppressors often
creates fear in the hearts of the oppressed. What could a small
band of slaves do against the armed might of a nation? Indeed
what can the oppressed blacks today do in order to break the
power of the Pentagon? Of course, we may "play" revolutionary
and delude ourselves that we can do battle against the atomic
bomb. Usually when the reality of the political situation dawns
upon the oppressed, those who have no vision from another
world tend to give up in despair. But those who have heard about
the coming of the Lord Jesus and have a vision of crossing on the
other side of Jordan, are not terribly disturbed about what
happens in Washington, D.C., at least not to the extent that their
true humanity is dependent on the political perspective of government officials. To be sure, they know that they must struggle
to realize justice in this world. But their struggle for justice is
directly related to the coming judgment of Jesus. His coming
presence requires that we not make any historical struggle an
end in itself. We struggle because it is a sign of Jesus' presence
with us and of his coming presence to redeem all humanity. His
future coming therefore is the key to the power of our struggle.
Black people can struggle because they truly believe that one day
they will be taken out of their misery. And they express it in song:

After 'while, After 'while,
Some sweet day after 'while,
I'm goin' up to see my Jesus,
O some sweet day after 'while.

Pray on! Pray on!
Some sweet day after 'while,
Prayin' time will soon be over,
O some sweet day after 'while.

Jesus Is Black

It is only within the context of Jesus' past, present, and future as these aspects of his person are related to Scripture, tradition, and contemporary social existence that we are required to affirm the blackness of Jesus Christ. I realize that many white critics of Black Theology question "blackness" as a christological title, because it appears to be determined exclusively by the psychological and political needs of black people to relate theology to the emergence of black power in the later 1960s. That is only partly true. The phrase "Black Christ" refers to more than the subjective states and political expediency of black people at a given point in history. Rather, this title is derived primarily from Jesus' past identity, his present activity, and his future coming as each is dialectically related to the others. But unless black theologians can demonstrate that Jesus' blackness is not simply the psychological disposition of black people but arises from a faithful examination of Christology's sources (Scripture, tradition, and social existence) as these sources illuminate Jesus' past, present, and future, then we lay ourselves open to the white charge that the Black Christ is an ideological distortion of the New Testament for political purposes.

Before moving to the substance of the Black Christ issue, it is necessary to unmask the subjective interests of white theologians themselves. When the past and contemporary history of white theology is evaluated, it is not difficult to see that much of the present negative reaction of white theologians to the Black Christ is due almost exclusively to their *whiteness*, a cultural fact that determines their theological inquiry, thereby making it almost impossible for them to relate positively to anything black. White theologians' attitude toward black people in particular and the oppressed generally is hardly different from that of oppressors in any society. It is particularly similar to the religious leaders' attitude toward Jesus in first-century Palestine when he freely associated with the poor and outcasts and declared that the Kingdom of God is for those called "sinners" and not for priests and theologians or any of the self-designated righteous people. The difficulty of white theologians in recognizing their racial interest in this issue can be understood only in the light of the social context of theological discourse. They cannot see the christological validity of Christ's blackness because their axiological grid blinds them to the truth of the biblical story. For example, the same white theologians who laughingly dismiss Albert Cleage's "Black Messiah" say almost nothing about the European (white) images of Christ plastered all over American homes and churches. I perhaps would respect the integrity of their objections to the Black Christ on scholarly grounds, if they applied the same vigorous logic to Christ's whiteness, especially in contexts where his blackness is not advocated.

For me, the substance of the Black Christ issue can be dealt with only on *theological* grounds, as defined by Christology's source (Scripture, tradition, and social existence) and content (Jesus' past, present, and future). I begin by asserting once more that *Jesus was a Jew*. It is on the basis of the soteriological meaning of the particularity of his Jewishness that theology must affirm the christological significance of Jesus' present blackness. He *is* black because he *was* a Jew. The affirmation of the Black Christ can be understood when the significance of his past Jewishness is related dialectically to the significance of his present blackness. On the one hand, the Jewishness of Jesus located him in the context of the Exodus, thereby connecting his appearance in Palestine with God's liberation of oppressed Israelites from Egypt. Unless Jesus were truly from Jewish ancestry, it would make little theological sense to say that he is the fulfillment of God's covenant with Israel. But on the other hand, the blackness of Jesus brings out the soteriological meaning of his Jewishness for our contemporary situation when Jesus' person is understood in the context of the cross and resurrection. Without negating the divine election of Israel, the cross and resurrection are Yahweh's fulfillment of his original intention for Israel to be

> a light to the nations,
> to open the eyes that are blind,
> to bring about the prisoners from the dungeon,
> from the prison those who sit in darkness.
>
> Isaiah 42:6-7 RSV

The cross of Jesus is God invading the human situation as the Elected One who takes Israel's place as the Suffering Servant and thus reveals the divine willingness to suffer in order that humanity might be fully liberated. The resurrection is God's conquest of oppression and injustice, disclosing that the divine freedom revealed in Israel's history is now available to all. The cross represents the particularity of divine suffering in Israel's place. The resurrection is the universality of divine freedom for all who "labor and are heavy laden." It is the actualization in history of Jesus' eschatological vision that the last shall be first and the first last. The resurrection means that God's identity with the poor in Jesus is not limited to the particularity of his Jewishness but is applicable to all who fight on behalf of the liberation of humanity in this world. And the Risen Lord's identification with the suffering poor today is just as real as was his presence with the outcasts in first-century Palestine. His presence with the poor today is not docetic; but like yesterday, today also he takes the pain of the poor upon himself and bears it for them.

It is in the light of the cross and the resurrection of Jesus in relation to his Jewishness that Black Theology asserts that "Jesus is black." If we assume that the Risen Lord is truly present with us as defined by his past history and witnessed by Scripture and tradition, what then does his presence mean in the social context of white racism? If Jesus' presence is real and not docetic, is it not true that Christ *must* be black in order to remain faithful to the divine promise to bear the suffering of the poor? Of course, I realize that "blackness" as a christological title may not be appropriate in the distant future or even in every human context in our present. This was no less true of the New Testament titles, such as "Son of God" and "Son of David," and of various descriptions of Jesus throughout the Christian tradition. But the validity of any christological title in any period of history is not decided by its universality but by this: whether in the particularity of its time it points to God's universal will to liberate particular oppressed people from inhumanity. This is exactly what blackness does in the contemporary social existence of America. If we Americans, blacks and white, are to understand who Jesus is for us today, we must view his presence as continuous with his past and future coming which is best seen through his present blackness.

Christ's blackness is both literal and symbolic. His blackness is literal in the sense that he truly becomes One with the oppressed blacks, taking their suffering as his suffering and revealing that he is found in the history of our struggle, the story of our pain, and the rhythm of our bodies. Jesus is found in the sociological context that gave birth to Aretha Franklin singing "Spirit in the Dark" and Roberta Flack proclaiming that "I told Jesus that it will be all right if he changed my name." Christ's blackness is the American expression of the truth of his parable about the Last Judgment: "Truly, I say to you, as you did it not to one of the least of these, you did it not to me" (Matt. 25:45). The least in America are literally and symbolically present in black people. To say that Christ is black means that black people are God's poor people whom Christ has come to liberate. And thus no gospel of Jesus Christ is possible in America without coming to terms with the history and culture of that people who struggled to bear witness to his name in extreme circumstances. To say that Christ is black means that God, in his infinite wisdom and mercy, not only takes color seriously, he takes it upon himself and discloses his will to make us whole—new creatures born in the spirit of divine blackness and redeemed through the blood of the Black Christ. Christ is black, therefore, not because of some cultural or psychological need of black people, but because and only because Christ *really* enters into our world where the poor, the despised, and the black are, disclosing that he is with them, enduring their humiliation and pain and transforming oppressed slaves into liberated servants. Indeed, if Christ is not *truly* black, then the historical Jesus lied. God did not anoint him "to preach good news to the poor" and neither did he send him "to proclaim release to the captives and recovering the sight to the blind to set at liberty those who are oppressed" (Luke 4:18f. RSV). If Christ is not black, the gospel is not good news to the oppressed, and Marx's observation is right: "Religion is the sign of the oppressed creature, the heart of a heartless world . . . the spirit of a spiritless situation. It is the opium of the people."[24]

I realize that my theological limitations and my close identity with the social conditions of black people could blind me to the *truth* of the gospel. And maybe our white theologians are right when they insist that I have overlooked the *universal* significance of Jesus' message. But I contend that there is no universalism that is not particular. Indeed their insistence upon the universal note of the gospel arises out of their own particular political and social interests. As long as they can be sure that the gospel is *for everybody,* ignoring that God liberated a *particular* people from Egypt, came in a particular man called Jesus, and for the particular purpose of liberating the oppressed, then they can continue to talk in theological abstractions, failing to recognize that such talk is not the gospel unless it is related to the concrete freedom of the little ones. My point is that God came, and continues to come, to those who are poor and helpless, for the purpose of setting them free. And since the people of color are his elected poor in America, any interpretation of God that ignores black oppression cannot be Christian theology. The "blackness of Christ," therefore, is not simply a statement about skin color, but rather, the transcendent affirmation that God has not ever, no not ever, left the oppressed alone in struggle. He was with them in Pharaoh's Egypt, is with them in America, Africa and Latin America, and will come in the end of time to consummate fully their human freedom.

VII.
THE MEANING
OF LIBERATION

If Jesus Christ, in his past, present and future, reveals that the
God of Scripture and tradition is the God whose will is disclosed
in the liberation of oppressed people from bondage, what then
is the meaning of liberation? In answering the question we begin by examining the theological presupposition upon which that
meaning is based.

Jesus Christ as the
Ground of Human Liberation

Because human liberation is God's work of salvation in Jesus
Christ, its source and meaning cannot be separated from Christology's sources (Scripture, tradition, and social existence) and
content (Jesus in his past, present, and future). Jesus Christ,
therefore, in his humanity and divinity, is the point of departure
for a black theologian's analysis of the meaning of liberation.
There is no liberation independent of Jesus' past, present, and
future coming. He is the ground of our present freedom to
struggle and the source of our hope that the vision disclosed in
our historical fight against oppression will be fully realized in
God's future. In this sense, liberation is not a human possession
but a divine gift of freedom to those who struggle in faith against
violence and oppression. Liberation is not an object but the
project of freedom wherein the oppressed realize that their fight
for freedom is a divine right of creation. This is what Anthony

Burns, an ex-slave, meant by saying that "God made me a *man*—not a *slave,* and gave me the same right to myself that he gave to the man stole me to himself."[1] A similar point was made by David Walker when he urged black slaves to remember that freedom is not a gift from white slave masters but a natural right of divine creation.

> Should tyrants take it into their heads to emancipate any of you, remember that your freedom is your natural right. You are men, as well as they, and instead of returning thanks to them for your freedom, return it to the Holy Ghost, who is your rightful owner. If they do not want to part with your labors, . . . and my word for it, that God Almighty, will break their strong band.[2]

The grounding of liberation in God's act in Jesus Christ is the logical consequence of any Christian theology that takes Scripture seriously as an important source for the doing of theology. According to Scripture, the human freedom to hope for a new heaven and a new earth is grounded in God's freedom. Divine freedom is not merely an affirmation of the self-existence of God, his complete transcendence over creaturely existence. It also expresses God's will to be in relation to his creatures in the social context of their striving for the fulfillment of humanity. That is, he is free to be for us. This is the meaning of the Exodus and the Incarnation. The biblical God is the God whose salvation is liberation. He is the God of Jesus Christ who calls the helpless and weak into a newly created existence. God not only fights for them but takes their humiliated condition upon the divine Person and thereby breaks open a new future for the poor, different from their past and present miseries. Here is the central meaning of the cross, dramatically revealed in the Markan account of Jesus' cry of dereliction: "My God, my God, why hast thou forsaken me" (15:34). These words show the depth of Jesus' agony and the pain of being abandoned by his Father. But because he was one with divinity and humanity, the pain of the cross was God suffering for and with us so that our humanity can be liberated for freedom in the divine struggle against oppression. This is why Ernst Käsemann says that "Jesus means freedom," and why Moltmann is correct in his contention that "the

Christian faith not only believes in freedom but is already freedom itself. It not only hopes for freedom but, rather, is itself the inauguration of a free life on earth."[3]

When God is revealed in history as freedom for us, he is disclosed as the God of hope. "Christian theology," writes Moltmann, "speaks of history *eschatologically*."[4] To speak of history eschatologically is to speak of the promise of God's Word of liberation, disclosed in his future, breaking into our present, and overthrowing the powers of evil that hold people in captivity. This theme is prominent in the black religious tradition with its claim that Jesus has not left black people alone in suffering. He is not only with them, "buildin' them up where they are torn down and proppin' them up on every leanin' side," but he is also "coming on the clouds of heaven" to take them "home to glory." Black people's faith in Jesus' future coming is the basis of their continued struggle against inexplicable evil in their present existence. They often expressed their faith in testimony. When the burdens of life became difficult and they could not offer a rational explanation of the pain they had to bear, the members of Macedonia could still affirm the meaning they found in black life. It might be expressed in language like this: "Sometimes the way gets difficult, and I don't know what to do. The burden of life gets heavy, and I often feel that I can't go anymore. But I tell you this *one* thing: I *know* that my Lord is coming again, and I want to be ready to put on my shoes, fasten up my robe, and walk around Zion. That's why I can't let a little trouble get me down. I can't quit, because I want to see my Jesus. 'O yes I'm going to eat at the welcome table some of these days, hallelujah!'" The courage and the strength to keep on fighting in this world are based on the hope that "de udder worl' is not like dis."

Black people can fight for freedom and justice, because the One who is their future is also the ground of their struggle for liberation. It does not matter what oppressors say or do or what they try to make us out to be. We know that we have a freedom not made with human hands. It is this faith that defines our person, and thus enables black people to sing when the world says that they have nothing to sing about, to pray when prayer seems useless to theologians and philosophers, and to preach when the world will not listen. For black people's singing, praying, and preaching are not grounded in any human potentiality but in the actuality of God's freedom to be with the oppressed as disclosed in the cross and resurrection of Jesus. Jesus is their freedom, the One they claim will "pick you up when you're fallin'" and will come to your rescue when you're in trouble." He is the One who gave our black mothers and fathers in slavery an "old time religion," that moved their consciousness back to the shores of Africa, and thus enabled them to use the resources of their heritage in the struggle for freedom. They could shout and dance to the rhythm of freedom because Jesus is the Lord of all creation who gives the little ones liberating visions in wretched places. That is why black people call him a "Balm in Gilead" who came "to make the wounded whole" and "to heal the sin-sick soul." With ecstatic praise they proclaim: "Lord, you've been so good to me. You stayed by my side when the world was against me. You are my rose of Sharon and the Prince of Peace," the One who breaks into the people's history, bestowing meaning upon their past, giving them courage to struggle in the present, and the will to hope that one day, "in that great gettin' up morning," it will "all be over with, all over this world."

Christ's salvation is liberation; there is no liberation without Christ. Both meanings are inherent in the statement that Jesus Christ is the ground of human liberation. Any statement that divorces salvation from liberation or makes human freedom independent of divine freedom must be rejected. From this starting point we proceed to examine the content of human liberation itself: as relation to God, as relation to self and community, as the practice of freedom in history and hope.

Liberation as Freedom To Be in Relation to God

Fellowship with God is the beginning and the end of human liberation. The liberated person is the one who encounters God in faith, that is, in conviction and trust that one's true humanity is actualized in God. This vertical dimension of faith is the essential response to the gospel and is thus the heart of liberation's meaning from the human side. This is why conversion, prayer, and community worship are dominant motifs in black religion—when the people testify that they met Jesus "early one Thursday morning" or "late one Friday evening," they are talking about the importance of the divine-human encounter. Seldom is the actual date, hour, or year very important, although some will claim that it is crucial to know when the Lord touched your soul. But theologically, the reality of conversion points to the vertical dimension of liberation which is often called "communion with God."

The conversion experience in black religion is a radical, transforming encounter with the One the people believe to be the foundation of their existence. One person speaks of this experience as being "hooked in the heart." Another says "God struck me dead," while another testifies that she was "split open from head to foot." Testimonies to these experiences, edited by Clifton H. Johnson of Fisk University, have an essential commonality: they speak of a divine-human encounter that meant death to the old life and the liberation to a new form of existence. One person put it this way:

> I was fifty-two years old when the Lord freed my soul. . . . I was killed dead and made live again. . .
>
> During the vision the voice said to me, "Here you must die." I truly died and saw my body. I had a temporal and spiritual body. My spiritual body had six wings on it, and when I was barked at by the hellhounds of the devil I arose and flew away.
>
> Ever since the Lord freed my soul I have been a new man. I trust in him to fight my battles, for he is a captain who has never lost a battle or been confounded with cares.[5]

In a more humorous vein, the same theme of conversion and its liberating effect was expressed by a nineteenth-century preacher who exhorted his converts at the water's edge, awaiting the ceremony of baptism.

> My brethren and sistren, hark to my words. 'Tain't 'nuff dat you should have songs of thanksgivin' on yo' lips. 'Tain't ample dat you

is shoutin' out hallelujas an' amens till yo' throats is hoarse an' yo' voices break in de middle. No suh! Onlessen you got de spirit of de Lawd pressin' heavy 'pon you an' de ol'-time 'ligion in yo' souls; onlessen you is filled wid happy hopes of de hereafter an' fear of ol' Satan; onlessen you feels dat de angels is lookin' down on you wid favor from heaven above an' dat cherubims is singin' sweet praise fo' yo' salvation an' de Pearly Gates is done swung wide open to welcome you ez worthy pilgrims an' de golden harps is tuned fo' you an' yo' wings is waitin' to be fitted onto yo' shoulders; onlessen you has all dese feelin's, you won't get nothin' when you is immersed 'cept wet![6]

After conversion, many blacks believe that prayer is needed in order to stay on what they call "the Lord's journey." Prayer is being able to communicate with God and to know that he cares for them. Most black prayers begin with an expression of thankfulness to God for having sustained the people in struggle. "Dear Lawd, we come befo' Thee and ask Thee ter stand by us. Thank Thee for ev'rything Thou's did for us." Because black families were brutalized and broken by slavery and oppression, God became the stabilizing and liberating force in their lives. Thus in prayer, God is often referred to as a "mother for the motherless" and a "father for the fatherless." God becomes everything that the people need in order to sustain their lives with dignity. He is the One that the people can "tell all about their troubles." And in the act of telling one's story to God, fellowship with the divine is established, and thus the believer becomes aware that God has not left him alone. Prayer is experiencing the power of God's presence and knowing that human liberation is based on divine revelation. This vertical sense of personal relationship with the God of Jesus is logically prior to the other components of human liberation. For without the knowledge of God that comes through divine fellowship, the oppressed would not know that what the world says about them is a lie. They would have to believe what they are *made* to believe through police sticks and guns. But if one has a relationship with the Resurrected One, then he can know that he has an identity that cannot be taken away with guns and bullets. This is what black people are affirming when they say: "Take it to the Lord in prayer." Prayer, therefore, is not an escape that leads to passivity. Rather, it is the beginning of the Christian practice of liberation. It is not only an expression of confidence in God's Word to effect a change in their history; it is also the start of their own action, the attempt of black people to take their history in their own hands on the basis of the gift of freedom made possible in and through divine fellowship. "To take one's troubles to the Lord in prayer" is to recognize that the One who said to Moses "I Am Who I Am" (Exod. 3:14 RSV) can cause being to replace nonbeing, merely through the assertion of his Word. Therefore to give one's allegiance to another authority than the divine Word of liberation is to negate divine fellowship. We are thus commanded to give our complete selves to him in prayer for the struggle of freedom. It is from the knowledge of this vertical divine-human relationship that the true struggle of liberation in history is based.

Community worship is also an important expression of the divine-human fellowship. Black worship itself is a liberating event for those who share the experience of the people that bears witness to God's presence in their midst. Through prayer, testimony, song, and sermon the people transcend the limitations of their immediate history and encounter the divine power, thereby creating a moment of ecstasy and joy wherein they recognize that the pain of oppression is not the last word about black life. It is not unusual for the people to get "carried away" with their feelings, making it difficult for an observer to know what is actually happening. But the meaning of this event, according to the people, is found in their liberating encounter with the divine Spirit. In this encounter, they are set free as children of God. To understand what this means for black people, we need only to remember that they have not known freedom in white America. Therefore, to be told, "You are free, my children" is to create indescribable joy and excitement in the people. They sing because they are free. Black worship is a celebration of freedom. It is a black happening, the time when the people gather together in the name of the One who promised that he would not leave the little ones alone in trouble. The people shout, moan, and cry as a testimony to the experience of God's liberating presence in their lives. "There is joy on the inside and it wells up so strong that we can't keep still," testifies an ex-slave. "It is fire in the bones. Any time fire touches a man, he will jump."[7]

Human liberation as fellowship with God also must be seen as the very heart of the theological concept of the "image of God," even though this point has often been obscured. In the history of theology, the image of God has frequently been identified with the human capacity to reason. By contrast, theologians since Karl Barth, taking their cue from the Reformation, have recognized the relational character of the image of God. But even Barth did not set forth the political and social implications of the divine-human encounter with sufficient clarity. His concern for the transcendent quality of God's presence obscured the obvious political import of his analysis, even though Barth himself never viewed his theology as separate from his political involvement in the world. It is within this context that the exchange between Barth and Martin Niemöller ought to be understood. According to George Casalis,

> Barth said to Niemöller, "You haven't the least idea what theology is all about, and yet how can I complain? For you think and see and do the right things!" To which Niemöller replied, "You can't stop thinking theologically for a moment, and yet how can I complain? For you think and see and do the right things too!"[8]

On the one hand, this exchange illustrates Barth's view that theology is relevant for life. But on the other, it also points out that Barth's exposition of the connection ought to be seen in a perspective in which theology is the exposition of the meaning of God's liberation. For to affirm that human beings are free only when that freedom is derived from divine revelation has concrete political consequences. If we are created for God, then any other allegiance is a denial of freedom, and we must struggle against those who attempt to enslave us. The image of God is not merely a personal relationship with God, but is also that constituent of humanity which makes all people struggle against captivity. It is the ground of rebellion and revolution among slaves.

The relational character of human liberation as grounded in the human struggle to be free is emphasized in the black spirituals. Black people sang that Jesus

>   Came down here and talked to me,
>   Went away and left me free.

They also sang:

>   You say the Lord has set you free,. . .
>   Why don't you let yo' neighbor be!

In both lyrics the theme is freedom in this world as an essential constituent of Jesus' redemption. Human fellowship with God is defined as Jesus' work of liberation ("Came down here and *talked* with me, Went away and left me free"). The freedom derived from Jesus' Incarnation is connected with having talked with Jesus. This talking is fellowship with him and thus is the foundation of freedom. It is the basis of the struggle to live in the world according to divine obedience. ("You say the Lord has set you free, Why don't you let yo' neighbor be!"). Liberation is not only a relationship with God but an encounter grounded in the historical struggle to be free. "The Christian faith is freedom in struggle, in contradiction, and in temptation."[9]

Liberation as Freedom in Relation to Self and the Community of the Oppressed

To affirm that liberation is an expression of the image of God is to say not only who God is but also who I am and who my people are. Liberation is knowledge of self; it is a vocation to affirm who I am created to be. Furthermore, it is clear from divine revelation as witnessed in Scripture that authentic liberation of self is attainable only in the context of an oppressed community in the struggle of freedom. Because God's freedom for humanity is the divine liberation of the oppressed from bondage, human freedom as response to God's gracious liberation is an act for our sisters and brothers who are oppressed. There can be no freedom for God in isolation from the humiliated and abused. There can be no freedom for God unless the hungry are fed, the sick are healed, and justice is given for the poor. This is the meaning of Bibilov's comment in Bernard Malamud's *The Fixer*: "Keep in mind that the purpose of freedom is to create it for others."[10] How can we claim to be liberated or in the process of liberation in the Christian sense, if the structure and meaning of liberation is not derived from the oppressed community in its struggle of freedom? No one can be truly liberated until *all* are liberated. And until that eschatological event happens, the measure of liberation achievable is limited to the consciousness of freedom as defined by the oppressed and downtrodden in their fight for justice. In an unjust society, freedom for Christ can be found only among those who are in chains.

In the dialectic of freedom and oppression as both are related to political praxis the black theological view of liberation emerges. On the one hand, oppression is the denial of freedom, and therefore the opposite of liberation. But on the other, in an unredeemed social existence no one can be free who is not oppressed, that is, identified with the struggle of the unfree. There is no way to avoid the paradox I have expressed elsewhere: "Freedom is the opposite of oppression, but only the oppressed are truly free."[11] We must affirm this paradox because Christ (in the dialectic of his death and resurrection) has connected his liberation with the struggles of the wretched of the earth. The Christian community, therefore, is that community that freely becomes oppressed, because they know that Christ himself has defined humanity's liberation in the context of what happens to the little ones. Christians join the cause of the oppressed in the fight for justice not because of some philosophical principle of "the Good" or because of a religious feeling of sympathy for people in prison. Sympathy does not change the structures of injustice. The authentic identity of Christians with the poor is found in the claim which the Christ-encounter lays upon their own life-style, a claim that connects the word "Christian" with the liberation of the poor. Christians fight not for humanity in general but for themselves and out of their love for concrete human beings.

This raises the question, Who are the oppressed? What does Black Theology mean by oppression? Is Black Theology saying that only black people are oppressed and, further, that oppression is limited to social, political, and economic reality? What about the obvious oppression of others not of African descent and also the oppression of oppressors themselves which may be described as mental or spiritual oppression? After all, are we not *all* oppressed, especially those who think that their freedom is found in social, political, and economic domination of others?

Although these questions point to an essential truth of the gospel of liberation, they have been used by oppressors for untruth. The untruth of these questions lies in the subjective and often undisclosed intention of the people who ask them. While pretending to be concerned about the universal character of the human condition, oppressors are in fact concerned to justify their own particular status in society. They want to be oppressors and Christians at the same time. Since the oppressed are the only true Christians, oppressors claim to be victims, not for the purpose of being liberated but for their own social interests in retaining a "Christian" identity while being against Jesus Christ. This is what Dietrich Bonhoeffer in another context called "cheap grace."[12] I call it hypocrisy and blasphemy.

While it is true that *all* are oppressed (and especially those who rule over others), *only* those whose existence (and thus consciousness) is defined by the liberation of people from social, political, and economic bondage can understand the dialectic of oppression and freedom in the practice of liberation. Therefore when white theological rulers claim, "We are all oppressed!" they are speaking the truth, although they do not understand the truth. To do so, the truth would have to be reflected in their struggle to free themselves from their culture in order to join the cultural freedom of the poor. Until their consciousness is born anew in the light of black liberation, the truth of the statement is limited to verbal propositions that may be interesting for academicians but of little consequences for the freedom of the poor.

The first task of theology is to recognize that truth is not contained in words. Truth is found in the dynamic of the divine-human encounter in social existence wherein people recognize the connections between historical struggle and ultimate reality. I do not believe that people can understand the truth of the statement that "all are oppressed" unless their consciousness is defined by that social existence that makes for understanding. In the context of biblical revelation, this means quite clearly the social existence of the poor. When therefore the question is asked, "Are not all oppressed?" one can easily discover the function of the question by unmasking the social interests that the questioner intends to represent. If the person is white and wants to find a justification for the continued existence of white suburban churches that obviously contradict the essence of Jesus' gospel of liberation, then the asking of the question and its implied affirmative answer is nothing but a clever theological trick to blur important *material* distinctions in social existence itself. For it is material reality (social, economic, and political existence with the poor) that makes for the proper understanding of spiritual reality ("all oppressed"). But when the spiritual reality really is made the point of departure of liberation; important material distinctions are lost in clouds of theological rhetoric that not only enhance confusion but contribute to the continued existence of oppression.

By putting physical oppression derived from unjust social structures in the same category with suburban loneliness, the white questioner implies that either one may be the point of departure for an understanding of the gospel of liberation. But that is not true. Of course everyone has problems, but those problems can be understood only from *one* social perspective, namely, the social perspective of the poor in the struggle of freedom. Those whose consciousness is defined by the oppressors cannot understand what liberation is. For the oppressors to understand liberation, they must be liberated from being political oppressors. When the dialectic of change in social existence meets the idea of liberation, liberation's content and form are thus radically changed. What was once merely spoken is now actualized in history, enabling the former oppressors to know that truth is embodied in the historical movement of the liberation and not in theology textbooks.

Because the phrase "all are oppressed" can be understood only from the perspective of the poor, only they are in a position to take seriously the *universal* dimension of the gospel of liberation. This places an awesome responsibility upon them, for when the dialectic of oppression and liberation is seen correctly, the oppressed recognize that their call is to be God's "Kingdom of priests" to all peoples of the earth. Election involves service, even to the oppressors. This is the significance of Jesus' refusal to define God's Kingdom in terms of the private advantage of anyone, not even himself. When James and John said to him, "Grant us to sit, one at your right hand and one at your left, in your glory," Jesus replied: "You do not know what you are asking. Are you able to drink the cup that I drink, or to be baptized with the baptism with which I am baptized?" (Mark 40:35-38 RSV). And to prove that they did not know what they were asking or recognize the connection between election and service, they said, "We are able" (10:39). Although Jesus' reply made clear that a place in God's Kingdom is not a popularity contest given out to special favorites but for those (i.e., the poor) for whom it has already been assigned, the other disciples still became indignant at James and John. At that point Jesus said:

> You know that those who are supposed to rule over the Gentiles lord it over them, and their great men exercise authority over them. But it shall not be so among you; but whoever would be great among you must be your servant, and whoever would be first among you must be slave of all. For the Son of man also came not to be served but to serve, and to give his life as a ransom for many.
>
> Mark 10:42-45 RSV

To be a "slave of all" is to recognize that the struggle of liberation is for all. This recognition does not make one submissive to unjust powers, but humble before Jesus Christ who is the Lord of all. His presence in our midst requires that we subordinate our personal interests to the coming liberation for all. Those who see God's coming liberation breaking into the present must live as if the future is already present in their midst. They must bear witness to humanity's liberation by freeing the present from the past and for the future. This means fighting for the inauguration of liberation in our social existence, creating new levels of human relationship in society. The struggle for liberation is the service the people of God render for all, even those who are responsible for the structure of slavery.

The assertion that liberation is for all does not mean that all will regard God's coming realm of freedom as good news. Even some oppressed people, having "made" it in the oppressors' world, will not always welcome the freedom that the liberation struggle inaugurates. Their mental enslavement to their few crumbs from the master's table often negates their desire to share in the freedom of humanity. Therefore, though oppressed, they do not share the consciousness that arises from the dialectic of oppression and liberation in the political praxis of the people. They thus must be liberated in spite of and against themselves.

It is the same for the oppressors: they never recognize that the struggle of freedom is for all, including themselves. As Ostrovsky, the lawyer in Bernard Malamud's *The Fixer*, says: "In a sick country every step to health is an insult to those who live on its sickness."[13] As bearers of liberation—of the realm of health in a sick society—the oppressed must therefore fight against the oppressors in order to fight for them. This is what Jesus meant when he said, "the Son of man . . . came not to be served but to serve, and to give his life as a ransom for many" (Mark 10:45 RSV). The service would not be understood and would lead to his death.

To recognize that liberation is for oppressors because it is for all people prevents hate and revenge from destroying the revolutionary struggle. This is one of the essential truths of Franz Fanon's insights on freedom. He saw that the struggle was for all. "For Europe, for ourselves and for humanity, comrades, we must turn over a new leaf, we must work out new concepts, and try to set afoot a new man."[14] Like Jesus in his attitude toward the oppressors of the first century, Fanon did not expect Europeans to recognize that Africa's liberation would be for Europe. Only those who are oppressed can see that the true liberation of self is found in the oppressed community in struggle of freedom.

Liberation as the
Project of Freedom in History

There is no true liberation independent of the struggle for freedom in history. History is the immanent character of liberation; it is the project of freedom. The immanence of liberation is "visible whenever the emancipation of [people] from the chains of slavery takes place in history."[15] There is no liberation without transformation, that is, without the struggle for freedom in this world. There is no liberation without the commitment of revolutionary action against injustice, slavery, and oppression. Liberation then is not merely a thought in my head; it is the sociohistorical movement of a people from oppression to freedom —Israelites from Egypt, black people from American slavery. It is the mind and body in motion, responding to the passion and the rhythm of divine revelation, and affirming that no chain shall hold my humanity down. This is what black slaves meant when they sang:

> I'm a chile of God wid my soul set free,
> For Christ hab bought my liberty.

A similar point is made in Scripture when divine revelation is connected with history, and salvation is defined in political terms. In the Old Testament salvation is grounded in history and is identical with God's righteousness in delivering the oppressed from political bondage. Salvation is a historical event of rescue. It is God delivering the people from their enemies and bestowing upon Israel new possibilities within the historical context of her existence. "This means that man's spiritual aims are inseparably connected with the transformation of society."[16]

The historical character of liberation as an essential ingredient in salvation is also found in the New Testament. Jesus' message centered on the proclamation of liberation for the poor, and his exorcisms clearly illustrated that he viewed his ministry as an engagement in battle with the powers of evil that hold people in captivity. The healing of the sick, feeding the hungry, and giving sight to the blind mean that Jesus did not regard salvation as an abstract, spiritual idea or a feeling in the heart. Salvation is the granting of physical wholeness in the concreteness of pain and suffering.

Liberation then cannot be separated from the historical struggle of freedom in this world. To be liberated is not simply "a status one has but an action one undertakes as a self-conscious subject."[17] Liberation means:

> Mammy, don't you cook no more,
> You are free, you are free!
>
> Rooster, don't you crow no more,
> You are free, you are free!
>
> Old hen, don't you lay no more eggs,
> You are free, you are free.

Any view of liberation that fails to take seriously a people's freedom in history is not biblical and is thus unrelated to the One who has called us into being. That is why black preachers from Richard Allen to Adam Clayton Powell and Martin Luther King, Jr., viewed slavery and oppression as a contradiction of the divine will. While white missionaries and preachers were saying, "The Freedom which Christianity gives is a Freedom from the Bondage of Sin and Satan, and from the Dominion of Men's Lust and Passions and inordinate Desires" but "does not make the least Alteration in Civil property,"[18] black preachers were taking their text from the book of Exodus and its account of Moses leading the Israelites from bondage. They also preached about Joshua and the battle of Jericho and John on the island of Patmos. Each of these biblical stories stressed God's will to make historical freedom a reality in the land of the oppressed.

Liberation as the fight for justice in this world has always been an important ingredient in black religion. Indeed black religion's existence as another reality, completely different from white religion, is partly related to its grounding of black faith in the historical struggle of freedom. Richard Allen, Absalom Jones, and other blacks walked out of St. George Methodist Church in 1787, and by 1816 Allen had become the first bishop in the newly organized African Methodist Episcopal Church. This church, like its sister church (African Methodist Episcopal Zion Church) became an important instrument of the attainment of black freedom during and after slavery. Independent black Baptist churches had a similar function in black life. During slavery black preachers were almost unanimous in pronouncing God's judgment on human servitude and in affirming that God created black people for freedom. According to the preachers, slaves must struggle to realize freedom in history by breaking the chains of slavery. While not all black preachers went as far as Henry Highland Garnet, he nonetheless represented the spirit of the black religious tradition when he identified obedience to God with the struggle against slavery. In an address to slaves, he said:

> Your condition does not absolve you from your moral obligation. The diabolical injustice by which your liberties are cloven down, neither God, nor angels, or just men, command you to suffer for a single moment. Therefore, it is your solemn and imperative duty to use every means, both moral, intellectual, and physical, that promises success.[19]

The identification of divine justice with civil justice became the central theme of the civil rights movement in the 1950s and 60s. This identification was consistent with black religious tradition and with the Bible. To justify his fight against injustice, Martin Luther King, Jr., referred not only to the Exodus and Jesus Christ but especially to the prophets of the Old Testament. He quoted Amos often: "Let justice roll down like waters, and righteousness like an ever-flowing stream" (5:24 RSV).

The historical character of liberation is also found in the spirituals and the blues. The spirituals stressed freedom from legal slavery, while the blues expressed the quest for freedom from the kind of oppression that emerged after the Civil War. Both the spirituals and the blues are inseparably connected with the social existence of a people trying to find self-expression in a world that placed severe limitations on black people. Liberation thus meant the breaking of the chains that held the people in servitude. This theme is expressed with poetic imagination by the contemporary black poet Mari Evans:

> I take my freedom
> lest I die
> for pride runs through my veins. . . .
> For I am he who
> dares to say
> I shall be Free, or dead
> today. . . .[20]

Liberation is not a theoretical proposition to be debated in a philosophy or theology seminar. It is a historical reality, born in the struggle for freedom in which an oppressed people recognize that they were not created to be seized, bartered, deeded, and auctioned. To understand the question of liberation, we need only hear the words, experience the mood, and encounter the passion of those who have to deal with the dialectic of freedom and oppression in the concreteness of their everyday existence.

> Standin' on de corner, weren't doin' no hahm,
> Up come a 'liceman an' he grab me by de ahm.
> Blow a little whistle an' he ring a little bell
> Heah come patrol wagon runnin' like hell.
>
> Judge he call me up an' ast mah name.
> Ah tole him fo' sho' Ah weren't to blame.
> He wink at 'liceman, 'liceman wink too;
> Judge say, "Nigger, you got some work to do!"
>
> Workin' on ol' road bank, shackle boun'.
> Long, long time 'fo' six months roll aroun'.
> Miserin' fo' my honey, she miserin' fo' me,
> But, Lawd, white folks won't let go holdin' me.

In this context, liberation is the opposite of the policeman, the judge, and that system which may be loosely described as "white folks" and in the New Testament is called the principalities and powers. Black people do not need a degree in theology or philosophy to know that something is not right about this world. Karl Marx may be helpful in providing a theoretical frame for an articulation of the consciousness of the masses who are victims of economic oppression. But blacks in America and some other places believe that the problem of oppression is much more complex than Marx knew. Any analysis that fails to deal with racism, that demon embedded in white folks' being, is inadequate.

> Diggin' in de road bank, diggin' in de ditch,
> Chain gang's got me, boss got de switch.
> All ah want's dese cold iron shackles off mah leg.
>
> Judge say, "Three days!" Ah turn aside.
> "And ninety nine more years!" Ah hung mah head an'
>   cried.
> All ah want's dese cold iron shackles off mah leg.

Of course, liberation is more than the recognition that iron shackles are inhuman; it is also the willingness to do what is necessary to break the chains. As Paulo Freire says: "Nor does the discovery by the oppressed that they exist in dialectical relationship with the oppressor . . . in itself constitute liberation. The oppressed can overcome the contradiction in which they are caught only when this perception enlists them in the struggle to free themselves."[21]

Also it is in the historical context of reflection and action that the oppressed recognize that God is struggling with them in the fight for liberation. This is the meaning of Jesus' lowly birth in Bethlehem, his healing of the sick and demon-possessed, and his death on the cross. God is making plain that his kingdom is not simply a heavenly reality; it is an earthly reality as well. Human beings were not created to work in somebody else's fields, to pick somebody else's cotton, and to live in ghettos among rats and filth. They were created for liberation—for fellowship with God and the projection of self into the future, grounded in historical possibilities. Liberation is self-determination in history and laying claim to that which rightfully belongs to humanity. As Mari Evans puts it:

I
am a black woman
tall as a cypress
strong
beyond all definition still
defying place
and time
and circumstance
assailed
  impervious
    indestructible
Look
  on me and be
renewed.[22]

And lest this struggle seem only grim and austere, the same poet sings of its present joy.

Who
can be born black
and not
sing
the wonder of it
the joy
the challenge
Who
can be born
black
and not exult![23]

Liberation as the Project of Freedom in Hope

While the meaning of liberation includes the historical determination of freedom in this world, it is not limited to what is possible in history. There is a transcendent element in definition of liberation which affirms that the "realm of freedom is always more than the fragments of a free life which we may accomplish in history."[24] As the writer of I John puts it, "Beloved, we are God's children now; it does not appear what we shall be, but we know that when he appears we shall be like him, for we shall see him as he is" (3:2). There is included in liberation the "not yet," a vision of a new heaven and a new earth. This simply means that the oppressed have a future not made with human hands but grounded in the liberating promises of God. They have a liberation not bound by their own strivings. In Jesus' death and resurrection, God has freed us to fight against social and political structures while not being determined by them. Black preachers expressed that truth with apocalyptic imagination:

> I know the way gets awful dark sometimes; it looks like everything is against us. Sometimes we wake up in the dark hours of midnight, briny tears flowing down our cheeks, crying and not knowing what we are crying about. But because God is our Captain and is on board now, we can sit still and hear the Word of the Lord. Away back before the wind ever blowed or before the earth was made, Our God had us in mind. He looked down through time one morning and saw you and me and ordained from the very beginning that we should be his children. You remember Old John the Revelator who claimed he saw a number that had come through hard trials and great tribulations and who had washed their robes in the blood of the lamb. Oh, brothers! Ain't you glad that you have already been in the dressing room, because it won't be long before we will take the wings of the morning and go where there will be no more sin and sorrow, no more weeping and mourning.[25]

This sermon makes clear that liberation is also beyond history and not limited to the realities and limitations of this world. God is the sovereign ruler and nothing can thwart his will to liberate the oppressed.

To persons who would be quick to define this kind of perspective on liberation as an opiate, I would suggest that the analysis of black eschatology as merely compensatory is too superficial and thus reflects the use of intellectual categories not derived from the social existence of black people. Harriet Tubman, Sojourner Truth, and Nat Turner are enough evidence that such language about God and heaven does not always lead to passivity. But when black scholars spend too much time and energy trying to show how "radical" and "revolutionary" black religion was or is, they often fall into the trap of defining the content of these words in the light of Marxism or some other theoretical frame that did not arise from the social existence of black people. While recognizing the possibility of overlap in human experience, I contend that black people's experience of liberation as hope for a new heaven and a new earth represents a new mode of perception, different from the experience of white people. When black people sing, "When the roll is called up yonder, I'll be there," they are referring to more than a metaphysical reality about heaven. For the "roll up yonder" is not about an object but about black subjects who have encountered liberation's future. The people are talking about an experience of freedom that has already broken into their present, and the signs of its presence are reflected in the rhythm and the dance of the people. Rhythm and dance point to the experience of liberation as ecstasy, that is, the ability of the people to step outside of their assigned place and to affirm their right to be other than what is now possible in history. To be able to dance to the rhythm of black life means that the people are moving with a sense of direction and artistry derived from the depths of the "not yet." To be sure, sometimes the people *have* to sing to keep from crying, but the fact that they can sing is an indication of their transcendence over the present and a step into the future.

Liberation as a future event is not simply *other*worldly but is the divine future that breaks into their social existence, bestowing wholeness in the present situation of pain and suffering and enabling black people to know that the existing state of oppression contradicts their real humanity as defined by God's future. Black people sometimes expressed the contradiction between their present slavery and the liberated future in folkloric tales. Consider the tale entitled "Swapping Dreams." The master told Ike: "I dreamed I went to Nigger Heaven last night, and I saw there a lot of garbage, some torn-down houses, a few old broken down, rotten fences, the muddiest, sloppiest streets I ever saw, and a big bunch of ragged, dirty Negroes walking around." But rather than accept the master's perspective about himself and his community, Ike responded with a comment that was deceptive and full of humor but liberating in its rejection of the present white value system. "Umph, umph, Massa," said Ike, "yah sho' musta et de same t'ing Ah did las' night, 'cause Ah dreamed Ah went up ter de white man's paradise, an' de streets wuz all ob gol' an' silvah, and dey was lots o' milk an' honey dere, an' putty pearly gates, but dey wuzn't uh soul in de whole place."[26] With this story, the statement about heaven becomes a revolutionary judgment against the system of oppression. The future becomes a present reality in the slave's consciousness, enabling him to struggle against the white system of injustice. Through story, black people created liberated structures of the future wherein they were able to encounter freedom's essence even though they were slaves.

It is important to note that Black Theology, while taking history with utmost seriousness, does not limit liberation to history. When people are bound to history, they are enslaved to what the New Testament calls law and death. If death is the ultimate power and life has no future beyond this world, then the rulers of the state who control the policemen and the military are indeed our masters. They have our future in their hands and the oppressed can be made to obey laws of injustice. But if the oppressed, while living in history, can nonetheless see beyond it, if they can visualize an eschatological future beyond the history of their humiliation, then "the *sigh* of the oppressed," to use Marx's phrase, can become a cry of revolution against the established order. It is this revolutionary cry that is granted in the resurrection of Jesus. Liberation then is not simply what oppressed people can accomplish alone; it is basically what God has done and will do to accomplish liberation both in and beyond history. Indeed, because we know that death has been conquered, we are set free to fight for liberation in history—knowing that we have a "home over yonder."

"The home over yonder," vividly and artistically described in the black slave songs, is a gift of divine freedom. If this "over-worldliness" in freedom is not taken with utmost seriousness, then there is no way for the oppressed to be sustained in the struggle against injustice. The oppressed will get tired and also become afraid of the risks of freedom. They will say as the Israelites said to Moses when they found themselves between Pharaoh's army and the sea: "Is it because there are no graves in Egypt that you have taken us away to die in the wilderness? What have you done to us, in bringing us out of Egypt?" (Exod. 14:11 RSV). The fear of freedom and the risks contained in the struggle are ever present realities in the fight for liberation. But the transcendence of freedom, granted in Jesus' resurrection, introduces a factor that makes a significant difference. The difference is not that we are taken out of history while living on earth —that would be an opiate. Rather, it is a difference that plants our being firmly in history for struggle, because we know that death is not the goal of history. It was this truth that enabled black slaves to survive humanely in a situation of extreme cruelty. To be sure, they sang about the fear of "sinking down" and the dread of being a "motherless child." They encountered death and expressed the agony of its presence in song:

> Soon one mornin', death comes a-creepin' in my room.
> O my Lawd, O my Lawd, what shall I do?

Death was not an abstract idea, to be debated in a philosophy seminar. Death was a personal experience of loss who appeared in the black situation of pain as "a little ole man," "tippin' in the room." Sometimes death was pictured as "a chariot swingin' low" and "a train a-blowin' at de station." That is why blacks sing

> Before this time another year,
> I may be gone;
> Out in some lonely graveyard,
> O Lord, how long.

But because black slaves believed that death had been conquered in Jesus' resurrection, they transcended death and interpreted freedom from death as a heavenly, eschatological reality.

> You needn't mind my dying,
> Jesus' goin' to make up my dying bed.
>
> In my room I know,
> Somebody is going to cry,
> All I ask you to do for me,
> Just close my dying eyes.

They could transcend death because they knew about Jesus' past, had encountered his presence, and thus were assured of his future coming. Jesus' future coming was the foundation of their faith, enabling them to express this truth in song: "Where shall I be when the first trumpet soun'; soun' so loud till it woke up de dead?" "One day, one day 'bout twelve o' clock, O this ol' earth goin' to reel an' rock." "O My Lord, what a morning, when the stars begin to fall!" "When the sun refuse to shine, when the moon goes down in blood!" "In dat great getting up morning," "de world will be on fire," and "you'll see de stars a-fallen', de forked lighting, de coffins bursting," and "de righteous marching." "The dumb will talk, the lame will walk, the blind will see, and the deaf will hear."

VIII.
DIVINE LIBERATION
AND BLACK SUFFERING

The reality of suffering challenges the affirmation that God is liberating the oppressed from human captivity. If God is unlimited both in power and in goodness, as the Christian faith claims, why does he not destroy the powers of evil through the establishment of divine righteousness? If God is the One who liberated Israel from Egyptian slavery, who appeared in Jesus as the healer of the sick and the helper of the poor, and who is present today as the Holy Spirit of liberation, then why are black people still living in wretched conditions without the economic and political power to determine their historical destiny? Why does the Holy One of Israel permit white people to oppress helpless black people when the Scripture says God came in Jesus Christ to set the captives free? The persistence of suffering seems to require us to deny either God's perfect goodness or his unlimited power. According to which view is adopted, God is either unwilling or unable to deliver the oppressed from injustice. William Jones's exploration of the question, "Is God a white racist?"[1] is a cogent example of the first alternative, while E. S. Brightman's "finite God" illustrates the second.

Black Theology, while recognizing the seriousness of the problem, cannot accept either logical alternative for solving it. It is a violation of black faith to weaken either divine love or divine power. In this respect Black Theology finds itself in company with all of the classic theologies of the Christian tradition. However, the problem is resolved differently in Black Theology, which takes the liberation of the oppressed as its starting point.

Suffering in the Bible

The best place to begin an examination of the problem of suffering is with the Bible. How does Scripture reconcile the suffering of the innocent and weak with its claim that "the Lord is a man of war" (Exod. 15:3 RSV) who "delivers [the poor] in the day of trouble" and "'protects him and keeps him alive" (Ps. 41:1-2 RSV)?

The Old Testament tells the story of Israel's faith in the faithfulness of God to liberate the lowly and downtrodden from the proud and the mighty. Israel's faith in the promise of God to be with the little ones in time of trouble is grounded in Yahweh having been with her in the Exodus–Sinai event, thereby disclosing his mighty power and unlimited love on behalf of the helpless. Because the Exodus was the decisive event in Israel's knowledge of God, the people naturally were troubled when historical events seemed to contradict their faith in God as the Liberator of the oppressed. The more they believed that God "heals the brokenhearted, and binds up their wounds" (Ps. 147:3 RSV), the more the suffering and the pain of the poor emerged as a problem in their religious consciousness. Since God is who the people know him to be, why then did he not always intervene to liberate his faithful servants? Why did the God of the oppressed permit the innocent to suffer?

On the one hand, Israel firmly believed that "the Lord is a great God" (Ps. 95:3 RSV), whose "steadfast love endures for ever" (Ps. 136 RSV) and who is the "great King above all gods" (Ps. 95:3 RSV). On the other hand, Israel could not ignore the obvious historical contradictions inherent in her faith, particularly when the wicked continued to "slay the widow and sojourner, and murder the fatherless" (Ps. 94:6 RSV). Consequently, the integrity of her faith in Yahweh's faithfulness was dependent upon her asking,

> O Lord, how long shall the wicked,
> how long shall the wicked exult?
> Psalm 94:3 RSV

This is not a theoretical question arising out of an intellectual concern about the content of divine justice. It is a practical question emerging out of the struggle of faith with the negative dimensions of human experience. Whatever else may be said about biblical faith, it did not affirm divine revelation in lieu of facing the reality of human suffering. Indeed it was not the mere presence of suffering that troubled Israel's faith. "The problem in Scripture is not why suffering exists, but why it afflicts some people and not others. The problem is not the *fact* of suffering but its *distribution*. Why do the wicked prosper, while those who try to keep faith with God suffer?"[2]

One of the simplest and most common responses to this problem was the suggestion that suffering was distributed in exact proportion to the sins committed.[3] This formula was applied both to the community in general and to the individual in particular. Suffering therefore was understood as the just punishment of God inflicted on those who had disobeyed his will. This view is directly related to the covenant experience at Sinai wherein Israel agreed to obey Yahweh's Law and to live according to his holy ways. To be sure, there were many instances of Israel's disobedience, and Yahweh did not always administer the punishment merited by the people. But that was due to God's grace and mercy which tempered his justice but did not negate it. Furthermore, the establishment of divine justice in Israel meant that those who keep the covenant will be rewarded, and those who disobey will be punished by God according to the extent of their disobedience.

> Tell the righteous that it shall be well with them,
>   for they shall eat the fruit of their deeds.
> Woe to the wicked! It shall be ill with him,
>   for what his hands have done shall be done to him.
>   Isaiah 3:10-11 RSV

This view is the theological assumption of Deuteronomy and the Deuteronomic theory of history as found in I and II Kings. It is also found in Proverbs.

> The fear of the Lord prolongs life,
>> but the years of the wicked will be short.
>>> Proverbs 10:27 RSV

Although the idea that suffering was the just punishment for
sins is clearly present in the Bible, that formula was often contradicted by history. It was not difficult for the people to see
that the wicked person did not always suffer for his wrongdoings,
and neither did the righteous one prosper. The opposite often
occurred. That is why Jeremiah complained:

> You have right on your side, Yahweh,
> when I complain about you.
> But I would like to debate a point of justice with you.
> Why is it that the wicked live so prosperously?
> Why do scoundrels enjoy peace?
>> Jeremiah 12:1 JERUSALEM BIBLE

And Habakkuk, who was concerned about the use of evil as an
instrument of divine purpose, also questioned the justice of God.

> Thou who are of purer eyes than to behold evil
>> and canst not look on wrong,
> why dost thou look on faithless men,
>> and art silent when the wicked swallows up
> the man more righteous than he?
>> Habakkuk 1:13 RSV

It is important to note that neither Habakkuk nor Jeremiah
received an answer to his perplexing question. Both prophets
illustrate how biblical religion, on the one hand, faced squarely
the reality of suffering but, on the other hand, refused to let evil
count decisively against Yahweh's sovereignty. That suffering is
real and thus contradicts Israel's knowledge of God is affirmed
throughout biblical history. But despite suffering, biblical faith
continued to insist on the sovereignty of Yahweh's justice and his
will to establish divine righteousness in human history. Indeed
it was the strength of Israel's monotheising faith in God's abso-

lute sovereignty, which finally (and canonically) excluded any form of metaphysical dualism, that created the seriousness of the problem of the distribution of suffering. Since evil was under the aegis of God's sovereignty and not an independent power co-eternal with him, why then does not God establish divine righteousness here and now, by distributing rewards and punishments in accordance with the obedience and disobedience of his creatures?

The people's failure to reconcile divine justice with human suffering in the present led some to attempt reconciliation by an appeal to the future. Habakkuk suggests this solution:

> For still the vision awaits its time;
>> it hastens to the end—it will not lie.
> If it seem slow, wait for it;
>> it will surely come, it will not delay.
> Behold, he whose soul is not
>> upright in him shall fail,
>> but the righteous shall live by his faith.
>> Habakkuk 2:3-4 RSV

The emphasis of facing the enigmas of history in faith, confident that God will make things clear in the future, is also implied in Jeremiah when he says, "the days are coming, says the Lord, when I will make a new covenant with the house of Israel and the house of Judah" (31:31 RSV). While Jeremiah and Habakkuk held onto belief in God's sovereignty in the context of injustice and suffering, looking forward to the inauguration of God's future establishment of divine righteousness, others before and after them insisted on the classical explanation, suggesting that the divine punishment of the wicked is only temporarily delayed.

> Better is a little that the righteous has
>> than the abundance of many wicked.
> For the arms of the wicked shall be broken;
>> but the Lord upholds the righteous.
>> Psalm 37:16-17 RSV;
>> cf. Proverbs 24:19f.

But the application of the Deuteronomic ethic of election to the case of individual suffering in Diaspora could not stand up against the facts of history, even with the appeal to future historical happenings. The wicked did not always get their punishment before death and neither did the righteous get their reward, as Psalm 37 in a simplistic application of the Deuteronomic formula insists. The basic Deuteronomic answer, thus applied, did not explain the problem of suffering, and its inadequacy was brought to a head in Job and Ecclesiastes. The latter not only rejects the Deuteronomic success formula as affirmed by the sages of the book of Proverbs, it says clearly that the problem of suffering is insoluble, completely beyond any rational or religious explanation.

> Vanity of vanities, says the Preacher,
> vanity of vanities! All its vanity.
> Ecclesiastes 1:2 RSV

With this affirmation, the central theme of Ecclesiastes is set in unambiguous opposition to the classical explanation of human suffering. The Preacher does not deny God's existence or his sovereignty, for "who can make straight what he has made crooked" (7:13)? Ecclesiastes merely contends that God is completely transcendent and thus his ways are hidden from human wisdom. Therefore the Preacher concludes that as far as human understanding goes:

> One fate comes to all, to the righteous and the wicked, to the good and the evil, to the clean and the unclean, to him who sacrifices and him who does not sacrifice. As to the good man, so is the sinner; . . . The race is not to the swift, nor the battle to the strong, nor bread to the wise, nor riches to the intelligent, nor favor to men of skill; but time and chance happen to them all. For man does not know his time. Like fish which are taken in an evil net, and like birds which are caught in a snare, so are the sons of men snared at an evil time, when it suddenly falls upon them.
> Ecclesiastes 9:2; 11-12 RSV

Job, while not embracing the skeptical and sometimes cynical attitude of Ecclesiastes, also wrestles with the problem of suffering, as that problem is directly related to human fellowship with God. Job is described as "blameless and upright, one who feared God, and turned away from evil" (1:1 RSV). According to the wise men's retribution dogma, his prosperity and good health were true indicators of his righteousness. But suddenly the situation changed, and Job lost everything he had: wealth, family, and good health. While the Job of the Prologue keeps the faith, the Job of the poetic sections becomes extremely defiant, cursing the day of his birth and insisting that he has done nothing to merit the punishment inflicted on him. He challenges God to a debate in order that his integrity might be vindicated. Job wrestles with suffering, not as a metaphysical problem but as a practical problem related to the life of faith. Like Ecclesiastes, this book is concerned with suffering insofar as it usurps life's meaning as defined by human fellowship with God. Because Job's friends accepted the dogma of retribution as the rule for measuring human fellowship with God, Job protested that their God was unjust.

> Far be it from me to say that you are right;
> till I die I will not put away my integrity from me.
> I hold fast to my righteousness, and will not let it go;
> my heart does not reproach me for any of my days.
> Job 27:5-6 RSV

Job concludes with an audacious challenge: "Let the Almighty answer me!" (31:35).

The Almighty answers, but not according to Job's definition of the problem of suffering. God transposes the issue to another level, emphasizing divine power and knowledge in contrast to human weakness and ignorance.

> Where were you when I laid the foundations of the earth?
> Tell me, if you have understanding.
> Job 38:4 RSV

After God's challenging confrontation, reminding Job of his ignorance, Job repents. Job's repentance is not due to his acceptance of his punishment as just when understood in the light of the retribution dogma. His contrition is due to his recognition that God's revelation transcends human comprehension. God cannot be defined by human logic. Consequently "prosperity and adversity *have no necessary connection* with goodness and wickedness."[4] Thus Job says:

> I have uttered what I did not understand,
>> things too wonderful for me, which I did not know. . . .
> I had heard of thee by the hearing of the ear,
>> but now my eye sees thee;
> therefore I despise myself,
>> and repent in dust and ashes.
>
> Job 42:3, 5-6 RSV

In addition to the idea that God's revelation cannot be limited to the dogma of retribution, the book of Job suggests two additional responses to human suffering. First, the Prologue suggests that Job's suffering was a test of his faith (1:6-12), a theme also found in Abraham's willingness to sacrifice Isaac (Gen. 22:1-19). Second, the Epilogue touches on the theme that suffering can be redemptive (42:10), a theme that is dominant in Second Isaiah. "By his suffering shall my servant justify many, taking their faults on himself" (Isaiah 53:11 JERUSALEM BIBLE).

Second Isaiah's contention that suffering can be redemptive was a new departure in biblical theodicy and requires further examination. The historical setting is Israel's exile in Babylon. Here Israel faced the most severe test of her faith. As the people whom Yahweh chose as his own, liberating them from Egyptian slavery and thereby bestowing upon them a sense of peoplehood, the people of Israel found it difficult to reconcile their faith in God as Savior and Liberator with their existence as exiles in a foreign land. To be sure, the people realized that they had sinned and thus their exile was partly justifiable in view of the orthodox dogma of retribution. Had not the prophets warned Israel to repent or suffer exile? But how was Yahweh justified in using the works of evil men to accomplish his purpose? And if we grant that the answer to the previous question lies in God's inscrutable will, the justice of God still has to face the fact that Babylon was pitiless in her oppression of Israel, and thus "showed them no mercy" (47:6 RSV).

> When the poor and needy seek water,
>   and there is none,
>   and their tongue is parched with thirst.
>   Isaiah 41:17 RSV

Why did Israel receive "*double* for all her sins" (Isa. 40:2 RSV)? It is not surprising that many Israelites concluded that Yahweh was either impotent (Isa. 40:28) or had cast them off. "My way is hid from the Lord," said Israel, "and my right is disregarded by my God" (Isa. 40:27 RSV). "The Lord has forsaken me, [and] my Lord has forgotten me" (Isa. 49:14 RSV).

In the context of despair and hopelessness, Second Isaiah emerges on the scene to proclaim that Israel's servitude is over, because Yahweh, the Creator and Redeemer of humankind, still loves his people. How absurd it is to think that Yahweh, the God of the poor, has forgotten about his people in Babylon. And how ridiculous it is to think that Yahweh, the everlasting God, has grown faint and weary. His power is unlimited and his love knows no bounds for those who are weak and helpless. Then the prophet moves beyond the simple moral coherence of the dogma of retribution and introduces the idea of the Suffering Servant. Israel's suffering must be understood, in the light of the purpose and sovereignty of God wherein old Israel became a new being, his servant for the redemption of the nations.

Although there has been much scholarly debate about the identity of the servant in Second Isaiah,[5] there are several passages where the servant is explicitly identified with Israel.

> And he said to me, "You are my servant,
>   Israel, in whom I will be glorified"
>   Isaiah 49:3 RSV

> But you Israel, my servant,
>   Jacob, whom I have chosen,
>   the offspring of Abraham, my friend;
>   Isaiah 41:8 RSV

Because Israel as a new being is Yahweh's servant, her mission is to "bring forth justice to the nations" (Isa. 42:1 RSV) by enduring the transgressions and sins of others (Isa. 53). The sins of others are placed upon Israel when she remains faithful to Yahweh, even though evil men inflict pain and suffering upon her. Her mission is to be Yahweh's people in the world by expressing the liberating presence of God among the nations. This act is the *vicarious* suffering of the innocent for the guilty. This is the meaning of Israel's double portion which she received from Yahweh's hand: expiation for her own sins, and transformation into a new being for the sake of others.

Two questions arise from this analysis of Israel's suffering: (1) Why should Israel suffer for others? and (2) What makes Israel's suffering redemptive? The answer to the first question is found in the meaning of divine election. To be chosen by Yahweh involves service, and thus the responsibility to participate in his will to establish justice in the world. To share in Yahweh's inauguration of divine righteousness involves the willingness to suffer in the struggle of freedom. Election therefore is not a privileged status that is given to favorite people. It is a call to serve, to suffer with God in the divine realization of justice in the world. And Yahweh's justice is not only for Israel but for all who hurt and inflict hurt in the world. For the oppressed, justice is the rescue from hurt; and for the oppressors it is the removal of the power to hurt others—even against their will—so that justice can be realized for all.

When viewed in the context of Yahweh's sovereignty and purpose, Israel's exile experience is not merely the fulfillment of the dogma of retribution. It is also the time when she receives a new vocation equal in importance to that of the Exodus, a higher vision of her calling as God's people. To be Yahweh's servant not only means that God will strengthen and help you and "will uphold you with [his] victorious right hand" (Isa. 41:10 RSV); it also means that Israel suffers with Yahweh in the divine establishment of justice in the land. There is no divine election without the call to suffer for justice.

But how can Israel's suffering become redemptive for others? Israel's suffering is redemptive, because she is suffering with and for her Lord who is always identified with the little ones in agony. Therefore, it is God who makes human suffering redemptive! For Yahweh takes upon himself the pain of the widow and orphans and transforms slavery into freedom. This is what a later Isaiah meant when he said:

> In all their affliction he was afflicted. . . .
> In his love and in his pity he redeemed them;
> he lifted them up and carried them all the days of old.
>
> Isaiah 63:9 RSV

As Yahweh's Suffering Servant, Israel becomes God's visible presence in the world, enduring suffering for the freedom of humanity. Her suffering is redemptive because Yahweh is present with her, bearing the pain of sin so that liberation will become a reality among all people.

Second Isaiah's description of Israel as Yahweh's Suffering Servant influenced Jesus' understanding of his ministry as presented in the synoptic Gospels and John. Mark opens his Gospel with a quotation from Second Isaiah, and says that John's preaching is the fulfillment of that prophecy (see Mark 1:1-3 and Isa. 40:3). Matthew and Luke refashion the same passage with their own distinctive approaches (Matt. 3:1-3; Luke 3:1-6). A unique and dramatic use of Isaiah 40:3 is also found in John 1:19-23. The heavenly voice, which combines Isaiah 42:1 and Psalm 2:7, not only occurs at Jesus' baptism[6] (Luke 3:21f.; Matt. 3:16f.; Mark 1:9f.) but also near the close of his ministry at the transfiguration (see Mark 9:7; Matt. 17:5; Luke 9:35). A reference is also made to the Suffering Servant theme in the important Q saying, the reply of Jesus to John (Luke 7:22; Matt. 11:5) and Jesus' direct reading from Isaiah 61 is found in Luke 4:18f. All these passages point to Jesus' acceptance of the role as the expected Messiah and his reinterpretation of messiahship in the light of the Suffering Servant of Second Isaiah. And in Mark 10:45, Jesus' identification of himself with the Suffering Servant of Isaiah 53 is made with unmistakable clarity: "For the Son of man . . . came not to be served but to serve, and to give his life as a ransom for many." The passion predictions[7] make a similar point, as well as the Fourth Gospel's reference to Jesus as "the Lamb of God, who takes away the sin of the world" (1:29, 36; cf. Isa. 53:4f., 7, 11).

Though Paul does not call Jesus the Servant of the Lord, his saying that "Christ died for our sins *in accordance with the Scriptures*" (I Cor. 15:3 RSV) has virtually the same meaning. Other echoes identifying Jesus with the Suffering Servant are found elsewhere in the New Testament.[8] "It is thus fair to say," writes Millar Burrows, "that from Acts on the identification of Jesus with the Suffering Servant of the Lord is constant in the New Testament and there is no compelling reason to doubt that Jesus himself originated the idea."[9]

But the theological question is, What does Jesus' acceptance of the role of the Suffering Servant of the Lord have to do with human suffering? The answer to this question is the crux of the biblical view of suffering. The approach to suffering is not derived from the philosophical definition of the problem of evil (If God is all-powerful and all-loving, why is there evil?), although the philosophical statement of the problem is relevant to the Bible, since philosophy emerges out of the culture to which the gospel seeks to speak. The weight of the biblical view of suffering is not on the *origin* of evil but on what God in Christ has done about evil. According to the New Testament, God became human in Jesus Christ, and defeated decisively the power of sin, death, and Satan, thereby bestowing upon us the freedom to struggle against suffering which destroys humanity. This is the meaning of Jesus' life, death, and resurrection. During Jesus' life, God became the Suffering Servant in Israel's place, and thus took upon the divine-self human pain.

> He was despised and rejected by men;
>   a man of sorrows and acquainted with grief;
> and as one from whom men hide their faces
>   he was despised, and we esteemed him not.
>   Isaiah 53:3 RSV

On the cross, God's identity with the suffering of the world was complete. This event was the actualization of Second Isaiah's prophecy.

> Surely he has borne our griefs
>   and carried our sorrows;
> yet we esteemed him stricken,
>   smitten by God, and afflicted.
> But he was wounded for our transgressions,
>   he was bruised for our iniquities;
> Upon him was the chastisement that made us whole,
>   and with his stipes we are healed.
>   Isaiah 53:4-5 RSV

In this context, Jesus' death was a sacrifice: "like a lamb that is led to the slaughter and like a sheep that before its shearers is dumb, so he opened not his mouth" (Isa. 53:7 RSV). Thus the reality and the depth of God's presence in human suffering is revealed not only in Jesus' active struggle against suffering during his ministry but especially in his death on the cross. The cross of Jesus reveals the extent of God's involvement in the suffering of the weak. He is not merely sympathetic with the social pain of the poor but becomes totally identified with them in their agony and pain. The pain of the oppressed is God's pain, for he takes their suffering as his own, thereby freeing them from its ultimate control of their lives. The oppressed do not have to worry about suffering because its power over their lives was defeated by God himself. God in Christ became the Suffering Servant and thus took the humiliation and suffering of the oppressed into his own history. This divine event that happened on the cross liberated the oppressed to fight against suffering while not being determined by it.

The resurrection ignites joy and excitement because it is the sign of God's victory over suffering on the cross. The oppressed are set free to struggle politically against the imposed injustice of rulers. The Suffering Servant was raised from the dead, and this means that God is now present not only with Israel but with all who fight for the realization of humanity. Without the resurrection, Jesus was just a good man who suffered like other oppressed people. There is no reason to believe that God was with Jesus and thus defeated suffering unless Jesus transcended death and is alive and present in the struggle of freedom. But if he is alive and present with God, then we have every reason to believe that we too will be raised from the dead and will be given the eternal freedom of communion with God. A foretaste of that freedom is already breaking into our present history and that is why the oppressed can struggle for freedom in this world. The freedom to struggle against suffering is the eschatological gift of a new humanity derived from Jesus' resurrection. For without this gift of new humanity, the oppressed would have no grounds for struggling against suffering. They would be defined by the limits of history. The resurrection, therefore, is God breaking into history and liberating the oppressed from their present suffering, thereby opening up humanity to a divine realization beyond history. That is why Paul says: "If Christ has not been raised, then our preaching is in vain. . . " (I Cor. 15:14 RSV). For his resurrection is the foundation of our freedom. "For freedom Christ has set us free" (Gal. 5:1 RSV).

Jesus' life, death, and resurrection render the orthodox law of retribution inadequate as an explanation of human suffering. God is not an even-handed Judge who inflicts punishment according to the crime. Rather, he is the Loving Father of Jesus, the crucified and risen One, who suffers on our behalf. The legalistic structure of the orthodox formula, therefore, fails to deal with the complexity of divine involvement in suffering and the divine call of freedom to the oppressed in their situation of injustice. The divine involvement in suffering, radically revealed in Jesus' cross, counts decisively against any suggestion that God is indifferent to human pain. Whatever else may be said about the philosophical difficulties that the problem of evil poses, whether in the traditional definition of classical philosophy or in Albert Camus's humanism or even in the more recent black humanism of William Jones, faith arising out of the cross and resurrection of Jesus renders their questions ("Is God evil?" or "Is God a white racist?") absurd from the biblical point of view. The absurdity of the question is derived from the fact that its origin ignores the very foundation of biblical faith itself, that is, God becoming the Suffering Servant in Christ in order that we might be liberated from injustice and pain.

However, the biblical view that God suffers for us and has defeated the powers of evil decisively in the cross and resurrection of Jesus does not mean that suffering no longer exists. The New Testament is clear that though the decisive victory has been won on the cross and through the resurrection of Jesus, the war against evil and suffering is still going on. The final victory will take place with the Second Coming of Christ. In the meantime, Christians are called to suffer with God in the fight against evil in the present age. This view gives us a new perspective on suffering. The oppressed are called to fight against suffering by becoming God's suffering servants in the world. This vocation is not a passive endurance of injustice but, rather, a political and social praxis of liberation in the world, relieving the suffering of the little ones and proclaiming that God has freed them to struggle for the fulfillment of humanity. Suffering therefore is reinterpreted in the light of Jesus' cross and resurrection and of our call to become liberated sufferers with God. There is joy in our suffering insofar as we have to suffer for freedom. There is joy not only because we know that God has defeated evil but also because God is present with us in our fight against suffering and will come again fully to consummate the freedom already given in Jesus Christ. Therefore when suffering is inflicted upon the oppressed, it is evil and we must struggle against it. But when suffering arises out of the struggle against suffering, as in the fight against injustice, we accept it as a constituent of our calling and thus voluntarily suffer, because there is no freedom independent of the fight for justice.

Suffering in the Western Theological Tradition

Regarding the definition of the problem of suffering, it is unfortunate that most of the exponents of the Western theological tradition have not paid sufficient attention to the biblical view.[10] Although the Bible makes the divine liberation of the oppressed its starting point in the analysis of the problem of suffering, the classical theological tradition generally and Euro-

American theology in particular have usually taken their clue from the speculations of Greek philosophy or from a naïve orthodox providential claim that "all things work together for good to them that love God, to them that are called according to his purpose" (Rom. 8:28 KJV). Both alternatives have contributed to a political conservatism that locates the resolution of the problem of suffering either in the logical structure of the rational mind or in the interior depths of the human heart, and thereby negates the praxis of freedom against the structures of injustice and oppression.

When theology defines the problem of suffering within the context of philosophical discourse, it inevitably locates the Christian approach to suffering in the wrong place. In philosophy, human suffering is an aspect of the problem of evil. Thus the crux of the problem is: How do we *rationally* reconcile a God unlimited both in power and in goodness with the presence of evil, moral and natural? Epicurus (341–270 B.C.) was probably the first to state the theoretical implications of this dilemma.

> God either wishes to take away evils, and is unable; or He is able, and is unwilling; or He is neither willing nor able, or He is both willing and able. If He is willing and is unable, He is feeble, which is not in accordance with the character of God; if He is able and unwilling, He is envious which is equally at variance with God; if He is neither willing nor able, He is both envious and feeble, and therefore not God; if He is both willing and able, which alone is suitable to God, from what source then are evils? or why does He not remove them.[11]

Whatever else may be said about this philosophical definition of the problem of evil, the political action against evil is not built into it. Thus the problem is basically theoretical and not practical. Here then is one of the essential differences between the Bible and Greek philosophy. The latter tends to be more concerned about the theoretical formulation of the problem and less concerned about its practical elimination. The Bible is the exact reverse. Its emphasis is on what God has done in Jesus's cross and resurrection to destroy the powers of evil and give the oppressed the freedom to struggle against humiliation and suffering. The Bible has little or no interest in rational explanations regarding the origins of evil. That evil exists is taken for granted. The focus is on what God has done, is doing, and will do to defeat the principalities and powers of evil. Thus God's past and present acts of liberation bestow upon the oppressed the freedom to fight against their slavery and oppression.

Because Western theology has been influenced too much by philosophy and too little by the Bible in its analysis of the problem of suffering, it has often contributed to the religious justification of unjust structures that oppress the poor. That is why theologians spend more time discussing metaphysical speculations about the origin of evil than showing what the oppressed must do in order to eliminate the social and political structures that create evil. By focusing on metaphysics, theologians make the problem of evil a matter of intellectual theory and more often than not end up suggesting solutions that have nothing to do with the liberation of the poor from bondage.

This is especially true of John Hick's analysis of the problem of evil. He accepts the classical definition of the problem: "If God is perfectly good, He must want to abolish all evil; if He is unlimitedly powerful, He must be able to abolish all evil: but evil exists. Therefore either God is not perfectly good or He is not unlimitedly powerful."[12] With this definition as his starting point, Hick proceeds to outline two classical approaches to the problem of evil in the Christian tradition: the Augustinian and the Irenean. He summarizes their difference as follows:

There is . . . to be found in Irenaeus the outline of an approach to the problem of evil which stands in important respects in contrast to the Augustinian type of theodicy. Instead of the doctrine that man was created finitely perfect and then incomprehensibly destroyed his own perfection and plunged into sin and misery, Irenaeus suggests that man was created as an imperfect, immature creature who was to undergo moral development and growth and finally be brought to the perfection intended for him by his Maker. Instead of the fall of Adam being presented, as in the Augustinian tradition, as an utterly malignant and catastrophic event, completely disrupting God's plan, Irenaeus pictures it as something that occurred in the childhood of race, an understandable lapse due to weakness and immaturity rather than an adult crime full of malice and pregnant with perpetual guilt. And instead of the Augustinian view of life's trials as a divine punishment for Adam's sin, Irenaeus sees our world of mingled good and evil as a divinely appointed environment for man's development towards the perfection that represents the fulfillment of God's good purpose for him.[13]

From a theological point of view, however, the differences between the two theories are not so significant as the similarities. Due to the influence of Greek philosophy, both are focused on the origin of evil rather than on the political structures that make for human suffering. The difference therefore between Irenaeus and Augustine does not lie in their political analysis of suffering. While Irenaeus stressed the biblical emphasis that Christ's work was primarily a victory over sin, death, and Satan, he fails to draw out the political significance of this theme. Augustine's analysis of suffering was unquestionably dependent on Neo-Platonism, a factor that surely de-emphasized the place of the Bible in his thinking. Thus he defined evil as the privation of the good, and not as a power independent of the human will. Although Irenaeus and Augustine differ in many respects, neither has much to say about God's empowerment of the oppressed to fight against injustice.

The same is true of theologians of Western Christianity who were influenced by them. Even John Hick, who seemed to be aware of the limitations of theoretical analyses of evil,[14] fails to add anything that would be relevant to the liberation of the oppressed. While I do not discount the value of the intellect in analyzing the problem of evil, Hick's analysis might have taken a different turn had he taken more seriously the distinction that Gabriel Marcel makes between the spectator and the victim.

> In reflecting upon evil, I tend almost inevitably, to regard it as a disorder which I view from outside and of which I seek to discover the causes or secret aims. Why is it that the "mechanism" functions so defectively? Or is the defect merely apparent and due to a real defect in my vision? In this case the defect is in myself, yet it remains objective to my thought, which discovers it and ob-

serves it. But evil which is only stated or observed is no longer evil which is suffered: in fact, it ceases to be evil. In reality, I can only grasp it as evil in the measure in which it *touches* me—that is to say, in the measure in which I am *involved*, as one is involved in a lawsuit. Being "involved" is the fundamental fact; I cannot leave it out of account except by an unjustifiable fiction, for in doing so, I proceed as though I were God, and a God who is an onlooker at that. [15]

It is hard not to conclude that the main reason theologians have said little that can be used in the struggle of the oppressed is due to the fact that they have been only spectators and not victims of suffering.

A similar criticism must be directed against the religious orthodox approach. It, like the philosophical approach, has too often been a spectator's viewpoint, contributing to the oppression of the poor by justifying the unjust status quo. One of the typical representatives of this approach is Emil Brunner. The key to his view of divine providence and thus the problem of theodicy, is found in his interpretation of Romans 8:28.

In the presence of the Cross we cease to talk about "unjust" suffering. On the contrary, as we look at the Crucified all suffering gains a positive significance. "To those who love God all things work together for good"—we know this as those who have perceived that the sufferings of Christ were for the good of the world. Now we may unite our sufferings with the sufferings of the Crucified; as those who are united with Him in faith we may conceive them as suffering with Christ, even when from the moral point of view our sufferings are well deserved. For us suffering loses its negative character; it becomes fruitful, as God's means of discipline, by means of which, in paternal severity, He draws us to Himself. This is the greatest transformation possible in the sphere of human experience. Without taking away the sting of suffering, without fostering a desire for suffering, suffering becomes a positive instead of a negative principle.

Finally, there is yet another result: "I reckon that the sufferings of this present time are not worthy to be compared with the glory which shall be revealed to us-ward" [Rom. 8:18]. The believer looks beyond his suffering to the final goal which it must serve;

compared with the promised glory, his suffering does not count. Suffering becomes the way to eternal life. Here, then, the theodicy problem is not solved *intellectually*, but by a real redemption, it is overcome. This does not mean that what is terrible becomes less terrible; terrible as it is, it is conquered by Him who permits us to bear this suffering, in order to purify us, and thus to prepare us for that life which no longer contains suffering. The real solution of the problem of theodicy is redemption.[16]

The difficulty with Brunner's antiphilosophical approach is not located in what he says but in what he fails to say, thereby negating the central meaning of biblical revelation which he intends to affirm. He rightly makes divine revelation the starting point of his analysis of the problem of suffering and also correctly concludes that redemption is the answer to that problem. But his analysis of biblical revelation and its meaning for the victim of suffering radically distorts God's self-disclosure in that he leaves out the divine will to liberate the oppressed from social and political bondage. According to the Bible, the cross and resurrection of Jesus are God's decisive acts against injustice, against the humiliation and suffering of the little ones. Indeed, it is because God disclosed himself as the Oppressed One in Jesus that the oppressed now know that their suffering is not only wrong but has been overcome. This *new* knowledge of God in Jesus grants the oppressed the freedom of fighting against the political structures of servitude which make for pain and suffering. Brunner seemed to have overlooked entirely God's gift of freedom to the oppressed for the struggle against injustice. He did not pay sufficient attention to the fact that God"s election involves the responsibility to struggle with him in the fight for justice. In this regard, theologians would do well to listen carefully to Ernst Käsemann's comment: "Every word, every deed, every demonstration is a denial of our Lord and ourselves, unless we test them from the point of view of whether they are opium of the people, or can be regarded and abused as such."[17] I contend that it is only in the struggle of an oppressed community for justice that problems of suffering and its relation to the gospel can be properly analyzed. For it is only in the fight for justice that God is encountered; and it is from this divine encounter in struggle that the oppressed also know that "the sufferings of this present time are not worth comparing with the glory that is to be revealed to us" (Rom. 8:18 RSV). But without struggle, this vision of a new heaven becomes a sedative that makes the victims of injustice content with servitude. Without struggle, the negative suffering inflicted by oppressors becomes positive and thus leads to passivity and submission. Without struggle, the idea of redemption becomes a human creation of oppressors designed to numb the pain and forestall challenges to the structures of injustice. Why is it that Brunner and many other contemporary Euro-American theologians have not recognized this danger? Why is it that white theologians in America have interpreted God's relation to black suffering in such a manner that the divine empowerment of the oppressed to fight actively against the evils of racism is absent from their analyses? Can this be due to anything else than the fact that the social existence of the oppressors inevitably distorts the biblical message? Only the oppressed can receive liberating visions in wretched places. Only those whose thinking emerges in the context of the struggle against injustice can see God's freedom breaking into unfree conditions and thus granting power to the powerless to fight here and now for the freedom they know to be theirs in Jesus' cross and resurrection.

Suffering in the Black Religious Tradition

In contrast to the spectator approach of the Western theological tradition, the black religious perspective on suffering was created in the context of the human struggle against slavery and oppression. Whether we speak of the spirituals or the blues, the prayers and sermons of black preachers or the folkloric tales of Br'er Rabbit and High John the Conqueror, black reflections about suffering have not been removed from life but *involved* in life, that is, the struggle to affirm humanity despite the dehumanizing conditions of slavery and oppression. Therefore, to understand the dynamic movement of black thought in relation to black suffering as black people attempted to make sense out of black life, it is necessary to keep in mind the social and political existence from which black thinking emerged. Black religious thought represents the theological response of an African people to their situation of servitude in North America.

On the one hand, the Bible says that the God of Jesus Christ is the Liberator of the oppressed from social and political bondage. Black people therefore concluded that just as God had delivered Moses and the Israelites from Egyptian bondage, Daniel from the lion's den, and the Hebrew children from the fiery furnace, he will also deliver black people from American slavery.

> Didn't my Lord deliver Daniel, deliver Daniel, deliver Daniel,
> Didn't my Lord deliver Daniel, An' why not every man.

But on the other hand, the continued existence of slavery and oppression seemed to contradict God's will and power to deliver black people from the power of white people. The more black people believed that "God is a God, God don't never change," the more difficult it was for them to reconcile their religious faith with their bondage. Black suffering was not so much a conflict in rational theory as a contradiction in black life. What is the meaning of black existence, and how do we reconcile black servitude and oppression with the biblical claim that "God is our refuge and strength, a very present help in trouble" (Ps. 46:1 RSV)?

For some black people, slavery was clear evidence that God either does not exist or, if he does, his existence is irrelevant to black suffering. If black people are to be liberated from white tyranny, it will be black people themselves, and not God, who will do the liberating. This perspective is found in the slave seculars and blues, in the work of black poets and novelists from the Harlem Renaissance to the 1970s, and more recently in black power and the black humanist philosophy of William Jones.

The slave seculars actually ridiculed the religious perspective of the spirituals. As Sterling Brown reports, some black slaves sang: "I don't want to ride no golden chariot; I don't want no golden crown; I want to stay down here and be, just as I am without one plea."

> One father, who is in heaven,
> White man owe me eleven and pay me seven,
> Thy kingdom come, thy will be done,
> And if I hadn't took that, I wouldn't had none. [18]

The blues, on the other hand, do not make many direct criticisms of the black religious faith. Yet they are clearly indifferent toward God and thus represent an attempt to create meaning out of life without reference to Jesus Christ. They are an expression of black people's recognition of the absurdity of black life in a white world, which regards blackness as nonbeing.

> They say we are the Lawd's children, I don't say that ain't true,
> They say we are the Lawd's children, I don't say that ain't true,
> But if we are the same like each other, ooh, well, well, why do they treat me like they do?

Because the Christian answer to that question was not satisfactory to many black poets and novelists of the twentieth century, they concluded that the God of Jesus Christ was an opiate for black people. As early as 1906, in response to the slaughter of black people in Atlanta, W.E.B. DuBois made his protest against the silence of God.

> Done at Atlanta, in the Day of Death, 1906.
> O Silent God, though Whose voice afar in mist and mystery hath left our ears an-hungered in these fearful days—
> Bewildered we are . . . mad with madness of a mobbed and mocked and murdered people; straining at the armposts of Thy Throne, we raise our shackled hands and charge Thee, God, by the bones of our stolen fathers, by the tears of our dead mothers, by the blood of Thy crucified Christ: *What meaneth this?* Tell us the Plan; give us the Sign!

Sit no longer blind, Lord God, deaf to our prayer and dumb to our dumb suffering. Surely Thou too art not white, O Lord, a pale, bloodless, heartless thing?[19]

By 1933 Langston Hughes had concluded not only that an appeal like DuBois's was pointless but that the entire history of black religion, particularly as characterized in the "sorrow songs," had contributed to black people's passivity and submission in the context of slavery and oppression.

> Bitter was the day
> When . . .
> . . . only in the sorrow songs
> Relief was found—
> Yet no relief,
> But merely humble life and silent death
> Eased by a Name
> That hypnotized the pain away—
> O, precious Name of Jesus in that day!
>
> That day is past.
>
> I know full well now
> Jesus could not die for me—
> That only my own hands,
> Dark as the earth,
> Can make my earth-dark body free.[20]

Some writers like Hughes and Richard Wright experimented with communism. But finding that white racism was not limited to white preachers and capitalists, they rejected the communist philosophy. However, the agony and depth of black suffering remained within their consciousness, and they expressed its contradiction with literary imagination. Without the reality of black suffering and its contradiction of life's meaning, Richard Wright would not have created Bigger Thomas[21] and neither would James Baldwin have felt the need to "Go Tell it on the Mountain" and to warn white America about the "Fire Next Time."[22] The fire about which he wrote erupted in Watts,

Detroit, and Newark; its political implications were set forth in Willie Rick's cry of "black power" in the summer of 1966. The poetic significance of black power was articulated by LeRoi Jones (Imamu Baraka), Don Lee, and Nikki Giovanni. These events and persons represented black people's revolutionary declaration that they will be free from white oppression "by any means necessary." The Christian faith came under severe attack because most black intellectuals viewed it as the white man's religion, used as an ideological justification of black passivity in the context of oppression. Although not written in the height of the black power revolution, William Jones' book *Is God a White Racist?* is a fitting climax to the black power mood. Using philosophical rather than political categories, Jones examines the claim of black Christians that God is involved in liberating black people. He contends that no evidence supports this claim, in particular that no "exaltation-liberation" event has taken place in black history to vindicate the black Christian faith in Christ the Liberator.[23] Therefore the work of liberation is left in the hands of black people alone.

Black humanism from the slave seculars to William Jones represents an appealing tradition. However, not all blacks accepted this perspective. Although many blacks rejected the claims of Christianity, they did not reject religion. Some substituted Allah for Yahweh, Mohammed for Jesus, Islam for Christianity. The most visible group of this persuasion is the Nation of Islam, often called the Black Muslims. In response to white people's oppression of blacks, they concluded that "the white man is the devil" whose destruction is inevitable at the hands of Allah. The Black Muslims expound an ideology that equates blackness with good and whiteness with evil, thereby fostering the belief that black people can be completely self-determining despite white oppression.

Another tradition in black history and culture is blacks who believed that black suffering would be eliminated through political activity alone. They did not directly deny the validity of religion but merely interpreted it as a matter of the soul and heart and not so much as a leverage in political change. Here are included Frederick Douglass, the National Association for the

Advancement of Colored People, the Congress of Racial Equality, and many of the past and present black officials at various
levels of government. These persons believe that the constitution
is the only foundation for black liberation. The struggle of freedom must be fought and won at the ballot box and through the
legal structures of the state and federal government.

But the vast majority of blacks are Christians who believe that
God is relevant for black life in a white society. Therefore,
unlike the already mentioned perspectives on black suffering,
black Christians are faced with an unavoidable paradox: How do
we explain our faith in God as the Liberator of the oppressed
when black people have been oppressed for more than three
centuries in North America? The importance of this question
cannot be overstated, and black theologians ought to be grateful
to William Jones for having brought this problem to our attention
so sharply.

Of course we are not the first black Christians to recognize the
significance of this problem. Bishop Daniel Payne of the A. M. E.
Church (elected 1852) agonized deeply over the problem of black
suffering.

> I began to question the existence of the Almighty, and to say,
> if indeed there is a God, does he deal justly? Is he a just God?
> Is he a holy Being? If so, why does he permit a handful of dying
> men thus to oppress us? . . . Thus I began to question the Divine
> government, and to murmur at the administration of his provi-
> dence. And could I do otherwise, while slavery's cruelties were
> pressing and grinding my soul in the dust, and robbing me and
> my people of these privileges which it was hugging to its breast,
> and giving thousands to perpetuate the blessing which was tearing
> away from us?[24]

Other black preachers had similar problems and they demanded
that God give an accounting of the divine behavior in the world.
Nathaniel Paul asked:

> Tell me, ye mighty waters, why did ye sustain the ponderous
> load of misery? Or speak, ye winds, and say why it was that ye
> executed your office to waft them onward to the still more dismal

state; and ye proud waves, why did you refuse to lend your aid
and to have overwhelmed them with our billows?. . . And, oh
thou immaculate God, be not angry with us, while we come into
this thy sanctuary, and make the bold inquiry in this thy holy
temple, why it was that thou didst look on with the calm indiffer-
ence of an unconcerned spectator, when thy holy law was violated, thy divine authority despised and a portion of thine own
creatures reduced to a state of mere vassalage and misery.[25]

What answers did blacks give to such questions? Some attempted to penetrate the mystery of black slavery and divine
liberation by appealing to divine providence. These persons
included Paul Coffee, Daniel Coker, Alexander Crummell, and
Edward Blyden. Generally, they sought to explain the mystery
of black servitude in North America with the idea that God willed
the enslavement of Africans in America so that the American
blacks could return to their native land from America and thus
lift "the veil of darkness from their less fortunate brethren and
[open] up the continent of Africa to modern political, economic,
and religious development."[26] According to Blyden, God has
spoken providentially to black people:

First, by suffering them to be brought here and placed in
circumstances where they could receive a training fitting them for
the work of civilizing and evangelizing the land whence they were
torn, and by preserving them under the severest trials and afflic-
tions. Secondly, by allowing them, not withstanding all the services they have rendered to this country, to be treated as strangers and aliens, so as to cause them to have anguish of spirit, as
was the case of the Jews in Egypt, and to make them long for some
refuge from their social and civil deprivations. Thirdly, by bearing
a portion of them across the tempestuous seas back to Africa, by
preserving them through the process of acclimation, and by
establishing them in the land, despite the attempts of misguided
men to drive them away. Fourthly, by keeping their fatherland
in reserve for them in their absence.[27]

Although we certainly can appreciate Blyden and others who
attempted to explain black slavery through an appeal to divine

providence, that explanation is inadequate today. Daniel Payne and Nathaniel Paul approached the problem in a way that is more useful. Payne's answer was grounded in his confidence that God would vindicate the sufferings of black people, appealing to the mystery of God's ways of acting in the world.

> But then there came in my mind those solemn words: "with God one day is as a thousand years and a thousand years as one day. Trust in him, and he will bring slavery and all its outrages to an end." These words from the spirit world acted on my troubled soul like water on a burning fire, and my aching heart was soothed and relieved from its burden of woes.[28]

Nathaniel Paul's answer was similar to Payne's. It focused on God's righteousness and will to be God and to establish justice according to his holy ways.

> Hark! while he answers from on high: hear Him proclaiming from the skies—Be still, and know that I am God! Clouds and darkness are round about me; yet righteousness and judgment are the habitation of my throne. I do my will and pleasure in the heavens above, and in the earth beneath; it is my sovereign prerogative to bring good out of evil, and cause the wrath of man to praise me, and the remainder of that wrath I will restrain.[29]

Although we may not fully accept these answers for our approach to the problem of suffering today, yet we cannot deny that their authors faced the problem and its extreme contradictions. They did not ignore history or encourage black passivity during slavery. Payne's stand against slavery began as early as 1839 when he said:

> I am opposed to slavery, not because it enslaves the black man, but because it enslaves *man*. And were all the slaveholders in this land men of color, and the slaves white men, I would be as thorough and uncompromising an abolitionist as I now am; for whatever and when ever I may see a being in the form of a man, enslaved by his fellowman, without respect to his complexion, I shall lift my voice to plead his cause, against all the claims of his proud oppressor; and I shall do it not merely from the sympathy which man feels towards suffering man, but because *God, the*

living God, whom I dare not disobey, has commanded me to open my mouth for the dumb, and to plead the cause of the oppressed.[30]

This same attitude was expressed by Nathaniel Paul who believed that the abolition of slavery in New York (1827) was a sign of God's liberating activity on behalf of black slaves. To be sure, we may not agree with his conclusion or with the similar contentions of David Walker, Henry Highland Garnet and other black Christians during slavery. But no careful student of black history can say that their views on black religion and suffering led to inactivity, particularly when the black Church and its ministers were the most visible activists against slavery. The same would be true of Harriet Tubman and Sojourner Truth, both of whom were active against slavery *because* they were believers in the God of Jesus Christ. This faith was the ground of their struggle against suffering, enabling Tubman to liberate more than three hundred slaves from bondage. Thus whatever else may be said about the truth claims of black religion, faith in Jesus Christ did not inevitably lead to black passivity.

Furthermore, when Payne and Paul appeal to God's mystery and sovereignty, they offer a valuable clue, though not a full answer, to the problem of black suffering. The ethos derived from this appeal has enabled countless people to survive and to give an account of their faith in the face of horrendous assault. Black humanism cannot do as well. Nevertheless, William Jones is right! There is no historical evidence that can prove conclusively that the God of Jesus is actually liberating black people from oppression. Thus he asks: Where is the decisive event of liberation in the experience of black people?

In responding to Jones, Christian theologians have to admit that their logic is not the same as other forms of rational discourse. The coming of God in Jesus breaks open history and thereby creates an experience of truth-encounter that makes us talk in ways often not understandable to those who have not had the experience. This statement is not meant to exclude my theological perspective from philosophical criticism. Rather, it is an honest attempt to give an account of black faith in the social context of a world that seems to contradict it. There is the experience of suffering in the world, and no amount of theological argument can explain away the pain of our suffering in a white racist society. But in the experience of the cross and resurrection, we know not only that black suffering is wrong but that it has been overcome in Jesus Christ. This faith in Jesus' victory over suffering is a once-for-all event of liberation. No matter what happens to us in this world, God has already given us a perspective on humanity that cannot be taken away with guns and bullets. Therefore, to William Jones' question, What is the decisive event of liberation? we respond: Jesus Christ! He is our Alpha and Omega, the one who died on the cross and was resurrected that we might be free to struggle for the affirmation of black humanity. I know that this answer will not satisfy Jones or others who view black humanity from another vantage point than Jesus Christ. But for blacks during slavery and its aftermath, Jesus was not a clever theological device to escape difficulties inherent in suffering. He was the One who lived with them *in* suffering and thereby gave them the courage and strength to "hold out to the end."

The idea that Jesus made blacks passive is simply a misreading of the black religious experience. He was God's *active* presence in their lives, helping them to know that they were not created for bondage but for freedom. Therefore, through sermon, prayer, and song black people expressed visions of freedom in a situation of servitude. When everything else in their experience said that they were nobodies, Jesus entered their experience as a friend and a helper of the weak and the helpless. His presence in the black experience was the decisive liberating event which bestowed dignity upon them. His presence enabled blacks to believe that they were on the "Lord's journey" despite the historical evidence that said otherwise. That is why blacks could sing and shout about freedom. They believed that God had not left them alone in suffering. To be sure, they could not rationally explain why they were slaves or why God permitted them to suffer so much. The meaning of black suffering remains a part of the mystery of God's will. But the presence of Jesus in their social existence did reveal that God was at work liberating them from bondage.

On the one hand, the faith of black people as disclosed in their sermons, songs and prayers, revealed that they faced the reality of black suffering. Faith in Jesus did not cancel out the pain of slavery.

Sometimes I'm up, sometimes I'm down,
Oh, yes, Lord!
Sometimes I'm almost to the ground,
Oh, yes, Lord!

But on the other hand, Jesus' presence in the experience of suffering liberated black people from being dependent upon the historical limitation of servitude for a definition of their humanity. Thus they began to project this new knowledge of themselves with future, apocalyptic imagination. They began to sing and preach about a "home in glory" where they would "sit at the welcome table." Heaven thus was not so much an opiate as it was a revolutionary judgment that black people made about American society on the basis of Jesus' presence in their lives. It was the "age to come" that had broken into the present age, giving black people a vision of freedom that enabled them to struggle now for the liberation of the little ones. It was this vision that enabled black preachers from Henry Highland Garnet to Martin Luther King, Jr., to struggle for freedom in the social context of oppression. King spoke of the vision in terms of the "mountain top" that enabled him to take the course of freedom even though he apparently knew that it would lead to his death. But suffering that arises in the context of the struggle for freedom is liberating. It is liberating because it is a sign of Jesus' presence in our midst. Black people, therefore, as God's Suffering Servant, are called to suffer with and for God in the liberation of humanity. This suffering to which we have been called is not a passive endurance of white people's insults, but rather, a way of fighting for our freedom.

Thus the real question is whether those who inflict suffering are the true definers of humanity. I contend that it is the opposite. Humanity's meaning is found in the oppressed people's fight for freedom, for in the fight for liberation God joins them and grants them the vision to see beyond the present to the future. Faith thus is God's gift to those in trouble. It bestows meaning in a meaningless situation, enabling the oppressed to believe that there is One greater than the power of the oppressors.

To summarize Black Theology's perspective on suffering, we can say it is based on the Scripture and the black Christian experience which claim that the God of Jesus is the Liberator of the oppressed from oppression. Although the continued existence of black suffering offers a serious challenge to the biblical and black faith, it does not negate it. The reason is found in Jesus Christ who is God's decisive Word of liberation in our experience that makes it possible to struggle for freedom because we know that God is struggling too.

IX.
LIBERATION AND
THE CHRISTIAN ETHIC

The black struggle for liberation involves a total break with the white past, "the overturning of relationships, the transformation of life and then a reconstruction."[1] Theologically, this means that black people are prepared to live according to God's eschatological future as defined by the reality of Christ's presence in the social existence of oppressed people struggling for historical liberation. This perspective informs black people's view of suffering and enables them to know that white people do not have the last word on black existence.

Because black liberation means a radical break with the existing political and social structures and a redefinition of black life along the lines of black power and self-determination, it is to be expected that white theologians and assorted moralists will ask questions about methods and means. Theologically and philosophically, they want to know whether revolutionary violence can be justified as an appropriate means for the attainment of black liberation. If Black Theology is Christian theology, how does it reconcile violence with Jesus' command to turn the other cheek and to go the second mile (Matt. 5:39)? Is it not true that violence is a negation of the gospel of Jesus Christ?

These are favorite *white* questions, and it is significant that they are almost always addressed to the oppressed and almost never to the oppressors. This fact alone provides the clue to the motive behind the questions. White people are not really concerned about violence in all cases but only when they are the victims. As long as blacks are beaten and shot, they are strangely silent, as if they are unaware of the inhumanity committed against the black community. Why didn't we hear from the so-called nonviolent Christians when black people were *violently* enslaved, *violently* lynched, and *violently* ghettoized in the name of freedom and democracy? When I hear questions about violence and love coming from the children of slave masters whose identity with Jesus extends no further than that weekly Sunday service, then I can understand why many black brothers and sisters say that Christianity is the white man's religion, and it must be destroyed along with white oppressors. What many white people fail to realize is that their questions about violence and Christian love are not only very naïve, but are hypocritical and insulting. When whites ask me, "Are you for violence?" my rejoinder is: "*Whose* violence?" "Richard Nixon or his victims?" "The Mississippi State Police or the students at Jackson State?" "The New York State Police or the inmates at Attica?"

If we are going to raise the question of violence and Christian love, it ought to be placed in its proper theological perspective. Violence is not primarily a theoretical question but a practical question, and it should be viewed in the context of Christian ethics generally and the struggle of liberation in particular. In this chapter, I intend to explore the theological foundation of the Christian ethic and its relation to divine liberation and the human struggle of freedom in an unjust society. I hope to lay to rest once and for all white people's obscene questions about whether we blacks ought to be violent in the attainment of our freedom.

The Interdependence of Theology and Ethics

The ethical question "What am I to do?" cannot be separated from its theological source, that is, what God has done and is doing to liberate the oppressed from slavery and injustice. Thus Christian theology is the foundation of Christian ethics. Theology is the Church's reflection upon the meaning of its faith-claim that

God's revelation is identical with the historical freedom of the weak and the helpless. Ethics derived from theology is that branch of the Church's reflection that investigates the implication of faith in divine liberation for Christian life in the world. Formally, Christian theology asks, "Who is God?" and ethics asks, "What must we do?" Although separate questions theoretically, in practice the answer to the theological question about God includes in it the answer to the ethical question about human behavior.

The close connection between theology and ethics is found not only in the current theologies of liberation but also in other theologies as well, even though this point has often been obscured by the influence of Greek philosophy. With the aid of philosophical categories, Christian theologians began to make exorbitant claims about the "universal" character of their discourse, and consequently failed to pay sufficient attention to the danger of divorcing theology from its biblical base. Thus it became easy to minimize the connection between theology and ethics. While the black answer to the God-question focuses on the divine liberation of the oppressed, and thus includes in it God's election of the oppressed for participation with him in the struggle of freedom, other theologies have viewed divine revelation and ethical obedience differently. In the history of Western theology, we seldom find an ethic of liberation derived from the God of freedom, but rather, an ethic of the status quo, derived from Greek philosophy and from the political interests of a church receiving special favors from the state. Sometimes this status-quo ethic was expressed in terms of a philosophical emphasis on reason. At other times, the theme was faith, understood either as assent to propositional truths or as a spiritual relationship with God. Whatever the variation of emphases on faith and reason, God's revelation was interpreted, more often than not, as consistent with the values of the structures of political oppression. Thus Constantine's participation in the Arian controversy influenced not only the Church's politics but also its theology and the ethical import of that theology. That was why the early Church Fathers could ask about the Son's relation to the Father and later the Holy Spirit's relation to both without connecting the question to the historical freedom of the oppressed. Since the Church and its bishops (during the age of Constantine and thereafter) were not slaves, it did not occur to them that God's revelation in Jesus Christ is identical with the presence of his Spirit in the slave community in struggle for the liberation of humanity. They viewed God in static terms and thus tended to overlook the political thrust of the gospel. This procedure was consistent with the God of Plotinus but not with the God of Moses and Amos. Consequently, the ethics of the fourth-century Fathers differed fundamentally from biblical revelation. Instead of standing unquestionably with the outcasts and downtrodden, as the God of the Bible does, their ethics did more to preserve the status quo than to change it. Whatever else the gospel of Jesus might be, it can never be identified with the established power of the state. Thus whatever else Christians ethics might be, it can never be identified with the actions of people who conserve the status quo. This was the essential error of the early Church. By becoming the religion of the Roman state, replacing the public state sacrifices, Christianity became the opposite of what Jesus intended.

The problem of identifying Christian ethics with the status quo is also found in Augustine and Thomas Aquinas. While they differed regarding the role of faith and reason in theological discourse, they agreed that the slave should not seek to change his civil status through political struggle. According to Augustine, slavery was due to the sinfulness of the slaves. Therefore he admonished "slaves to be subject to their masters . . .," serving "them with a good-heart and a good-will. . . ."[2] For Thomas, slavery was a part of the natural order of creation. Thus "the slave, in regard to his master, is an instrument. . . . Between a master and his slave there is a special right of domination."[3]

The identification of the will of God with the values of the status quo was not limited to early Christianity and the Middle Ages. In Protestant Christianity, this emphasis is found in Martin Luther's definition of the state as the servant of God. That was why he condemned the Peasant's Revolt, saying that "nothing can be more poisonous, hurtful, or devilish than a rebel." He equated the killing of a rebel with the killing of a mad dog.[4]

An ethic of the status quo is also found in Calvinism and Methodism, despite John Calvin's emphasis on divine sovereignty and John Wesley's *Thoughts on Slavery.* Calvinism seemed especially suited for America with its easy affinity with capitalism and slavery. And Wesley's condemnation of slavery notwithstanding he still appeared to be more concerned about a warm heart than an enslaved body.

Of course, it could be argued that the Church's ethical error in relation to the oppressed and their slavery was due to the historical limitation of thought and that this limitation and its subsequent ethical error did not affect the essential truth of the Church's theology. It is not fair, so runs the argument, for us to stand in the twentieth century, with the benefit of the Enlightenment, Marx, and Fanon, and criticize Luther and Wesley for not being revolutionary in their interpretation and implementation of the gospel.

This argument is only partly valid. It is correct in emphasizing the social determination of ethical discourse in the Church's history. The Church's ethics from its beginnings to the present day has been historically determined by its social and political setting. But the argument is wrong when it suggests that the historical determination of church ethics did not affect the essential truth of church theology. When church theologians, from the time of Constantine to the present, failed to see the ethical import of the biblical God for the liberation of the oppressed, that failure occurred because of defective theology. To understand correctly the Church's ethical mistake, we must see it in connection with a prior theological mistake. The basic problem with theological ethics cannot be solved through a debate of the deliberative, prescriptive, and relational motifs of ethical norms. Neither can it be solved through a discussion of the relative merits of the institutional, operational, and intentional motifs in the implementation of ethical decisions,[5] although these issues are important for Christian ethics. Rather, we must unmask this error by analyzing its theological origin. The matter may be put this way: *Theologians of the Christian Church have not interpreted Christian ethics as an act for the liberation of the op-*

pressed because their views of divine revelation were defined by philosophy and other cultural values rather than by the biblical theme of God as the Liberator of the oppressed. If American theologians and ethicists had read the Scripture through the eyes of black slaves and their preachers, then they would have created a different set of ethical theories of the "Good." For it is impossible truly to hear the biblical story as told in the songs and sermons of black people without also seeing God as the divine power in the lives of the oppressed, moving them toward the fullness of their humanity. An ethic derived from this God, then, must be defined according to the historical struggle of freedom. It cannot be identified with the status quo.

We cannot say that Luther, Calvin, Wesley, and other prominent representatives of the Church's tradition were limited by their time, as if their ethical judgments on oppression did not affect the essential truth of their theologies. They were wrong ethically because they were wrong *theologically*. They were wrong theologically because they failed to listen to the Bible—with sufficient openness and through the eyes of the victims of political oppression. How ironic it is that he who proclaimed *sola scriptura* as one of the guiding lights of his reformation did not really hear the true meaning of that proclamation. For to hear the message of Scripture is to hear and see the truth of God's liberating presence in history for those who are oppressed by unjust social structures. Luther could not hear God's liberating Word for the oppressed because he was not a victim. He could only see God's liberation in terms of the individual, "religious" oppression of sin and guilt. Any time God is not derived from the biblical theme of liberation of the oppressed, it is to be expected that Christian ethics will be at best indifferent toward the oppressed struggle of freedom.

That Luther's ethical error is much more serious than the fact that he lived during the sixteenth century and not the twentieth can be shown through an examination of contemporary American discourse on ethics. If Luther's error was due to the *time* in which he lived, then one would not expect to find similar ethical errors today. But that is just what one does find. Herbert Edwards' essay, "Racism and Christian Ethics in America"[6]

shows, with unmistakable clarity, that white ethicists, from Reinhold Niebuhr to James Gustafson, reflect the racism current in
the society as a whole. Here racism appears in the form of
invisibility. White theologians and ethicists simply ignore black
people by suggesting that the problem of racism and oppressi)n
is only one social expression of a larger ethical concern. This error
in contemporary ethical discourse is no different from Luther's
error. It is an ethics of the status quo, primarily derived from an
identity with the cultural values of white oppressors rather than
the biblical theme of God's liberation of the oppressed. Thus the
great theologian Reinhold Niebuhr can speak of black people in
terms of "cultural backwardness," and then conclude: "We must
not consider the Founding Fathers immoral just because they
were slaveholders."[7] What else can this ethical judgment mean
than that Niebuhr derived his ethics from white culture and not
biblical revelation? Despite slavery, lynchings, sit-ins, and boy-
cotts, white ethicists have not made the problem of racial oppression a central issue in their theological discourse. Most ethicists
limit the issue to one or two paragraphs with no more visibility
than the problem of stealing a ten-cent bar of candy. And when
they do say more, as with Paul Ramsey's *Christian Ethics and the
Sit-in*, they spend more time informing black people about the
"proper respect for law and order" than in unmasking the system-
ic order of white injustice. Thus Ramsey says that "simple and
not so simple injustice alone has never been a sufficient justification for revolutionary change."[8] This blindness of Christian ethicists is not merely a cultural accident. As with Luther and others
in the Western theological tradition, it is due to a *theological*
blindness. White ethicists take their cue from their fellow theologians: because white theologians have not interpreted God as the
Liberator of the oppressed, it follows that white ethicists would
not make liberation the central motif of ethical analysis.

Paul Lehmann is one contemporary American theologian and
ethicist who recognizes that there is a problem in the theology-
ethics relationship, even though he fails to locate its essential
solution. Lehmann's chief mistake, in his *Ethics in a Christian
Context*, is related to his excessive dependence upon the six-
teenth-century Protestant reformers for the starting point of

ethical analysis, without recognizing their theological limitation. Luther and Calvin did not interpret God in the light of the liberation of the oppressed, even though Lehmann's emphasis on God's politics in history comes very *close* to saying just that. And perhaps he would have said it, if he had listened less to the Reformation and more to Scripture. But in getting close to the truth of the gospel, Lehmann naturally sensed the contradiction of contemporary discourse on ethics and theology and expressed it in terms of their separation. Lehmann put it this way:

> Without ethical analysis and criticism the dynamics of the divine activity are obscured rather than expressed. This happens whenever the concern of theology with and for dogma becomes an end in itself and hardens into dogmatism. This does not mean that there is no liturgical action, no service of God appropriate to God as he is in himself. Nor does it mean that there is no theology as such, no distinguishable and indispensable concern with and about dogma. Liturgy and theology are not devoured by ethics. Without ethical analysis and criticism, however, the political thrust of divine activity attested by the biblical story and its images is insufficiently discerned and responded to in the liturgical and theological life of the *Koinonia*.[9]

Lehmann's instinct is right but his substantive analysis of the problem is wrong. The absence of the political thrust in theological analysis of divine activity is not due to its divorce from ethics. Christian ethics is a natural child of theology, and the two have really never been separated. The problem is more complex than Lehmann dares admit, for such an admission would lead him to see the defect of both Reformation theology and his own theological thrust. Though Lehmann must be given credit for calling theology and ethics back to its christological base, he did not carry that point to its logical conclusion. He stops short of saying what must be said in order to remain faithful to the biblical story: namely, that God is not simply the God of politics but the God of the politics of the oppressed, liberating them from bondage. And I contend that if he had encountered that biblical truth, he would have also recognized that theology's problem is not its separation from ethics but its separation from the Scripture and its claim that God is the Liberator of the poor. The problem of Christian ethics is its dependence on a theology that does not know the God of the oppressed.

Christian theology's failure to ground its analysis of God in the biblical story of the divine liberation of the oppressed has led to a similar error in Christian ethics. Both theologians and ethicists tend to listen more to philosophy and culture, thereby reflecting the cultural interests of oppressors. Unfortunately, this mistake is found in a fellow black ethicist, Preston Williams. In an article entitled "James Cone and the Problem of a Black Ethic," he pleads for the place of rationality in ethics, which, he contends, I have discarded. He writes:

> To the person who does not share Cone's presuppositions or interpretation of world events [his] account is not likely to be very appealing. Urging to decide this day whom you shall serve will strike both blacks and whites as being beside the point. More importantly neither blacks nor whites who affirm this will have any evidence for their conclusions other than that they accept Cone's views about race, scripture, and God's activity in spite of what they see and hear. In brief, Cone's evidence can be seen as such only after one adopts his perspective. . . . Rational debate and reasonable conclusions have to be foregone. . . . Like Cone, I believe that racism is endemic to white America, but I would prefer victory or defeat to be decided by concrete facts, not by arbitrary reading of God's acts in history. Our basic concern, then, is with *rational discussion of issues and decision-making based upon fact.*
>
> *Our alternative relies upon beliefs and values associated with the Christian faith and American constitutional principles.* . . . [*It*] *is determined by reliance upon some prima-facie duties acknowledged by the generality of mankind.*[10]

It is hard to believe that Williams could be so grossly misguided. I contend that his distortion of the issue is not due to his dependence on rationality but is a consequence of his reliance on *white theological irrationality.* Williams' mistake was that he allowed white theological ethicists, like James Gustafson, to define the content and method of his perspective on rational discourse. But as a *black* person and scholar who has been a victim of racism in and outside the sanctuary of the Church and the halls of academia, Williams should know better than that. White theologians and ethicists are in no position to tell black people what rational discourse in ethics means. Indeed, what they call "rationality" invariably means absurdity for black people, for our history is replete with their high-sounding phrases of "freedom" and "democracy" that meant death to our mothers and fathers. Apparently Preston Williams has been reading too much from white moral teachers and too little of the tales, sermons, and songs of black people. For if he had truly listened to the mothers and fathers of black history, then he would have known the dangerous ground he was treading. Sis Goose demanded a fair (rational) trial from Br'er Fox but found only "fox-justice," because all in the courthouse were foxes. To which black people concluded! "Now, my chilluns, listen to me, when all de folks in de cotehouse is foxes, and *you* is des' er common goose, der ain't gwine to be much jestice for you pore cullud folks."[11] This tale is no less true today when white theologians and ethicists plead for rational discourse and disinterestedness in the analysis of human behavior. If Williams really believes that "racism is endemic to white America,"[12] why then does he plead for a form of ethical discouse that is acknowledge by white racists? For racism lives on irrationality, and it is silly for its victim to expect the racist to adhere to values that will change the structures of oppression. Preston Williams is inviting black people to make the same mistake that Sis Goose made. And if we do, our end will also be the same. White theologians and ethicists will convene the court of rationality, and then they will convict and execute us, just as the foxes did Sis Goose.[13]

White people use such terms as "rationality" and "law" as they suit their interests. They frequently discard or ignore their own definitions when they are no longer applicable to their political interests. Preston Williams should have encountered enough white academic trickery to know that. For even if he could get whites, in a particular discussion, to agree with blacks on a common acceptance of law and rationality, what is there to keep them from conveniently forgetting it when the occasion no longer suits their immediate welfare. Again I think Professor Williams ought to get back to the tales, for there is found the truth about which I speak. The Fox told the Goose to "come down, and don't be afraid" because the animals "passed a *law* that no animal must hurt any other animal." But just when "the Goose was about to fly down, way off in the woods they heard a 'woo-wooh! woo-wooh,'" and "the Fox started to sneak off; and the Goose said, 'Fox, you ain't scared of that Dog, is you? Didn't all the animals pass a law at the meeting not to bother each other any more?' 'Yes,' replied the Fox as he trotted away quickly, 'the animals passed the law; but some of the animals round here ain't got much respec' for the law.'"[13] How true this tale is for the lives of black people! But despite our experience of white deceit that killed our mothers and fathers, Preston Williams would have us to come down from our ethical exclusivism and sit at the table of white rationality. I am simply amazed that he could make such a suggestion.[14]

Unlike Preston Williams, who begins with white rationality and American constitutional principles, I contend that the black Christian ethic must start with Scripture and the black experience. We must read each in the light of the other, and then ask, "What am I to do?" We cannot afford to let white people interpret the meaning of Scripture for us. Inevitably they will interpret the biblical story according to their racial interests. We black people must read the Bible in the light of our story to survive and God's promise to set the captives free. With the Bible in one hand and High John the Conqueror in the other, we must investigate the ethical truths of our lives. How shall we behave with a life-style that is both Christian and black? That is a difficult question, and James Gustafson and other white ethicists cannot help us, for they are part of the reason that we are faced with the problem. They would have us believe that black people's ethical dilemmas are similar to those of whites. But experientially, we know that that is not the case. Thus if we black theologians are to probe the depth of black existence and begin to create ethical structures that are consistent with our historical strivings to be faithful to the "God of our weary years, the God of our silent tears" who "hast brought us thus far on the way," we must *step over* James Gustafson and begin to take theological risks that will call into question everything white theologians and ethicists have said about the "right" and the "good." We must not be afraid to call on the "black and unknown bards of long ago" who created ethical patterns of behavior in song and story as they accepted the risks to fight for freedom. Their words may not be neatly structured to command the interests of white ethicists at Harvard Divinity School or Union Theological Seminary. But their truth is contained in the living reality of black people and not in philosophical and theological textbooks. In black people's sayings and tales, songs and sermons, are found the black ethicists' only starting point. We must take these black realities and place them alongside biblical revelation, and then ask, "What are we black people to do?"

Toward a Black Ethic of Liberation

Because the ethical question "What am I to do?" cannot be separated from its theological base, Christian ethics is, to use Lehmann's phrase, "koinonia ethics."[15] But unlike Lehmann, I contend that the koinonia is limited to the victims of oppression and does not include the oppressors. The ethical behavior of Christians, therefore, is defined in and by the oppressed community whom God has called into being for freedom. To ignore the historical context of the oppressed community and speak of God's politics in universal terms without specificity of words and deeds of the victims in struggle of freedom, is to distort the theological enterprise and the ethical dynamics of God's presence in the world "to make and to keep human life human" (Lehmann's phrase). Thus we can say that Christian ethics is meaningless apart from God's election of the oppressed for freedom in this world. Indeed, apart from divine liberation, there would be no community and thus no Christian ethics.

Contrary to Preston Williams, the behavior of Christians is not decided by rational principles that all people accept as good and right. It is decided by God's act of liberation in Jesus Christ to set the captives free. This divine act of liberation is the ground of the possibility and the actuality of human freedom. Because of Jesus Christ, our behavior can now be defined by divine behavior. Since God's revelation is an act of liberation for the weak and the helpless, the constituents of the koinonia inaugurated by that event are oppressed people who now know that what the world says about their personhood is not true. The encounter of God's liberating presence includes hearing the call to be obedient to the claim of divine freedom. Christian behavior is basically the behavior that arises out of the oppressed community in response to God's call to be obedient to his will.

But the will of God is not a set of rules and principles of behavior derived from a philosophical study of the "Good." We cannot know or hear the will of God apart from the social context of the oppressed community where Jesus is found calling us into being for freedom. The divine will come in an indicative form and not as an imperative. God enters into the social context of oppression and liberates the people into a new existence. At the precise moment that divine liberation happens, a divine claim is laid upon the oppressed to be what God has made them. That is why "ought" is not an accurate way of speaking of Christian ethics. Ought suggests an obligation that is placed upon people that is independent of divine revelation. But according to Scripture, it is the divine event of liberation in the lives of the oppressed that makes covenant-obedience possible. To live as a Christian simply means being what God has made us, namely, liberated creatures committed to the freedom of humanity.

Therefore the answer to the ethical question "What am I to do?" can be stated simply: be a liberator of Christ, because that is what you are! But then how does this work out in one's concrete social existence? How do I begin to develop criteria of ethical judgment? We begin answering this question by stating once more: because the oppressed community is the place where one encounters God's liberating deed, it is also the only place where one can know the will of God. We cannot be what we are apart from what God has done and is doing in the oppressed community. Thus the criteria of ethical judgment can only be hammered out in the community of the victims of injustice. But since God's will does not come in the form of absolute principles applicable for all situations, our obedience to the divine will involves the risk of faith. The risk of faith means that the oppressed are not infallible. They often do not do the will of God which they know, and do not know the will of God which they proclaim. Thus being a member of the oppressed community does not grant one immunity from error and sin. However, it can grant one the knowledge that God is present with them in struggle despite their frailty. God takes their meager actions and transforms them into liberating signs that the divine kingdom is coming. This knowledge lets the oppressed know that what they do is not in vain. From a relationship with the divine One and with the little ones who have encountered God in struggle, Christians are granted the risk of faith to hammer out the meaning of ethical obedience in the social context of human existence. Thus the difference between Christian ethics and non-Christian ethics does not lie in particular acts but in the *source* from which the acts arise. For Christians, Jesus is the source for what we do; without his power to make life human, our behavior would count as nothing. For Jesus is the criterion of our ethical judgment. We do not simply ask, "What would Jesus do?" as if he is an ethical principle to be applied without the risk of faith. We ask, "What is he doing *now* in America and elsewhere to heal the sick and to liberate the prisoners?" This is not an easy question. Therefore our answer to that question must be tested by *other* oppressed people who are involved in the struggle of freedom. We must carve out the answer for every new situation *in dialogue* with Scripture and tradition, as well as with other victims in our social existence. But even this dialogue does not grant the certainty of the truth of our answer. The only certainty we are permitted to know is that the Scripture claims that Jesus will be with us in our struggles. And for those who have met him, this divine promise is enough to hold them together so that they can fight to make the world a humane place to live.

The grounding of Christian ethics in the oppressed community means that the oppressor cannot decide what is Christian behavior. Intuitively and experientially black slaves recognized this basic truth, because their mental and physical survival was at stake. They rejected the white masters' view of morality, but they did not reject *law* and *morality*. Rather, they formulated a *new* law and a *new* morality that was consistent with black strivings for freedom. Right and wrong were not abstract philosophical truths but existential and historical realities defined by black survival and liberation in the social context of servitude. For black slaves, to do the right thing was to do what was necessary to stay alive in bondage with dignity. It had little to do with intellectual discussions about Immanuel Kant's categorical imperative or John Stuart Mill's utilitarianism. Black slaves did not discuss the logic of ethical theory but created ethical structures for behavior in the struggle of survival. What sense would it make for black people to talk about an absolutist ethic in relation to stealing with people who stole them from African and enslaved them in North America? Thus black slaves made a distinction between "stealing" and "taking." Stealing meant taking from a fellow slave, and slave ethics did not condone that. But to take from white folks was not wrong, because they were merely appropriating what was in fact rightfully theirs. Olmstead reports an incident that clarifies the distinction.

> A housemaid who had the reputation of being especially devout was suspected by her mistress of having stolen from her bureau several trinkets. She was charged with the theft, and vociferously denied it. She was watched and the articles discovered openly displayed on her person as she went to church. She still on her return, denied having them—was searched and they were found in her pockets. When reproached by her mistress and lectured on the wickedness of lying and stealing, she replied with the confident air of knowing the ground she stood upon, ". . . don't say I'm wicked . . . its alright for us poor colored people to appropriate whatever white folks' blessings the Lord puts in our way."[16]

Few slaves regarded "stealing" from white people as ethically wrong, because white people were not a part of their community. Indeed, whites were the enemy whom the slaves had to struggle against in order to survive. Blacks did not believe that they were morally bound to people who had reduced them to servitude. An ex-slave, Charles Ball, put it this way:

I was never acquainted with a slave who believed that he violated any rule of morality by appropriating to himself anything that belonged to his master if it was necessary to his comfort. The master might call it theft and brand it with the name of crime; but the slave reasoned differently when he took a portion of his master's goods to satisfy his hunger, keep himself warm, or to gratify his passion for luxurious enjoyment. [17]

The idea that many slaves did not feel themselves bound to white morality is a prominent theme in folklore. When the master found out that one of his yearlings had been taken, he told the black preacher to preach "hell out of the congregation that Sunday so whomever stole that yea'ling would confess having it." John revealed his ethical disposition toward his master when he said:

"Mr. Preacher, I understand you to say, Judgement Day, the man who stole Old Marster's yea'ling will be there, Old Marster will be there, yea'ling will be there, yea'ling will be staring you in the face."

Preacher says, "That's right."

John replied then, "Let Old Marster git his yea'ling on Judgement Day. That'll be time enough."[18]

Another essential ingredient of slave ethics was deception. To survive in an oppressive society, it is necessary to outsmart the oppressors, and to make them think you are what you *know* you are not. Oppressors like happy slaves, especially so-called Christian oppressors. They do not like "uppity" slaves, those who openly expressed their discontentment with servitude. Thus the slaves' survival was sometime dependent upon their ability to make slave masters believe that they accepted their limitations as an authentic form of slave existence. As Henry Bibb said: "The only weapon of self defense, I could use successfully, was that of deception."[19] The same theme is echoed by Lusford Lane:

Ever after I entertained the first idea of being free, I had endeavored so to conduct myself as not to become obnoxious to the white inhabitants, knowing as I did their power, and their hostility to the colored people. The two points necessary in such a case I had kept constantly in mind. First, I had made no display of the little property or money I possessed, but in every way I wore as much as possible the aspects of slavery. Second, I had never appeared to be even so intelligent as I really was. This all colored people at the south, free and slave, find it peculiarly necessary for their comfort and safety to observe.[20]

The theme of deception is also found in folklore and the songs of black slaves. When blacks sang about heaven and told tales about Br'er Rabbit, most whites did not know that they were sometimes referring to Africa and Canada and the need of black slaves to outwit the power of white masters. Whites believed what they wanted to believe, and they wanted to believe that blacks were contented. As one former Mississippian put it: "They find themselves first existing in this state, and pass through life without questioning the justice of their allotment, which, if they think at all, they suppose a natural one."[21] What he failed to understand was that contentment was a form of survival, and slaves often said what the master wanted to hear while thinking other thoughts.

Black people's limitation of ethics to their community and using deception in relation to white people does not mean that they reduce moral behavior to absolute relativity. It only means that liberation is not a theoretical principle limited to Marxian analysis. Liberation is a reality to be created and defined in struggle. Sometimes it may mean standing one's ground and shouting, as Stokely Carmichael once did, "Hell No, We won't go!" Then again it might mean saying, as many slaves did, "No massa, me no want to be free, have good massa, take care of me when I sick, never 'buse nigger; no me no want to be free."[22] Both statements can be valid. The decision must be made by the oppressed, engaged in life-or-death struggle. Both affirmations can be wrong if they are used for selfish gains without regard to the oppressed community. The absolute to which these statements ought to refer is the freedom of the oppressed. Everything else is secondary. When the slave says, "No massa, me no want to be free," to be true to black life, it must be a deception, a trick to survive for the moment so that he can later say, "Hell no, we won't go!" If the slave fails to say the latter to himself and his community at the same time the former is being articulated in the presence of whites, then it is likely that he has internalized what he is not. This is always a danger because the risks of freedom are so great. Thus to be true to the ethic of liberation, the "no massa" syndrome must be a temporary deception and its authenticity clearly dependent upon what is to follow—the "hell no" syndrome. But when the slave says the latter, he must have his "shit together" and be ready to do battle with the powers of evil. For the oppressors will not grant freedom merely through shouting. The oppressed must have the power to take it.

What we are to do, therefore, is not decided by abstract principles but is defined by Jesus' liberating presence in our community. The oppressed community is the place where we are called to hammer out the meaning of Jesus' presence for Christian behavior. This is a risk of faith, because there are no universal guarantees that our decision will be ethically consistent with our freedom in Christ. Therefore we must be in constant dialogue with each other about what we should and should not do in the struggle. No brother or sister can claim to have the whole truth and nothing but the truth. People can only bear witness to the truth they know, always remaining open for further instruction on the truth from other brothers and sisters. When any brother claims to speak the *last* word about our struggle, we can be sure that he is misguided. This guideline applies to Christians and non-Christians, integrationists and nationalists. We may speak to and about white oppressors in that manner as if there could be no doubt about our actions, because they do not deserve our trust or respect. And they probably would not know it if they received it. But in the black community, where everyone bears the scars of struggle, and everyone will have to bear the consequences of a particular course of action, there can be no popes who speak *ex cathedra* on the matter of black liberation. To be sure, there are leaders but *not* self-appointed ones. They must be chosen by the people and thus accountable to the people. This accountability is disclosed in the leader's recognition of his or her fallibility. The function of the leader is to lead the people toward a collective action for the struggle of all. Here is where true liberation ethics is born. What we are called to be and do is revealed in relation to each other in the common struggle of freedom. We may not always agree on a common action in regard to the means of liberation. But our common knowledge that we are enslaved by the structures of injustice binds us together and forces us to fight the good fight so that our children will have a more humane place in which to live.

Black people must be watchful of leaders that do not recognize their fallibility. Thus it is the people's task to inform these self-appointed prophets that their lack of openness to other perspectives on liberation renders them inoperative in the struggle. Their close-mindedness is a shameful display of their failure to take black people's humanity seriously; it shows contempt for the very community they claim to represent. We must tell them that their behavior is no different from white people who always think and act as if they are divine. These persons must be made to know that they do not represent the community, and the only people who can tell them are black people themselves. Leadership is born in struggle and conferred by the community engaged in liberation. Leadership is not conferred by private revelations or visions. One is not called to do a task through ESP but by the community itself, because they see a certain person especially equipped for a particular task. And it is not always a person who has been in the depths of the community's struggle.

We can create our ethic only in dialogue in the struggle of freedom. Anyone who lacks respect for the people's intelligence and has to assume that he or she knows everything, because of college and graduate degrees, does not deserve the people's trust. We black theologians and preachers must be especially sensitive to this point. It is easy for us to think that just because we have read Barth and Tillich or Henry Garnet and David Walker we know what is best for the people. It is easy for us to think that because we know more about the language and origin of biblical writings, we also know more about the gospel of Jesus. Not so! Black people learned a long time ago that there is no connection between education and Christian living. That much they picked up from observing white people who intellectually knew much about God but whose behavior made them children of the devil. We must be careful that we do not fall into the same trap as our oppressors when we are involved in the life of the community. We must be *truly* open to hearing and seeing the truth, even though it is not expressed in language learned in seminary. We must unlearn our slavery to the conceptualization of words and begin to see the black manifestation of truth in the rhythm of black life. It may be revealed when a deacon lines a hymn or when a beautiful sister struts down the aisle of the church, knowing that God was in a good mood when he created her. That is a theological truth you have to see in order to appreciate, for it is difficult to express this reality in words. To see black sisters and brothers relate to each other in community as they feel and touch each other with love means that white sexual morality should not and cannot apply to us. What it must be can only be hammered out in dialogue with each other, respecting each other's personhood. There is no place for male dominance of females. There can only be equality, an equality of power defined in the context of struggle. The task of the black ethicist is to formulate our values so that we can measure our behavior in relation to our proclamations.

We must probe our history, deep into its African roots, and ask about the relationship between the African shout and the Baptist moan, the river of Jordan in the spirituals and the river spirits of West African religion. What is the relationship of African behavior and slave behavior? In what sense did our survival in slavery depend upon liberating structures of behavior derived from Africa? And to what extent does our survival today depend upon our recognition of the essential African structure of our lives and the building of the liberation program upon that structure? A black Christian ethic cannot ignore the fact that we are an African people, and that heritage must be recognized in ethical analysis if we are going to suggest moral directions to black people that do not violate the very substance of our being. The exact extent that African culture should play in the black analysis of ethics is still being debated.[23] But there should be no debate that we are African and not European, even though we may not agree upon the fullest meaning of that affirmation. The meaning will emerge in struggle, as it should.

Another important element in a black Christian ethic is openness to people who are struggling for black freedom but whose perspective is non-Christian or even anti-Christian. I believe that Jesus Christ is at the heart of the black experience in North America. When black people's "road got rocky" and the "way became narrow," they told Jesus about it. He was the *ethical* difference in their lives that enabled them "to press on to higher ground." I am sure that it was he who gave slave preachers the power to proclaim freedom as the essence of the gospel. "Free indeed," Henry Clay Bruce recalls a black preacher saying, "free from death, free from hell, free from work, free from white folks, free from everything."[24] However, other blacks—rationalist or existentialist intellectuals, Marxians, Muslims, nationalists, and others—believe that Christianity retards the struggle for freedom. They rightly observe that the name of Jesus was on the lips of slaveholders, too. These people, in the view of black Christians, are mistaken in putting black and white Christianity in the same boat. Black people took the Jesus that white people knew by name only and reinterpreted him in the light of the Bible, Africa, and the struggle in North America. The difference between black Christians and other blacks must not be permitted to weaken the struggle. The dialogue on how to approach this issue must remain open. Christians must not beat nationalists over the head with Jesus, and neither should nationalists turn their noses up at black Christians. It matters little to white oppressors whether we are nationalists or Christians. As brother Malcolm X taught us:

What you and I need to do is to forget our differences. When we come together, we don't come together as Baptists or Methodists. You don't catch hell because you are a Baptist, and you don't catch hell because you're a Methodist or Baptist, you don't catch hell because you're a Democrat or a Republican, you don't catch hell because you're a Mason or an Elk, and you sure don't catch hell because you're an American; because if you were an American, you wouldn't catch hell. You catch hell because you're a black man. You catch hell, all of us catch hell for the same reason. [25]

Malcolm's message is still true today. The crucial point is that we are *black*, and that fact alone ought to keep us open to each other, not for the purpose of conversion, but for shared participation in finding out the best means of struggle. This openness is the crux of our authentic recognition of each other as brothers and sisters.

The logical extension of the failure to be open to each other leads to that phenomenon that is so detrimental to our struggle and pleasing to white people—namely, blacks killing blacks. We can destroy each other mentally and physically, because we are afraid to deal with the real oppressive forces in our community. Thus the drug-pushers, the pimps, and other self-seeking persons are detrimental to our struggle. When we kill each other with drugs and guns, that means that we are doing the oppressor's job. This phenomenon is the result of mental enslavement to the values that are meant to destroy us. Therefore at the same time that we must create ethical structures that will help us fight white oppressors, we must also find ways to create a black society that makes pimps and drug-pushers a thing of the past. This can be done by destroying white oppressive structures that create the conditions which make it so easy for blacks to kill and maim each other. Here we need all the available resources in the black community for the waging of war against all forces that seek to destroy us. The black ethicists must help to create the dialogue in the black community so that we can move toward the freedom that will appear only if we take the risk to claim it.

White oppressors must be excluded from this black ethical dialogue, because they cannot be trusted. To those whites who continually proclaim their goodwill, despite the long history of racism, the most blacks can say: "There may be a place for you, but you will have to do what we say, without suggesting that you know what is best for our liberation." Few if any whites can accept this. They will say that it is neither fair nor Christian. But we do not need to debate the meaning of fairness or Christianity with our oppressors. For they, of all people, have not earned the right even to utter these words. Our task is to be what we are in spite of white people, because we have seen the vision of freedom, and it is calling us to put the world in shape.

Ethics, Violence, and Jesus Christ

With an authentic ethic of liberation as our point of departure, it is now possible to say a word about violence. Because the oppressed have been victims of mental and physical dehumanization, we cannot make the destruction of humanity, even among oppressors, an end in itself. Such a procedure contradicts the struggle of freedom, the essence of our striving. Our intention is not to make the oppressors the slaves but to transform humanity, or, in the words of Fanon, "set afoot a new man." Thus hatred and vengeance have no place in the struggle of freedom. Indeed, hatred is a denial of freedom, a usurpation of the liberation struggle. The ethic of liberation arises out of love, for ourselves and for humanity. This is an essential ingredient of liberation without which the struggle turns into a denial of what divine liberation means.

However, the radical rejection of hatred and vengeance does not mean that we accept white people's analysis of violence and nonviolence. We are well aware that they derive their analysis of these terms from a theological and political interest that supports the status quo, whereas we must analyze them in accordance with our struggle to be free. We cannot let white rhetoric about nonviolence and Jesus distort our vision of violence committed against black people. Therefore, one of the tasks of the black ethicist is to untangle the confused and much discussed problem of violence and nonviolence and Jesus' relationship to both. At least three points ought to be made. (1) Violence is not only what black people do to white people as victims seek to change the structure of their existence; it is also what white people *did* when they created a society for white people only, and what they *do* in order to maintain it. Violence in America did not begin with the black power movement or with the Black Panther Party. Neither is it limited to the Symbionese Liberation Army. Contrary to popular white opinion, violence has a long history in America. This country was born in violent revolution (remember 1776?), and it has been sustained by the violent extermination of red people and the violent enslavement of black people. This is what Rap Brown had in mind when he said that "Violence is American as cherry pie."

White people have a distorted conception of the meaning of violence. They like to think of violence as breaking the laws of their society, but that is a narrow and racist understanding of reality. There is a more deadly form of violence, and it is camouflaged in such slogans as "law and order," "freedom and democracy," and "the American way of life." I am speaking of white-collar violence, the violence of Christian murderers and patriot citizens who define right in terms of whiteness and wrong as blackness. These are the people who hire assassins to do their dirty work while they piously congratulate themselves for being "good" and "nonviolent." The assassins are the policemen who patrol our streets, killing our men, women, and children.

I contend, therefore, that the problem of violence is not the problem of a few black revolutionaries but the problem of a whole social structure which outwardly appears to be ordered and respectable but inwardly is "ridden by psychopathic obsessions and delusions"[26]—racism and hatred. Violence is embedded in American law, and it is blessed by the keepers of moral sanctity. This is the core of the problem of violence, and it will not be solved by romanticizing American history, pretending that Hiroshima, Nagasaki, and Vietnam are the first American crimes against humanity. If we take seriously the idea of human dignity, then we know that the annihilation of Indians, the enslavement of Africans, and (Reinhold Niebuhr notwithstanding) the making of heroes out of slaveholders, like George Washington and Thomas Jefferson, were America's first crimes against humankind. And it does not help the matter at all to attribute black slavery to economic necessity or an accident of history. America is an unjust society, and black people have known that for a long time.

(2) If violence is not just a question for the oppressed but *primarily* for the oppressors, then it is obvious that the distinction between violence and nonviolence is an illusory problem. "There is only the question of the justified and unjustified use of force and the question of whether the means are proportionate to the ends";[27] and the only people who can answer the problem are the victims of injustice. It would be the height of stupidity for the victims of oppression to expect the oppressors to devise the means of liberation.

It is important to point out that no one can be nonviolent in an unjust society. The essential fallacy of the much debated issues of violence versus nonviolence is that the proponents of the latter have merely argued that issue from a perspective that accepted the oppressors' definitions. Too often Christian theologians have made the specious distinction between violence and force. "The state is invested with force; it is an organism instituted and ordained by God, and remains such even when it is unjust; even its harshest acts are not the same thing as the angry or brutal deed of the individual. The individual surrenders his passions, he commits violence."[28] This distinction is false and merely expresses an identification with the structures of power rather than with the victims of power. I contend that every one is violent, and to ask, "Are you nonviolent?" is to accept the oppressors' values. Concretely, ours is a situation in which the only option we have is that of deciding whose violence we will support—that of the oppressors or the oppressed. Either we side with oppressed blacks and other unwanted minorities as they try to redefine the meaning of existence in a dehumanized society, or we take a stand with the President or whoever is defending the white establishment for General Motors and U.S. Steel. There is no possibility of neutrality, the moral luxury of being on neither side. Neither the powers that be nor their victims will allow that! The U.S. government demands support through taxes and the public allegiance to the American flag. The oppressed demand commitment to the struggle of freedom and the willingness to take the risk to create a new humanity. We know that "sometimes [we are] tossed and driven," and "sometimes [we] don't know where to roam." But we've "heard of a city" where

"Jesus is the King," and we are struggling "to make it [our] home." Sometimes the city is called heaven, and we speak of it as "crossing the river Jordan" and as the "New Jerusalem." But this vision is the guide to our revolutionary fight to make this world a sign of its coming reality. People who want to join our struggle must relinquish their commitment to the structure of injustice. They cannot be for us and oppressors at the same time.

Of course, I realize that the choice for the oppressed has its own ambiguities. Insofar as we pay taxes and work in the system, are we not on the side of the oppressors? True enough. Well then, what is the difference between Gerald Ford and any black person? The difference is analogous to the distinction between the redeemed sinner and the unredeemed sinner. Ford is the latter, and the oppressed person in struggle of freedom is the former. One recognizes that, despite his participation in it, the world is unjust, and he must be committed to its liberation. The other believes that the world is in good hands, and he enjoys his participation in it. This distinction is crucial, because one participation is by force and the other is voluntarily. Thus the hope for the creation of a new society for all is dependent upon those people who know that struggle is the primary means by which a new age will be inaugurated. If they participate in injustice, they know that it is not right, and thus the system must be changed. There will be no change from the system of injustice if we have to depend upon the people who control it and believe that the present order of injustice is the best of all possible societies. It will be changed by the victims whose participation in the present system is against their will. Indeed, while they are participating in it involuntarily, *voluntarily* they are preparing for its destruction. They are living double lives, one part of which they are seeking to destroy because it contradicts the true self that is being made anew in struggle. Every sensitive black person knows what this means, and it is the source both of our being and not-being. Ethics in this context is a terrible risk, an existential and historical burden that must be borne in the heat of the day. It is this burden that made our ancestors create songs of sorrow and joy. Both realities are combined in this spiritual:

Nobody knows the trouble I've seen,
Nobody knows my sorrow.
Nobody knows the trouble I've seen,
Glory, Hallelujah!

At Macedonia A. M. E. Church, this spiritual was repeatedly sung as an expression of the people's struggle. DuBois' "twoness," the American and the Negro, the sorrow and the joy, was present in the very fabric of their existence. But this conflict did not create passivity; it was used by the people as the means of struggle. They put into action the saying that "you got to take what you got and use what you can," and that they did every chance they got. It is this *living* truth embodied in the lives of black people that makes the comparison of Ford's predicament with blacks utterly ridiculous. Oppressed blacks and other people of color are the only signs of hope for the creation of a new humanity in America.

From the foregoing analysis of violence and nonviolence, it is obvious that I do not share Martin Luther King, Jr.'s explication of this issue, although I agreed with much of the actual program-matic thrust of his leadership. His dependence on the analysis of love found in liberal theology and his confidence that "the universe is on the side of justice"[29] seem not to take seriously white violence in America. I disagreed with his conceptual analysis of violence versus nonviolence, because his distinctions between these terms did not appear to face head-on the historical and sociological complexities of human existence in a racist society. Thus much of King's writings reflect theological and philosophical discourse that had little to do with his actual creative thinking and acting. The source of the latter is not Gandhi or Bostonian personalism, despite his implied claims to the contrary. King's creative thought and power in the struggle of freedom were found in his black Church heritage. This was the heritage that brought him face to face with agony and despair but also hope and joy that somewhere in the bosom of God's eternity, justice would become a reality "in the land of the free and the home of the brave." This was the source of King's dream and his anticipation that "trouble won't last always." With black sermonic style and rhythm and with theological imagination, he attempted to explicate the content of his vision: "I have a dream," he said at the March on Washington in 1963, "that one day my children will no longer be judged by the color of their skin but by the content of their character." And the night before his assassination in Memphis, he reiterated a similar hope: "I may not get there with you, but I want you to know tonight that we as a people will get to the promised land." The idea that hope is created in the context of despair and oppression is what made King such a creative activist and a great preacher. It is also what makes my theology very similar to King's, despite our apparent difference on violence and nonviolence. For we both recognize that a fight is on and black survival and liberation are at stake. Therefore, we do not need to debate the relative merits of certain academic distinctions between violence and force or violence and nonviolence. The task is what King demonstrated so well in his life and thought, to try to replace inhumanity with humanity.

(3) If violence versus nonviolence is not the issue but, rather, the creation of a new humanity, then the critical question for Christians is not whether Jesus committed violence or whether violence is theoretically consistent with love and reconciliation. We repeat: the question is not what Jesus *did,* as if his behavior in first-century Palestine were the infallible ethical guide for our actions today. We must ask not what he did, but what is he *doing* —and what he did becomes important only insofar as it points to his activity today. To use the Jesus of history as an absolute ethical guide for people today is to become enslaved to the past, foreclosing God's eschatological future and its judgment on the present. It removes the element of risk in ethical decisions and makes people slaves to principles. But the gospel of Jesus means liberation; and one essential element of that liberation is the existential burden of making decisions about human liberation without being completely sure what Jesus did or would do. This is the risk of faith.

My difficulty with white theologians is their use of Jesus' so-called "nonviolent" attitude in the Gospels as primary evidence that the oppressed ought to be nonviolent today.[30] Not only have

Rudolf Bultmann and other Form Critics demonstrated that these are historical difficulties in the attempt to move behind the kerygmatic preaching of the early Church to the real Jesus of Nazareth, but the procedure is ethically questionable, especially from white defenders of the status quo. It is interesting that many white scholars are skeptical about the historical validity of practically everything that the Gospels record about Jesus' ministry *except* his political involvement. They are sure that he preached love, which they invariably interpret to mean an acceptance of the political status quo. His gospel, they contend, was spiritual or eschatological but had nothing to do with political, revolutionary struggle. This is a strange form of logic, especially since they are the same scholars who adhere *rigidly* to the form-critical method and also *universally* proclaim that the Kingdom about which Jesus preached included the whole of reality. Why is it that they do not express the same skepticism when dealing with Jesus' politics as they do with everything else? How can they be so sure that Jesus was not violent? Why is it that they say that Jesus preached the Kingdom, *an all-encompassing reality*, but suggest that it had nothing to do with politics? How can they say that the God of Jesus was Yahweh of the Old Testament, but shy away from his political involvement on behalf of the oppressed? How could Jesus be God's representative on earth, and not be concerned about social, economic, and political injustice? I think the answer to these questions is obvious. White theologians' exegesis is decided by their commitment to, and involvement in, the social structures of oppression. They cannot see the radial and political thrust of Jesus' person and work because their vision is committed to the very structures that Jesus despised. They are the contemporary representatives of the scribes and lawyers who cannot recognize the essential fallacy of their perspective.

However, even if it could be shown that Jesus was not a revolutionary zealot, that in itself would not be evidence that the risen Christ is not involved in the oppressed's struggle of freedom today. For the resurrected Christ is not bound by first-century possibilities. Though the Jesus of yesterday is important for our ethical decisions today, we must be careful where we locate that importance. It is not found in following in his steps, slavishly imitating his behavior in Palestine. Rather, we must regard his past activity as a *pointer* to what he is doing now. His actions were not as much examples as *signs* of God's eschatological future and the divine will to liberate all people from slavery and oppression. In Jesus' exorcisms and in his eating and drinking with the oppressed, he was pointing to the new age that was breaking into the present, disrupting the order of injustice. The new age of the coming Kingdom means a revolutionary usurpation of the present value system. The last shall be first and the first last. Herein is the ethical import of Jesus' words and deeds. They were concrete *signs* that the new age is dawning right in the social context of the people. They mean nothing to those who do not have the eyes of faith to see that something revolutionary is taking place in the midst of the people. The truth of Jesus' ethical presence is not found through a rational investigation of his deeds or words. It is found in what they bear witness to, namely, God's will to liberate the weak and the helpless.

Therefore if we today want to understand the meaning of Jesus' past existence in relation to his present existence with us, we must approach the problem not with the method of philosophy but from that perspective of faith which arises from the dispossessed, because their social existence bears witness to the vision of a coming new age. As Christians, who have seen the signs of the liberating Kingdom, we are commanded not to follow philosophical principles but to discover the will of God in a troubled and dehumanized world. Concretely, we must decide not between good and evil, right and wrong, but between the old and the new age, the former being represented in the oppressors and the latter in the struggle of the little ones to be free. We must ask and answer the question, "Whose actions, those of the oppressed or the oppressors, are consistent with God's work in history?" Either we believe God's will to be revealed in the status quo of America or in the actions of those who seek to change it.

Accepting the risk of faith and the ethical burden of making decisions about life and death without an infallible guide, I contend that God is found among the poor, the wretched, and the sick. "God chose what is foolish in the world to shame the wise [wrote Paul], God chose what is weak in the world to shame the strong, God chose what is low and despised in the world, even the things that are not, to bring to nothing things that are. . . ." (I Cor. 1:26 f. RSV) That was why God elected Israelite slaves and not Egyptian slave masters, the weak and poor in Israel and not the oppressors. As the Gospels' portrayal of Jesus demonstrates, the God of Israel is the God whose will is made known through his identification with the oppressed and his activity is always identical with those who strive for a liberated freedom.

If this message means anything for our times, it means that God's revelation is found in black liberation. God has chosen what is black in America to shame the whites. In a society where white is equated with good and black is defined as bad, humanity and divinity mean an unqualified identification with blackness. The divine election of the oppressed means that black people are given the power of judgment over the high and mighty whites. What else can a Christian ethic say than that the oppressed in struggle are the concrete signs of God's presence with us today?

X.
LIBERATION AND RECONCILIATION

When black people emphasize their right to defend them-selves against those who seek to destroy the black community, it never fails that so-called white Christians then ask, "What about the biblical doctrine of reconciliation?" "What about Christian forgiveness?" "Can't black people find it in their hearts to forgive us?" White people who ask these questions should not be surprised if blacks turn and walk away in disgust. The difficulty is not with the reconciliation-forgiveness question itself but with the people asking it. Like the question of violence, this question is almost always addressed *to* blacks *by* whites, as if we blacks are responsible for the demarcation of community on the basis of color. They who are responsible for the dividing walls of hostility, racism and hatred, want to know whether the victims are ready to forgive and forget—without changing the balance of power. They want to know whether we have any hard feelings toward them, whether we still love them, even though we are oppressed and brutalized by them. What are we to say to a people who insist on oppressing us but get upset when we reject them?

Because black liberation is the point of departure of my analysis of the gospel of Jesus, I cannot accept a view of reconciliation based on white values. The Christian view of reconciliation has nothing to do with black people being nice to white people as if the gospel demands that we ignore their insults and their humiliating presence. It does not mean discussing with whites what it means to be black or going to white gatherings and displaying what whites call an understanding attitude—remaining cool and calm amid racists and bigots.

To understand the biblical view of reconciliation, we must see it in relation to the struggle of freedom in an oppressed society. In America, that means seeing reconciliation in the social context of black liberation. As black theologians who have lived in the social context of racial oppression, we must not be afraid to ask the hard questions. In a society dominated by white people, what does Paul mean when he says that Christ is "our peace, who has made us . . . one, and has broken down the dividing wall of hostility," reconciling us to God "in one body through the cross, thereby bringing the hostility to an end" (Eph. 2:14-15 RSV)? Are we to conclude that the hostility between blacks and whites has been brought to an end? If so, I wish somebody would tell white folks in America and elsewhere in the world, because they sure don't act like it. If blacks and whites have been reconciled, how come white racists are still oppressing blacks in South Africa, Rhodesia, and elsewhere on that continent? How come white racists are still being elected to public office in America, thereby continuing their dehumanization of black people in the name of God and country? How come white churches still support racial oppression either through silence or through their public defense of the order of injustice? How can we black people take seriously the unity in Christ Jesus when there is no unity in politics or religion?

These are the questions that must inform a black theological analysis of reconciliation, and they cannot be answered by spiritualizing Christ's emphasis on love, as if his love is indifferent to social and political justice. We black theologians must refuse to accept a view of reconciliation that pretends that slavery never existed, that we were not lynched and shot, and that we are not *presently* being cut to the core of our physical and mental endurance. But with the words of Melvin Tolson, I ask rhetorically:

> Oh, how can we forget
> Our human rights denied?
> Oh, how can we forget
> Our manhood crucified?

> When Justice is profaned
> And plea with curse is met,
> When Freedom's gates are barred,
> Oh, how can we forget?[1]

The truth of the matter is that we dare not forget, for the only limit to our oppression is our power against it. In this final chapter, my purpose is to evaluate the Christian doctrine of reconciliation in the light of black people's unwillingness to forget the pains of their existence, and to relate it to biblical history.

The Objective Reality of Reconciliation

According to the Bible, reconciliation is primarily an act of God. "God was in Christ reconciling the world to himself," says Paul in II Corinthians 5:19 (RSV). And in Ephesians 1:10, emphasizing a similar point, he concludes that God has sent Jesus Christ "to unite all things in him, things in heaven and things on earth" (RSV). In both passages, Paul stresses the objective reality of reconciliation, grounded in God's initiative and affecting the entire cosmos. Reconciliation is not a human quality or potentiality, although it affects human relationships. It is a divine action that embraces the whole world, changing our relationship with God and making us new creatures. Formerly we were slaves; but reconciliation means that we are free. Formerly we were separated from God, alienated from his will and enslaved to the evils of this world. Now we are reconciled; fellowship with God is now possible, because Christ through his death and resurrection has liberated us from the principalities and powers and the rulers of this present world. Formerly our knowledge of our identity was defined by those who had power over life and death in this world. Now God has redeemed and reconciled us, so that we know that true life is found only in him who conquered death on the cross and was resurrected on the third day.

In the Bible the objective reality of reconciliation is connected with divine liberation. This means that human fellowship with God is made possible through his activity in history, setting people free from economic, social, and political bondage. God's act of reconciliation is not mystical communion with the divine; nor is it a pietistic state of inwardness bestowed upon the believer. God's reconciliation is a new relationship with *people* created by his concrete involvement in the political affairs of the world, taking sides with the weak and the helpless. Israel, reflecting on her covenant relationship initiated by divine action, summed up its meaning in a liturgical confession:

> My father was a homeless Aramaean who went down to Egypt with a small company and lived there until they became a great, powerful and numerous nation. But the Egyptians ill-treated us, humiliated us and imposed cruel slavery upon us. Then we cried to the Lord the God of our fathers for help, and he listened to us and saw our humiliation, our hardship and distress; and so the Lord brought us out of Egypt with a strong hand and outstretched arm, with terrifying deeds, and with signs and portents. He brought us to this place and gave us this land, a land flowing with milk and honey.
> Deuteronomy 26:5-10 NEB

The point if clear: Israel's covenant relationship with God is made possible because of God's liberating activity. Israel is Yahweh's people, and he is their God because, and only because, he has delivered them from the bondage of political slavery and brought them through the wilderness to the land of Canaan. There could have been no covenant at Sinai without the Exodus from Egypt, no reconciliation without liberation. Liberation is what God does to effect reconciliation, and without the former the latter is impossible. To be liberated is to be delivered from the state of unfreedom to freedom; it is to have the chains struck off the body and mind so that the creature of God can be who he is. Reconciliation is that bestowal of freedom and life with God which takes place on the basis of God's liberating deeds. Liberation and reconciliation are tied together and have meaning only through God's initiative. They tell us that man cannot be man, and God refuses to be God unless the creature of God is delivered from that which is enslaving and dehumanizing.

If we take seriously the objective reality of divine liberation as a precondition for reconciliation, then it becomes clear that God's salvation is intended for the poor and the helpless, and it is identical with their liberation from oppression. That is why salvation is defined in political terms in the Old Testament and why the prophets take their stand on the side of the poor within the community of Israel. As we have demonstrated, throughout the biblical story, God takes his stand with the weak and against the strong. Thus fellowship with God is made possible by his righteous activity in the world to set right the conditions for reconciliation. His setting right the conditions for divine-human fellowship is liberation, without which fellowship would be impossible. To speak of reconciliation apart from God's liberating activity is to ignore the divine basis of the divine-human fellowship.

The close relationship between reconciliation and liberation is also found in the New Testament. Christ is the Reconciler because he is first the Liberator. He was born in Bethlehem and "laid in a manger, because there was no place in the inn" (Luke 2:7 RSV). He was baptized with the sinners, the poor and the oppressed, because he was the Oppressed One sent from God to give wholeness to broken and wretched lives. Christ lived and worked among them, and on the cross he died for them. In him God entered history and affirmed the condition of the oppressed as his own existence, thereby making clear that poverty and sickness contradict the divine intentions for humanity. The cross and the resurrection are God's defeat of slavery. We are now free to be reconciled with God because he has destroyed the power of death and sin. We do not have to be afraid of death anymore. Our existence is reconciled with the Creator's existence.

Unfortunately this essential connection between liberation and reconciliation is virtually absent in the history of Christian thought. Theologians emphasized the objectivity of reconciliation, but they lost sight of the fact that reconciliation is grounded in history. This tendency is undoubtedly due partly to the influence of Greek thought and the Church's political status after

Constantine. The former led to rationalism and the latter produced a "gospel" that was politically meaningless for the oppressed. Reconciliation was defined on timeless "rational" grounds and was thus separated from God's liberating deeds in history. The political status of the post-Constantinian church, involving both alliance and competition with the state, led to definitions of the atonement that favored the powerful and excluded the interests of poor.

Anselm, the famous archbishop of Canterbury, is a case in point. He asked the soteriological question: *"Cur deus homo?"* (Why the God-man?). And he answered that question from a rationalistic viewpoint that was meaningless for the oppressed. His theory has been summarized as follows:

> Man, by sin, has done dishonor to God. His debt is to God alone. God's nature demands "satisfaction." Man, who owes obedience at all times, has nothing wherewith to make good past disobedience. Yet, if satisfaction is to be made at all, it can be rendered only by one who shares human nature, who is himself man, and yet as God has something of infinite value to offer. Such a being is the God-man. Not only is his sacrifice a satisfaction, it deserves a reward. That reward is the eternal blessedness of his brethren.[2]

A neat rational theory but useless as a leverage against political oppression. It dehistoricizes the work of Christ, separating it from God's liberating act in history.

The same is true of Anselm's critic, Abelard, who rejected the satisfaction theory and opted for what has been called the "moral influence" theory. In his perspective, God sent Jesus Christ as a revelation of his love to sinful people and as a teacher and example. And through his life, which became the ground of the forgiveness of sins, faith and love are aroused in sinful people. Abelard not only de-emphasized the objective reality of divine reconciliation, he apparently failed to grasp the radical quality of evil and oppression.

More recently Gustaf Aulén[3] revived what he calls the "classical" theory of the atonement with its emphasis on God's victory over the principalities and powers, Satan and his demons. He contends that this is the view of the New Testament, the early Church Fathers and also of Martin Luther. Here the focus is upon the objective reality of reconciliation as defined by God's victory over Satan and his powers. Reconciliation means that sin, death, and Satan—objective realities holding people in bondage—have been decisively defeated on the cross. We are now free to have fellowship with God.

Although Aulén's concern is "motif-research," which is itself nonpolitical, the classical theory offers contemporary theology an opportunity to return to the biblical emphasis on God's victory over the powers of evil. The difficulty with Aulén's analysis is that his theological method (motif-research) limits the contemporary applications of his findings as they might be related to oppressed peoples. (This may be due to his own political situation of Sweden in which the church and state have similar interests.) But if the classical theory is radicalized politically, then liberation and reconciliation can once again be grounded in history and related to God's fight against the powers of enslavement. The principalities and powers of evil, mythically expressed in the figure of Satan, represent not only metaphysical realities but earthly realities as well. They are the American system, symbolized in Gerald Ford and other government officials, who oppress the poor, humiliate the weak, and make heroes out of rich capitalists. The principalities and powers are that system of government symbolized in the Pentagon, which bombs and kills helpless people in Vietnam and Cambodia and attributes such obscene atrocities to the accidents of war. They are that system, symbolized in the police departments and prison officials, which shoots and kills defenseless blacks for being *black* and for demanding their right to exist. As long as Atticas exist and George Jacksons are killed, then we know that Satan is not dead. He is alive in those who do his work. Satan is present in those powers, visible and invisible, that destroy humanity and enslave the weak and the helpless. And it is against Satan and his powers that Christ has given his life. Because Christ has been raised from the dead, we know that the decisive victory has been won. We have been redeemed, that is, set free from the powers of slavery and death. This is the objective side of the biblical view of reconciliation.

The Subjective
Reality of Reconciliation

Because God has liberated the oppressed from bondage, thereby making freedom possible, the oppressed must now accept their freedom by joining God in the fight against injustice and oppression. Reconciliation then is not only what God does in order to deliver oppressed people from captivity; it is also what oppressed people do in order to remain faithful to their new gift of freedom. Reconciliation is not only justification, God's righteous deliverance of slaves from bondage; it is sanctification, the slaves' acceptance of their new way of life, their refusal to define existence in any other way than in freedom. Reconciliation is not simply freedom *from* oppression and slavery; it is also freedom *for* God. That is why Paul says: "For freedom Christ has set us free." (Gal. 5:1 RSV)

The objective reality of reconciliation cannot be separated from its subjective appropriation. They both belong together as "different 'moments' with a different bearing"[4] of the one divine act of reconciliation. God did not simply deliver Israel from Egypt and let it go at that. "If you *obey* my voice and keep my covenant, you shall be my own possession among all peoples" (Exod. 19:5 RSV). Yahweh demanded obedience. Israel must live as a liberated people.

Commenting on the indissoluble relation between justification and sanctification, Barth writes: "'I will be your God' is the justification of man. 'Ye shall be my people' is his sanctification."[5] Here Barth rightly sees that God's decision to be for man involves simultaneously man's decision (through the work of the Holy Spirit) to be for God. Dietrich Bonhoeffer made a similar point with his distinction between "cheap grace" and "costly grace." "Cheap grace is grace without discipleship, grace without the cross, grace without Jesus Christ, living incarnate." Costly grace is the opposite. It recognizes that reconciliation is bound up with repentance and that there is no "justification of sin without the justification of the sinner."[6] And "when Christ calls a man, he bids only him come and die."[7]

It is in the context of costly grace that we must understand the biblical view of reconciliation. When Paul says that Christ is "our peace, who has made us both one [Jew and Gentile, male and female, black and white] and has broken down the dividing wall of hostility," he is writing about the objective reality of reconciliation, accomplished through the cross and the resurrection of Jesus. But when Jew and Gentile, male and female, black and white begin to live on the basis of that reality, raising theological rhetoric to political reality—that is sanctification, the subjective appropriation of divine liberation. When Paul says, "For by grace you have been saved . . . and this is not your own doing" but "is a gift of God" (Eph. 2:8 RSV), that is justification, God's act of freedom for his people. But when he continues, "We are his workmanship, created in Christ Jesus for good works" (Eph. 2:10 RSV), that is sanctification, man's response to God's gift of freedom.

Because God's act for man involves man's liberation from bondage, man's response to God's grace of liberation is an act for his oppressed brothers and sisters. There can be no reconciliation with God unless the hungry are fed, the sick are healed, and justice is given to the poor. The justified person is at once the sanctified person, one who knows that his freedom is inseparable from the liberation of the weak and the helpless.

This is the meaning of Jesus' parable of the Last Judgment (Matt. 25:31ff.). People are placed on the right and on the left according to their ministering to the neighbor. Because the ones on the right met the needs of the oppressed, they were accepted into the Kingdom—even though they were not consciously trying to get there. For them the neighbor was an end in himself and not a means to an end. The ones on the left, who were rejected, were surprised at their rejection because they wanted to make it into the Kingdom. They failed to recognize the connection between the poor and the Son of man. For if they had known that the despised were, in fact, Jesus, they would have been prepared to help them, because they just wanted to be in the Kingdom. That is why they said, "Lord, when did we see thee hungry or thirsty or a stranger or naked or sick or in prison, and did not minister to thee?" (Matt. 25:44 RSV). The answer was simple: "Truly, I say to you, as you did it not to one of the the least of these, you did it not to me" (Matt. 25:45 RSV).

Reconciliation: Black and White

Theologians write these days about reconciliation, explaining its relationship to justification and sanctification, but they seldom get to the core of the issue. New Testament scholars can tell us whether Jesus uttered this or that saying, and whether it is a variation of an earlier saying in Deuteronomy, Psalms, or Second Isaiah. That is good. Systematic theologians can tell us about the philosophical influences in this or that theology from Justin and Origen to Karl Barth and Paul Tillich. And that too is to be commended. But they seldom seem to be able to get to the point that makes the gospel *the* gospel, in the light of which all of their scholarly investigations must be evaluated. I want to know why they spend time writing about these things, and what it all means in the light of the cross and the resurrection. Specifically, I want to know how reconciliation is related to Asia, Africa, Latin America, and every other section of this human globe where people are oppressed socially, politically, and economically. What does reconciliation have to do with Macedonia A.M.E. Church where the people still claim that they are "on their way to the promised land"? What are we to make of this doctrine, subjectively and objectively, in a society where black people define the promised land as a liberation from white oppression?

(1) From God's side, reconciliation between blacks and whites means that God is unquestionably on the side of the oppressed blacks struggling for justice. His justification is his righteous and total identification with black existence, taking it upon himself and revealing that he will not tolerate the wrong committed against his people. As he delivered the Israelites from Egypt, he will also deliver black people from white oppression. Black slaves expressed that truth in song:

> Slavery chain done broke at last, broke at last, broke at last,
> Slavery chain done broke at last,
> Going to praise God till I die.

Reconciliation means that God enters into black history and breaks down the hostility and racism of white people. It means the end of "driver's driving," "Master's hollering," and "missus' scolding." Thus black slaves sang with confidence:

> Children, we shall be free
> When the Lord shall appear.
> Give ease to the sick
> Give sight to the blind,
> Enable the cripple to walk;
> He'll raise the dead from under the earth,
> And give them permission to talk.

God's reconciliation means destroying all forms of slavery and oppression in white America so that the people of color can affirm the authenticity of their political freedom.

We must keep in mind that when Paul said, "God was in Christ reconciling the world unto himself," he was not making a sentimental comment on race relations. God's reconciling act is centered on the cross, and it reveals the depths of divine suffering for the reconciliation of enslaved humanity. On the cross, God encounters evil and suffering, the principalities and the powers that hold people in captivity; and the resurrection is the sign that these powers have been decisively defeated, even though they are still very active in the world. But the victory in Jesus' resurrection is God's liberating act that makes possible human reconciliation with God. We have been given the gift of freedom to fight with God in the liberation struggle. We can now be reconciled with God because he has removed the conditions of alienation as represented in the powers of evil.

When this biblical message is translated into twentieth-century America, the meaning is obvious. The principalities and powers that are still active in the world, despite God's victory in Jesus' resurrection, are represented concretely in the structures of injustice that oppress the weak and humiliate the poor. They are the demonic forces of white racism that enslave black, red, and brown people in the name of freedom and liberty. In this social context, then, God's reconciliation is his liberating work against these powers. Divine justification is the removal of oppressed black people from the control of white power, thereby making it possible for the enslaved to be free.

While divine reconciliation, for oppressed blacks, is connected with the joy of liberation from the controlling power of white people, for whites divine reconciliation is connected with God's wrathful destruction of white values. Everything that white oppressors hold dear is now placed under the judgment of Jesus' cross. This is a difficult pill for the white theologians and church people to swallow, because they have so much invested in the status quo. And it is likely that they will continue to rationalize the meaning of divine reconciliation in "spiritual" and nonpolitical terms. But God's will to liberate the little ones and to bring them "home to glory" will not be defeated by white piety or rhetoric. The new age is coming in, and through God's will to reconcile the oppressed to himself. This faith stands at the center of black religious experience. Though blacks were enslaved and oppressed by white people, blacks still continued to sing that "we'll soon be free, when the Lord will call us home." Despite the present condition of suffering, their present reconciliation with God enabled them to see God's future, and they expressed it in song:

> When I gets to heaven, gonna be at ease,
> Me an' my God gonna do as we please.

Here divine reconciliation was both a future and a present reality. It was God breaking into the conditions of servitude and destroying white definitions of black existence. Anselm is right: the atonement means that God takes our place, and does for us what we could not do for ourselves. However, the problem of sin is not a legalistic issue connected with God's honor in abstract theory. The problem of sin is an alienation from God that is always connected with injustice and oppression. Thus the atonement of Jesus Christ represents God taking the place of the oppressed in history so that they might be given the freedom to create a new future as defined by the liberation struggle in history. Instead of black people having to accept the consequence of white oppression, Jesus takes our place and undergoes the depth of the pain of being black in a white racist society and thereby transforms the condition of alienation into the possibility and the actuality of reconciliation. Through his taking our place and becoming black in a white racist society, black people's existence is radically transformed *objectively*. This objective act of God in Jesus Christ's present existence with us means that God has performed a reconciling act of liberation quite independently of our faithful response. God's reconciliation is real because Jesus is real. He is the power of divine presence in our world that makes freedom possible, whether we accept it or not. It was black people's knowledge of what God has done for them that enabled them to sing and preach about the certainty of their reconciliation even though their present existence was characterized by slavery. They merely lived the truth of this song:

> Don't be weary, traveller,
> Come along home, come home.
> Don't be weary, traveller,
> Come along home, come home.
>
> My head is wet with the midnight dew,
> Come along home, come home.
> The mornin' star was a witness too,
> Come along home, come home.
>
> Keep a-goin', traveller,
> Come along home, come home.
> Keep a-singin' all the way,
> Come along home, come home.

(2) On the human side, reconciliation means that we blacks must accept our new existence by struggling against all who try to make us slaves. We must refuse to let whites define the terms of reconciliation. Instead, we must participate in God's revolutionary activity in the world by changing the political, economic, and social structures so that the distinctions between rich and poor, oppressed and oppressors, are no longer a reality among people. To be reconciled with white people means fighting against their power to enslave, reducing masters to the human level, thereby making them accountable to black liberation. We must let them know that there can be no communication between masters and slaves until the *status* of master no longer

exists. The task of black people is to rebel against all white masters, destroying their pretensions to authority and ridiculing the symbols of power. White people must be made to realize that reconciliation is a costly experience. It is not holding hands and singing "Black and white together" and "We shall overcome." Reconciliation means *death*, and only those who are prepared to die in the struggle for freedom will experience new life with God.

Unfortunately, my black colleague, J. Deotis Roberts, has distorted the Christian view of black-white reconciliation precisely at this point. He implies that black people ought to forget their slavery and oppression and be prepared to join hands, in Christian love, with white oppressors. He writes:

> Christians are called to be agents of reconciliation. We have been able to love and forgive. . . . The assertion that all are "one in Christ Jesus" must henceforth mean that all slave-master, servant-boss, inferior-superior frames of reference between blacks and whites have been abolished.[8]

I simply cannot accept either the theological or the sociological basis of Roberts's analysis of reconciliation. In his concern to make reconciliation a central theme in Black Theology, he not only distorts its Christian meaning, but contradicts his own argument. On the one hand, Roberts says quite clearly that "*liberation* is a proper precondition for reconciliation in the area of race relations";[9] on the other, he insists that blacks "must hold up at all times the possibility for black-white interracial fellowship and cooperation."[10] If liberation is the precondition of reconciliation, why then should enslaved blacks assure white oppressors that we are ready to be reconciled when the latter have no intention of loosing the chains of oppression? Either liberation is the foundation of reconciliation or it is not. Roberts will have to make a decision about his theological perspective. It is not the case that I have overlooked reconciliation, as Roberts implies,[11] but rather, that I refuse to let white people define its terms. I contend that only black people can define the terms on which our reconciliation with white people will become real. I cannot say, as Roberts does:

A Black Theology that takes reconciliation seriously must work at the task of inter-communication between blacks and whites under the assumption that for those who are open to truth, there may be communication from the inside out, but at the same time there may be communication from the outside in. In the latter sense, white Christians may be led to understand and work with blacks for liberation and reconciliation on an interracial basis.[12]

Because a man is black and poor does not mean that he is heaven bound. Neither does whiteness and great wealth bar a man from the Kingdom.[13]

In these quotations and in the book as a whole, Roberts opens the door not only for white people to be oppressors and Christians *at the same time,* but also for them to participate in black liberation and to set the *terms* of our reconciliation with them. This assumption is unbiblical and unhistorical. Indeed, in black history, reconciliation and liberation on white terms have always meant death for black people.

Whenever black people have entered into a mutual relation with white people, with rare exceptions, the relationship has always worked to the detriment of our struggle. From the abolitionist movement of the nineteenth century to the recent civil rights struggle of the 1950s and 60s, whites demonstrated that they cannot follow but must always lead. Thus there was a split between Frederick Douglass and William Garrison, Henry Garnet and Maria Chapman. Garnet's reply to Maria Chapman's attack on his perspective should be stamped on the consciousness of all blacks who are optimistic about black-white reconciliation.

I was born in slavery, [wrote Garnet] and have escaped, to tell you and others, what the monster has done, and is still doing. It, therefore, astonishes me to think that you should desire to sink me again to the condition of a *slave,* by forcing me to think as you do. My crime is, that I have dared to think, and act, contrary to your opinion. . . . If it has come to this, that I must think and act as you do, because you are an abolitionist, or be exterminated by your thunder, then I do not hesitate to say that your abolitionism is abject slavery.[14]

Whether for us or against us, white people seem to think that they know what is best for our struggle. It was this white attitude that led to the rise of black power and the exclusion of white people from the civil rights struggle in the 1960s. Black people came to realize that our liberation depends solely on our actions and decisions and not on white folks. From the black power consciousness emerged Black Theology, a theological enterprise defined of, for, and by black people in the struggle of freedom.

Whether we like it or not, the days of integration are over, although this does not mean that we blacks are *for* separation. It means that separation is a fact of life. The ghettos of this country are ample proof that white folks intend to keep it that way. Thus it is absurd to talk about reconciliation to people who are determined to separate us for the purpose of oppression. Our task, then, is to begin to develop structures of behavior that do not depend on white folks' goodwill. We must recognize that our liberation begins and ends with the decisions we make and the actions we take to implement them. All talk about reconciliation with white oppressors, with mutual dialogue about its meaning, has no place in black power or Black Theology.

I am not ruling out the *rare* possibility of conversion among white oppressors, an event that I have already spoken of in terms of white people becoming black. But conversion in the biblical sense is a *radical* experience, and it ought not to be identified with white sympathy for blacks or with a pious feeling in white folks' hearts. In the Bible, conversion is closely identified with repentance, and both mean a radical "reorientation of one's whole life and personality, which includes the adoption of a new ethical line of conduct, a forsaking of sin and a turning to righteousness."[15] Or, as Günther Bornkamm puts it: "Repentance . . . means: to lay hold on the salvation which is at hand, and to give up everything for it."[16] Thus Jesus speaks of the Kingdom as a "treasure hidden in a field, which a man found and covered up; then in his joy he goes and sells all that he has and buys that field" (Matt. 13:44 RSV). The point is that everything must be sacrificed for the reality now present in the midst of human existence. The person who repents is the one who sells all and redefines his life in commitment to the Kingdom of God. That is why, in the Bible and the black religious experience, repentance is connected with *death*. It means dying to sin and alienation and being born anew in Jesus Christ and thus living in faithful obedience to his will to make whole the brokenness of human existence. Therefore, there can be no forgiveness of sins without repentance, and no repentance without the gift of faith to struggle with and for the freedom of the oppressed.

When whites undergo the true experience of conversion wherein they die to whiteness and are reborn anew in order to struggle *against* white oppression and *for* the liberation of the oppressed, there is a place for them in the black struggle of freedom. Here reconciliation becomes God's gift of blackness through the oppressed of the land. But it must be made absolutely clear that it is the black community that decides both the *authenticity* of white conversion and also the place these converts will play in the black struggle of freedom. The converts can have nothing to say about the validity of their conversion experience or what is best for the community or their place in it, *except* as permitted by the oppressed community itself. As is true of every member of the black community, accountability remains an essential ingredient of all who share in the struggle of freedom. But white converts, if there are any to be found, must be *made* to realize that they are like babies who have barely learned how to walk and talk. Thus they must be told when to speak and what to say, otherwise they will be excluded from our struggle. What is always ruled out is white converts using their experience in our community as evidence *against* blacks, claiming that reconciliation with whites is possible. Whites must be made to realize that they are not only accountable to Roy Wilkins but also to Imamu Baraka. And if the latter says that reconciliation is out of the question, then nothing the former says can change that reality, for both are equally a member of the black struggle of freedom. Unless whites can get every single black person to agree that reconciliation is realized, there is no place whatsoever for white rhetoric about the reconciling love of blacks and whites. For if whites are truly converted to our struggle, they know that reconciliation is a gift that excludes boasting. It is God's gift of blackness made possible through the presence of the divine in the social context of black existence. With the gift comes a radical change in life-style wherein one's value system is now defined by the oppressed engaged in the liberation struggle.

Black people must be aware of the extreme dangers of speaking too lightly of reconciliation with whites. Just because we work with them and sometimes worship alongside them should be no reason to claim that they are truly Christians and thus a part of our struggle. Every mistake we make regarding white integrity will lead to the further entrenchment of our oppression by white people. This problem is quite obvious in Roberts's treatment of reconciliation. He seems to think that merely through proper theological analysis, according to white rules, white people would come to see the truth of what he was trying to say. He apparently did not realize that in his call for reconciliation alongside the theme of liberation, whites would hear *only* the former but completely disregard its connection with the latter. That is why liberation *must* be expressed in uncompromising language and actions, for only then can the conditions be created for reconciliation. A word about reconciliation too soon or at the wrong time to the oppressors only grants them more power to oppress black people. Roberts said what should *not* have been said, because he should have known that, despite his honest intention to face the truth of the gospel, white oppressors are not prepared to hear the truth, much less do it, because truth would condemn them. Thus his proclamation that we need reconciliation was in bad taste for blacks struggling for freedom, since it was obvious that whites were not prepared to hear what he was trying to say. On white ears, his call for reconciliation in opposition to my theological emphasis on liberation would merely mean that whites would be granted permission by a black theologian to separate love from justice, reconciliation from liberation, despite Roberts's feeble attempt to hold them together. That accounts for the enthusiastic response to his book among the white church establishment, both liberal and conservative. When white conservatives, the people who have been most blatant in their oppression of blacks, begin to support his theological work, then it should be obvious to brother Roberts that he is on the wrong theological track.[17]

It is appropriate to conclude this book with a restatement of the call to black theologians to speak the truth to the people. Again we must be reminded that truth is not a concept or an idea to be discovered in a theology or philosophy textbook. Truth is a *liberating event,* a divine happening in the lives of the people. It is that reality that breaks into black existence and gives the people the strength and courage to "keep on pushing," so that they can realize in their present what they see coming on the horizon of the future. To do theology in the light of this black truth, we black theologians must recognize the conceptual limitations of white academic categories—whether in theology, philosophy, or history of religions. This black truth has its own uniqueness and thus cannot be truly understood with a conceptual framework from Karl Barth or Mircea Eliade. The categories for an analysis of black truth must be derived from the socioreligious context of the people who live on the basis of its reality. If the black theologian is to interpret black truth correctly, he must be convicted by this truth, for only then can he understand what black people are talking about when they testify that the God of Jesus "picked them up and turned them around and placed their feet on solid ground." If we make the mistake of listening too much to white theologians and too little to black witnesses of the truth, our theology will be black in name only, because it will not represent the hopes and dreams of the people. Thus everything we do and say in theology must be defined by God's liberating presence as witnessed in the Scriptures, the songs, and the tales of black people.

When the question is asked, "What does reconciliation mean?" we must not consult the theological treatises of Euro-American theologians for the answer. These theologians cannot tell us what reconciliation means in black-white relations, because their consciousness is defined by the political structures responsible for our humiliation and oppression. To know what reconciliation means in the black perspective, we must investigate the black sources of the truth—the sermons, prayers, tales of our people. Here we will find that reconciliation is not a theological idea but a human struggle, a fight to create dignity in an inhuman situation. Reconciliation is not sitting down with white liberals and radicals, assuring them that we don't have any hard feelings toward them. Rather, it is that vision of God's presence in our lives that lets us know that the world will be changed only through our blood sweat, and tears. It is that feeling of togetherness with our brothers and sisters in struggle, knowing that "we shall overcome" "in that great gettin' up mornin'."

From the experience of divine truth in our social existence, we now know that reconciliation must start *first* with black brothers and sisters who have suffered the pain of a broken community. Therefore as black theologians, we must begin to ask, *not* about black people's reconciliation with white oppressors, but about our reconciliation with each other. We must unmask the social and political structures that make us kill and shoot each other. Reconciliation, like love, must begin at home before it can spread abroad. As long as the oppressor can keep us divided and fighting among ourselves, his task of keeping black people oppressed is made that much easier. In this context, reconciliation *precedes* liberation. For unless we are reconciled with each other and begin to join hands in the struggle of black freedom, we black people will not be able to survive in this troubled world. Unless we can create structures that will bring us together so that our unity with each other will lay the foundation for talk about reconciliation with others, we will not survive to be unified with others.

It is therefore black people's reconciliation with each other, in America, Africa, and the islands of the sea, that must be the black theologians' primary concern. For unless we can get together with our African brothers and sisters for the shaping of our future, then white capitalists in America and Europe will destroy us. We must not forget that we are engaged in a struggle of survival and liberation, and our children are counting on us to prepare the world for them for living. We must not fail them, because they are depending on us to give an accountability of our words and deeds. Thus if we black theologians are going to interpret correctly the meaning of the black people's struggle, we cannot be concerned with what white theologians are going to say about our theological perspective. Black theologians are not called to interpret the gospel in a form acceptable to white oppressors. Our calling is derived from the people who have been through the trials and tribulations of this world. Our task is to interpret their struggle in the light of God's presence with them, liberating and thus reconciling the oppressed to himself. We must let white oppressors know that we are on the "battle-field of the Lord," and are determined through God's grace to fight until we die. We must make clear to them that we will not be distracted from our liberation with their obscene talk about "love" and "forgiveness." And to white people who insist that we blacks are preaching hatred, we merely say to whites, with Joseph Cotter:

Brothers, come
And let us go unto our God
And when we stand before him
I shall say—
Lord, I do not hate,
I am hated.
I scourge no one,
I am scourged.
I covet no lands,
My lands are coveted.
I mock no peoples,
My people are mocked.
And [white boy] what shall you say?[18]

Notes

Chapter I

1. Richard Wright, *White Man Listen!* (New York: Doubleday 1964), p. 83.

2. Paul Holmer, "Remarks Excerpted from 'The Crisis in Rhetoric,'" in *Theological Education*, Vol. VII, No. 3 (Spring 1971), p. 211. See also an important reply to Holmer by Charles S. Rooks in the same issue, "Response to Paul Holmer," pp. 215-218.

3. Abraham Heschel, *The Prophets*, Vol. I (New York: Harper Torchbooks, 1969), p. xiv.

4. Feuerbach, cited in Herbert Marcuse, *Reason and Revolution* (Boston: Beacon Press, 1960), p. 270

5. Karl Marx and Friedrich Engels, *On Religion* (New York: Shocken Books, 1964), pp. 74-75.

6. Cassandra, cited in H. A. Baker, Jr., *Long Black Song* (Charlottesville: University of Virginia Press, 1972), p. 116.

Chapter II

1. Mari Evans, *I Am a Black Woman* (New York: William Morrow, 1970), p. 91.

2. Baraka, cited in Don L. Lee, *Dynamite Voices*, Vol. I (De-

troit: Broadside Press, 1971), p. 14. Baraka's concern was to critique the so-called "objectivity" in poetry and other art forms. The same critique applies to other human expressions, especially theology.

3. Tertullian, "On Prescription against Heretics", in *The Ante-Nicene Fathers*, Vol. III, ed. A. Roberts and J. Donaldson (Grand Rapids, Mich.: Wm. B. Eerdmans, 1951), p. 246.

4 Bissainthe, cited in John V. Taylor, *The Primal Vision* (London: SCM Press, 1963), p. 16.

5. Cited in J. Mason Brewer, *American Negro Folklore* (Chicago: Quadrangle Books, 1968), p. 140.

6. Cited in Langston Hughes and Arna Bontemps (eds.), *Book of Negro Folklore* (New York: Dodd, Mead, 1958), pp. 234-235. This is an excellent collection of sermons, prayers, songs, and other folkloric material. Perhaps the earliest and the best study of old-time black preaching is William H. Pipes, *Say Amen, Brother!* (Westport, Conn.: Negro Universities Press, 1970; originally published in 1951). See also James W. Johnson's excellent book, *God's Trombones* (New York: Viking Press, 1927). Another excellent study and collection of folkloric material in general and sermons in particular is J. Mason Brewer, *American Negro Folklore*. See also Bruce A. Rosenberg, *The Art of the American Folk Preacher* (New York: Oxford University Press, 1970); Henry H. Mitchell, *Black Preaching* (Philadelphia: Lippincott, 1970). However the best introduction to the black sermon is through the black preacher himself at a black church on any given Sunday morning. Failing that possibility, I would recommend the recordings of the Rev. C. L. Franklin, who perhaps represents in his tradition what his daughter, Aretha, represents in hers. He has recorded more than fifty sermons at New Bethel Baptist Church in Detroit and they are available on Chess long-playing records. For a listing of these sermons, see his album, "The Inner Conflict," sermon No. 43, Chess Producing Corporation, 320 East 21st St., Chicago, Ill. For other black sermons, see the Rev. Clay Evans's "A Foolish Sale"; Evans, from whom the records are available, is pastor of the Fellowship Baptist Church, Chicago, Ill., 45th Place and Princeton Ave.; see also the sermons by the Rev. George A. Weaver, Witnessing Recording Agency, Kansas City, Kan.; Weaver is pastor of New Mt. Olive Baptist Church, Fort Lauderdale, Fla.; and by Rev. C. A. W. Clark, pastor of Good Street Baptist Church, Dallas, Tex., Witnessing Recording Agency.

7. James W. Johnson, *God's Trombones*, pp. 4-5.

8. Some interpreters have misunderstood the black preacher because of the limitations of their conceptual tools of evaluation. I have reference to Bruce Rosenberg's *The Art of the American Folk Preacher*. The importance of this book is perhaps limited to its inclusion of valuable texts of sermons. From my viewpoint and concern, the chief defect of this work was Rosenberg's failure to take seriously, as an *interpretive tool*, the socioreligious consciousness of the preachers under investigation.

9. Cited in J. Mason Brewer, *American Negro Folklore*, p. 139.

10. *Ibid.*, p. 140. Like the sermon, the best source for black prayers is the black church on a given Sunday morning or a Wednesday night prayer service. The next best sources are the recordings found in many sermon albums. See, the Rev. C. L. Franklin, "Rev. C. L. Franklin Sings," LP-33, Chess Producing Corporation. Written prayers are found in Hughes and Bontemps, *Negro Folklore;* J. W. Johnson, *God's Trombones;* J. Mason Brewer, *American Negro Folklore;* and William H. Pipes, *Say Amen, Brother!*

11. Cited in Hughes and Bontemps, *Negro Folklore*, pp. 156-157.

12. Cited in Zora Neal Hurston, *Mules and Men* (New York: Harper Perennial Library, 1970), p. 44.

13. Sources and texts of the spirituals are numerous. For an interpretation of the theological significance of the spirituals, see my *The Spirituals and the Blues* (New York: Seabury Press, 1972); see also Howard Thurman, *The Negro Spiritual Speaks of Life and Death* (New York: Harper & Row, 1947), and *Deep River* (Port Washington, N.Y.: Kennikat Press, 1969). The best collection of the text and music of the spirituals is James W. Johnson and J. Rosamond Johnson, *The Books of American Negro Spirituals* (New York: Viking Press, 1925). See also John W. Work, *American Negro Songs and Spirituals* (New York: Bonanza Books, 1940). The earliest book collection of slave songs is William F. Allen, Charles P. Ware, and Lucy McKim Garrison, *Slave Songs of the United States* (New York: A. Simpson & Co. 1867). One of the best and most comprehensive studies on the spirituals is John Lowell, Jr., *Black Song: The Forge and the Flame* (New York: Macmillan Co., 1972).

   Unfortunately, the gospel songs have not been studied as seriously as the spirituals. The best volume I know of is *The Gospel Sound* by Tony Heilbut (New York: Simon and Schuster, 1971). For the lyrics, see L. Hughes and A. Bontemps, *Negro Folklore*, Chap. XII. See especially the special issue on Thomas Dorsey, "Father of Gospel Music," in *Black World*, July 1974.

Again, the best introduction to the black song is the black church. Failing that, I would suggest the recordings by Mahalia Jackson, James Cleveland, Clara Ward, and Paul Robeson. I strongly suggest Aretha Franklin's recent album entitled "Amazing Grace," with James Cleveland and the Southern California Community Choir (Atlantic Recording Corporation, New York, 1972).

14. Brewer, *American Negro Folklore*, pp. 3-4. For authenticity, most scholars still regard Joel Chandler Harris, *Uncle Remus: His Songs and His Sayings* (New York: Houghton, Mifflin and Co., 1881) as the most significant. On Br'er Rabbit and other animal tales, see also L. Hughes and A. Bontemps, *Negro Folklore*, Chaps. I and II.

15. Cited in William F. Cheek, *Black Resistance before the Civil War* (Beverly Hills, Calif.: Glencoe Press, 1970), p. 51.

16. *Ibid.*

17. Cited in Hughes and Bontemps, *Negro Folklore*, pp. 67-68.

18. For an account of the tales about High John the Conqueror, see Zora Neal Hurston, "High John De Conquer", in Hughes and Bontemps, *Negro Folklore*, pp. 93-102; see also her excellent work, *Mules and Men* (New York: Harper & Row, 1970), originally published in 1935. See J. Mason Brewer, *American Negro Folklore*; Julius Lester, *Black Folktales* (New York: Grove Press, 1969).

19. Zora N. Hurston, "High John De Conquer," in Hughes and Bontemps, *op. cit.*, pp. 93-94.

20. *Ibid.*

21. *Ibid.*

22. *Ibid.*, p. 96.

23. The blues have been given much study. For an introduction to the theological implications of the blues, see my *The Spirituals and the Blues*, Chap. VI. The best one-volume work on the blues and jazz is LeRoi Jones, *Blues People* (New York: William Morrow, 1963); see also Charles Keil, *Urban Blues* (Chicago: University of Chicago Press, 1966); Paul Oliver, *The Meaning of the Blues* (New York: Collier Books, 1963), *The Story of the Blues* (Philadelphia: Chilton Book Co., 1969).

24. For an introduction to slave and ex-slave narratives, see Arna Bontemps, *Great Slave Narratives* (Boston: Beacon Press, 1969); W. L. Katz (ed.), *Five Slave Narratives* (New York: Arno Press, 1969), B. A. Botkin, *Lay My Burden Down* (Chicago: University of Chicago Press, 1945); Norman R. Yetman, *Life Under the "Peculiar Institution"* (New York: Holt, Rinehart and Winston, 1970). See also Frederick Douglass's autobiography, *Life and Times of Frederick Douglass* (New York: Collier Books, 1962), reprinted from the revised edition of 1892. See also the very important *God Struck Me Dead*, ed. Clifton H. Johnson (Boston: Pilgrim Press, 1969).

25. This comment was made by the celebrated ex-slave Ellen Craft; see her letter in Carter G. Woodson, *The Mind of the Negro as Reflected in Letters during the Crisis, 1800–1860* (New York: Russell and Russell, 1969), p. 265, originally published in 1926.

26. Claude McKay, "If We Must Die," in *Black Voices*, ed. Abraham Chapman (New York: New American Library, 1968), pp. 372-373. For a critical evaluation of the Harlem Renaissance of the 1920s and early 30s, see Nathan I. Huggins, *Harlem Renaissance* (New York: Oxford University Press, 1971). See also Alain Locke, *The New Negro* (New York: Atheneum, 1969), originally published in 1925.

27. *Ibid.*, p. 273.

28. Countee Cullen, "Yet Do I Marvel," in *Black Voices*, p. 383.

29. Billy Taylor and Dick Dallas, "I Wish I Knew How It Would Feel to Be Free," in *The Poetry of Soul*, ed. A. X. Nicholas (New York: Bantam Books, 1971), p. 57.

30. LeRoi Jones (Imamu Amiri Baraka), *Home* (New York: William Morrow, 1966), p. 251. For an analysis of the black poets of the 1960s see Don L. Lee, *Dynamite Voices*, Vol. I (Detroit: Broadside Press, 1971). See also, Abraham Chapman (ed.), *New Black Voices* (New York: New American Library, 1972).

31. J. Mason Brewer, *American Negro Folklore*, p. 6.

32. Barnwell, cited by Adam Small "Black Versus Nihilism: Black Racism Rejected," in *Black Theology: The South African Voice* (London: C. Hurst & Co., 1973), p. 14.

33. See Richard Allen, *The Life Experience and Gospel Labors*

of the Rt. Rev. Richard Allen (Nashville: Abingdon Press, 1960).

34. See Walker, *Appeal and an Address to the Slaves of the United States of America by H. H. Garnet* (New York: Arno Press, 1969).

35. See H. M. Turner, "God is a Negro," in J. H. Bracey, Jr., A. Meier, and E. Rudwick (eds.), *Black Nationalism in America* (New York: Bobbs-Merrill, 1970), pp. 154-155; Howard Thurman, *Jesus and the Disinherited* (Nashville: Abingdon Press, 1949); M. L. King, Jr., *Why We Can't Wait* (New York: Signet Books, 1963).

36. Paul makes a similar point in I Cor. 1:26f.: "To shame the wise, God has chosen what the world counts weakness. He has chosen things low and contemptible, mere nothings, to overthrow the existing order."

37. *God Struck Me Dead*, ed. Clifton H. Johnson, p. 170.

38. My theological emphasis on Scripture as a source of Black Theology and Jesus Christ as its content has led some black theologians to charge me with merely the blackenization of white Christian theology. Therefore Gayraud Wilmore asks: "Is Black theology simply the Blackenization of the whole spectrum of traditional Christian theology, with particular emphasis upon the liberation of the oppressed, or does it find in the experience of the oppression of Black people, as *black*, a singular religiosity, identified not only as Christianity, but with other religions as well?" (*Black Religion and Black Radicalism* [Garden City, N.Y.: Doubleday, 1972], p. 296). Wilmore goes on to suggest three sources of Black Theology: (1) "the existing Black community, where the tradition of Black folk religion is still extant and continues to stand over against the institutional church" (p. 298); (2) "the writings and addresses of the Black preacher and the public men of the past" (p. 300); and (3) "the traditional religions of Africa" (p. 302). I am sympathetic to Wilmore and other black theologians' concern to broaden the scope of Black Theology's meaning. Indeed the present work is an attempt to hear their critiques of my previous writing which failed to take seriously enough the black experience in the construction of a Black Theology. But I do not agree with their implication that the use of Scripture as a critical source and of Jesus Christ as the content of Black Theology is simply to make *black* what white people have been doing for two thousand years. The real test of whether any given articula-

tion of Black Theology is *black* does not depend on what Wilmore, Cone, or any other theologian say; rather, it depends upon whether the particular theology is consistent with what black people believe to be the basis of their struggle. Therefore we will have to wait and see how black people respond to what we say. Their response is the only test. At this writing, I cannot change my emphasis on Jesus Christ and Scripture, because the emphasis seems to be a decisive ingredient of the black experience as I and others have lived it in North America. I cannot change my point of departure merely because of the *intellectual* persuasion of a few black theologians who know more about Africa than the masses of black people. Either Black Theology is a theological expression of the hopes and dreams of black people, or it is an articulation of the intellectual interests of black professors. If the former, as I think it must be, then its meaning must be decided by the people about whom it claims to speak. The black theologian cannot claim to know what the people *ought* to believe or claim to have a "secret" knowledge that transcends the faith of the community. Thus what I write as Black Theology is what I believe to be the faith of the black church community which claims my allegiance. This means that I am persuaded that Black Theology is *Church* theology. It is this community about whom it seeks to speak. To be sure, there are blacks who reject the Church and thus do not regard it as a liberating agent. I simply disagree and take my stand with Richard Allen and James Varick. Their faith is my faith, and that is why I cannot exclude Jesus Christ and his witness in the Scripture, although I insist that Jesus' person must be defined by the oppressed of the land. Of course I believe that Black Theology must listen to other elements in our experience that are not specifically Christian; but these other elements cannot be the point of departure or the norm of Black Theology. The norm is Jesus Christ as witnessed in Scripture and the black experience. My problem with Gay Wilmore and others who stress the uniqueness of Black Theology is their failure to define clearly enough the *norm* for the interpretation of the sources they suggest for Black Theology. Our disagreement is not at the point of the *sources* of Black Theology but in its norm. I say the norm is Jesus Christ, and Wilmore disagrees; but, and this is important, *he does not tell us what the norm is*. It is not very helpful to reject my point of departure and fail to offer an alternative starting point.

39. Mari Evans, *I Am a Black Woman*, p. 92.

Chapter III

1. Niebuhr, *The Meaning of Revelation* (New York: Macmillan Co., 1941), p. 35.

2. *Ibid.*, p. 10.

3. Ludwig Feuerbach, *The Essence of Christianity*, trans. George Eliot (New York: Harper Torchbooks, 1957), p. xxx-vii.

4. *Ibid.*, pp. 11, 8.

5. *Ibid.*, pp. 17, 12.

6. See Karl Barth's penetrating introductory essay in *ibid;* see also Sidney Hook, *From Hegel to Marx* (Ann Arbor: University of Michigan Press, 1950); Herbert Marcuse, *Reason and Revolution* (Boston: Beacon Press, 1960); Robert Tucker, *The Philosophy and Myth in Karl Marx* (Cambridge, Eng.: Cambridge University Press, 1961); and H. R. MacKintosh, *Types of Modern Theology* (New York: Charles Scribner's, Sons, 1937).

7. Karl Marx and Friedrich Engels, *The German Ideology*, ed., with an introduction, by C. J. Arthur (New York: International Publishers, 1970), p. 60. See also Marx and Engels, *Basic Writings on Politics and Philosophy*, ed. Lewis S. Feuer (Garden City, N.Y.: Doubleday Anchor Books, 1959), p. 243.

8. *Ibid.*, p. 64.

9. I have in mind Marx's often-quoted eleventh thesis on Feuerbach: "The philosophers have only *interpreted* the world, in various ways; the point however, is to *change* it." See Marx and Engels, *Basic Writings*, ed. Feuer, p. 245.

10. See Marx's second thesis in *ibid.*, p. 243.

11. Cited in Ernst Bloch, *On Karl Marx*, trans. John Maxwell (New York: Herder and Herder, 1971), p. 59.

12. Marx and Engels, *Basic Writings*, ed. Feuer, p. 244 (4th thesis).

13. Marx and Engels, *The German Ideology*, p. 47.

14. *Ibid.*, p. 118.

15. The term "sociology of knowledge" was used in Germany by Max Scheler during the 1920s and was popularized in the English-speaking world by Karl Mannheim. For a brief

background on the development of this discipline, see Berger and Luckmann's, *The Social Construction of Reality* (Garden City, N.Y.: Doubleday Anchor Books, 1967); for a more detailed analysis of the different perspectives on this discipline, see Stark, *The Sociology of Knowledge* (London: Routledge and Kegan Paul, 1958). See also Mannheim, *Ideology and Utopia*, trans. Louis Wirth and E. Shils (New York: Harcourt, Brace and World, 1936); Peter Berger, *Sacred Canopy* (Garden City, N.Y.: Doubleday Anchor Books, 1969).

16. Stark, *The Sociology of Knowledge*, p. ix.

17. Marx and Engels, *The German Ideology*, p. 51.

18. Marx and Engels, *Basic Writings on Politics and Philosophy*, p. 244.

19. Stark, *The Sociology of Knowledge*, pp. 16, 7f.

20. In chap. IV and V, we will discuss "Biblical Revelation and Social Existence" and the relation between "Theology and Ideology." Here we will argue that the social a priori of biblical revelation is incompatible with the axiological perspective of the ruling class. Therefore any theology that fails to make God's liberation of the oppressed from political bondage its point of departure for an exposition of the gospel is *ipso facto* not Christian. It also follows, as we will seek to demonstrate in Chapter V, that ideological thinking, or what the Bible calls false prophecy, is thought that ignores the liberation of the poor as the decisive ingredient of the gospel. But the point in this chapter is merely to demonstrate the social context of all thinking.

21. More than any of his American theological contemporaries, H. Richard Niebuhr has investigated the problem of the relativity of theological knowledge. The influences of Troeltsch, Weber, and Tawney are obvious. Cf. *The Social Sources of Denominationalism* (New York: Meridian Books, 1957), originally published in 1929. See also his *The Kingdom of God in America* (New York: Harper & Row, 1937); *The Meaning of Revelation* (New York: Macmillan Co., 1941); *Christ and Culture* (New York: Harper & Row, 1951). On social existence and color, see his *Social Sources:* Chap. IX discusses "Denominationalism and the Color Line." It is an excellent analysis, except for one very obvious weakness. Niebuhr suggests that the division of the church along the racial line was due not to theology but to social realities. "The causes of the racial schism," he writes, "are not difficult

to determine. Neither theology nor polity furnished the occasion for it. The sole source of this denominationalism is social." Not so! For that statement assumes that the theology of the socially racist was adequate and that depraved social views did not affect theological doctrine. He fails here to recognize the dialectic relation between social reality and theological reflection. The fact that racism affected the white churches' doctrinal statements is most clearly shown in the *absence* of any reference in them to color and prejudice. The importance of this for black churches, from the perspective of doctrine (despite Niebuhr's insulting reference to "the lack of theological speculation among the Negroes") is the choice of name as a description of their places of worship, namely the *African* Methodist Episcopal Church, the *African* Methodist Episcopal Zion Church, etc. The A.M.E. Church chose a motto which expressed their doctrinal stand: "God Our Father, Christ Our Redeemer, Man Our Brother." I think Niebuhr's cultural definition of theology caused him to overstate his case. Niebuhr's failure to see the doctrinal issue involved in racism is perhaps the reason he does not regard the white church as existing in the state of apostasy. He still seems to think that racism is a terrible thing and ought to be removed but not so terrible as to deny the essence of the gospel. The white church can be racist and Christian—at the same time! Perhaps this explains why Niebuhr never bothered to discuss the matter seriously after 1929.

22. Van Harvey, *The Historian and the Believer* (New York: Macmillan Co., 1966), p. XI.

23. Marx, *The German Ideology*, p. 103.

24. Marx and Engels, *Basic Writings on Politics and Philosophy*, pp. 24, 26.

25. Cited in H. Shelton Smith, *In His Image, But . . . : Racism in Southern Religion, 1780–1910* (Durham: Duke University Press, 1972), pp. 6f. See especially the sermons by Mather and Bacon in Gilbert Osofsky, *The Burden of Race* (New York: Harper Torchbooks, 1968), pp. 35–44.

26. Cited in H. S. Smith, *In His Image, But . . .*, p. 37.

27. *Ibid.*, p. 38.

28. *Ibid.*, p. 45.

29. Cf. William and Jane Pease (eds.), *The Antislavery Argument* (New York: Bobbs-Merrill, 1965).

30. Leon F. Litwack, *North of Slavery* (Chicago: University of Chicago Press, 1961), p. 227.

31. See Herzog, *Liberation Theology* (New York: Seabury Press 1972); Lehmann, *Ethics in a Christian Context* (New York: Harper & Row, 1963); Schaull, *Containment and Change*, coauthored with Carl Oglesby (New York: Macmillan Co., 1967); Braaten, *The Future of God* (New York: Harper & Row, 1969). Another important contribution to theology is Peter Hodgson, *Children of Freedom* (Philadelphia: Fortress Press, 1974). Unfortunately that book was published after I had completed this work. It is an example of the kind of dialogue needed if white theologians expect to break out of their cultural limitations. Another recent work, Paul Lehmann's, *The Transfiguration of Politics* (New York: Harper and Row, 1975) is even more important than Hodgson's in laying a foundation for conversation between black and white theologians. I am sorry it was published too late for me to address it in this book.

32. Cf. the "Introduction" in *Liberation Theology*, pp. 1–22.

33. Niebuhr, *Social Sources*, p. 16.

34. DeWolf, *A Theology of the Living Church* (New York: Harper & Row, 1953), p. 18.

35. Tillich, *Systematic Theology*, Vol. I (Chicago: University of Chicago Press, 1951), p. 3.

36. Marx, *On Religion* (New York: Schocken Books, 1964), pp. 74–75.

37. Bloch, *A Philosophy of the Future*, trans. J. Cumming (New York: Herder and Herder, 1970), pp. 2f.

38. Cited in Langston Hughes and Arna Bontemps (ed.), *Book of Negro Folklore* (New York: Dodd, Mead & Co., 1958), p. 234.

39. Zora Neale Hurston, *Mules and Men* (New York: Harper Perennial Library, 1970), pp. 18–19.

Chapter IV

1. Bernhard W. Anderson, *Understanding the Old Testament* (Englewood Cliffs, N.J.: Prentice-Hall, 1957), pp. 289–290.

2. Gerhard von Rad, *Old Testament Theology*, Vol. I, trans. D.M.G. Stalker (New York: Harper & Row, 1962), p. 41.

3. Anderson, *Understanding the Old Testament*, p. 377.

4. Although few New Testament scholars question the historical validity of Jesus' baptism by John, yet the question of the accessibility of the historical Jesus has undergone much discussion in the twentieth century. Since the publication of Albert Schweitzer's *The Quest of the Historical Jesus* (1906) and the rise of Form Criticism shortly thereafter, it was commonplace to hear distinctions drawn between the Jesus of history and the Christ of faith. The former referred to the person accessible to the tools of historical scholarship, and the latter to the proclamation and teachings of the early Church. It was generally assumed by Rudolf Bultmann that practically nothing can be known of the Jesus of history. See his *Jesus and the Word*, trans. L. P. Smith and E. H. Lantera (New York: Charles Scribner's Sons, 1934), where he says: "I do indeed think that we can now know almost nothing concerning the personality of Jesus" (p. 8). That view tended to dominate New Testament scholarship in Germany until the 1950s when many of Bultmann's followers began to speak of the New quest for the historical Jesus. These persons (who included Ernst Käsemann, Günther Bornkamm, Hans Conzelmann, and Ernst Fuchs) recognized that Bultmann's historical skepticism not only had scientific flaws but also, and more importantly, threatened the foundation of the faith itself. Käsemann expressed it well: "Only if Jesus' proclamation decisively coincides with the proclamation about Jesus is it understandable, reasonable, and necessary that the Christian kerygma in the New Testament conceals the message of Jesus; only then is the resurrected Jesus the historical Jesus. From this perspective we are required, precisely as theologians, to inquire behind Easter. . . . By this means we shall learn whether he stands behind the word of his church or not, whether the Christian kerygma is a myth that can be detached from his word and from himself or whether it binds us historically and insolubly to him" (cited in Wolfhart Pannenberg, *Jesus—God and Man*, trans. L. L. Wilkins and D. A. Priebe [Philadelphia: Westminster Press, 1968], p. 56). For a detailed discussion of this problem, see James Robinson, *The New Quest of the Historical Jesus* (London: SCM Press, 1959); also Hugh Anderson, *Jesus and Christian Origins* (New York: Oxford University Press, 1964).

It should be made clear that this chapter (and the book as a whole) is being written on the assumption that there is no radical distinction between the Jesus of history and the

Christ of faith. I have discussed elsewhere this issue and have located the indispensable historical datum (without which the gospel is no longer valid) as Jesus' identification with the oppressed (A *Black Theology of Liberation*, Chap. VI). The key, therefore, to the baptism incident (and others reported in the Gospels) for our purposes is not only "Did it really happen?" but also "What is the theological meaning embedded in it?" Although history *qua* history is the place where revelation happens, it is not revelation. Revelation is the disclosure of God in the social context of history but is not identical with it. Since I content that the Jesus of the Gospels cannot be separated from the "real" Jesus, and have discussed the reasons for this conclusion elsewhere, there is no need here to enter into the critical discussion about the old and new quests for the historical Jesus. The text of the New Testament serves not only as a theological check on what we theologians are permitted to do with Jesus; it also serves as a *historical* check against contemporary historians.

5. There has been much discussion about Jesus' probable attitude toward John the Baptist. Jesus certainly saw his ministry connected with John's, and there is evidence from the Fourth Gospel that he received his first disciples from John (1:35-39). For a discussion of John's relation to Jesus, see Joachim Jeremias, *New Testament Theology*, trans. John Bowden (New York: Charles Scribner's Sons, 1971), pp. 43ff.

6. One of the few exceptions is Ernst Käsemann whose writings disclose an unusual sensitivity to the use of the gospel as an opiate of the oppressed. "Every word, every deed, every demonstration is a denial of our Lord and ourselves, unless we test them from the point of view of whether they are opium of the people, or can be regarded and abused as such." (*Jesus Means Freedom*, trans. Frank Clarke [London: SCM Press, 1969], p. 13). See also his *New Testament Questions of Today*, trans. W. J. Montague (Philadelphia: Fortress Press, 1969); *Perspectives On Paul*, trans. Margret Kohl (Philadelphia: Fortress Press, 1971.)

7. See J. Jeremias, *New Testament Theology*, p. 103f.

8. *Ibid.*, p. 112.

9. *Ibid.*, p. 116.

10. For the exegetical support of the exclusive interpretation of Matt. 21:31, see J. Jeremias, *New Testament Theology*, p. 117. "The Προαγουσιν ʿυμας . . . does not denote a priority in time, but an exclusive displacement of the others."

Chapter V

1. H. Richard Niebuhr, *Christ and Culture* (New York: Harper Torchbooks, 1956), p. 2,. originally published in 1951.

2. Niebuhr, p. 45.
3. Niebuhr, p. 41.
4. Niebuhr, p. 83.
5. Niebuhr, pp. 41–42.
6. Niebuhr, p. 145.
7. Niebuhr, p. 151.
8. Niebuhr, p. 191.
9. Niebuhr, p. 192.
10. Niebuhr, p. 194.
11. Niebuhr, p. 195.
12. Niebuhr, p. 14.
13. Niebuhr, p. 32.
14. Mannheim, *Ideology and Utopia*, trans. Louis Wirth and E. Shils (New York: Harcourt, Brace and World, 1936), pp. 56–57.

15. Cited in Carol George, *Segregated Sabbaths: Richard Allen and the Emergence of Independent Black Churches, 1760–1840* (New York: Oxford University Press, 1973), p. 160.

16. L. Hughes and A. Bontemps (eds.), *Book of Negro Folklore* (New York: Dodd, Mead & Co., 1958), p. 13.

17. Words from a black prayer, in *ibid.*, p. 256.

18. Lyrics of the gospel songs "Move on up a Little Higher" by Mahalia Jackson and Theodore Frye, in *ibid.*, pp. 323–325.

Chapter VI

1. Included in *Kerygma and Myth*, ed. H. W. Bartsch and trans. R. H. Fuller (New York: Harper Torchbooks, 1961), pp. 1–44. Bultmann's essay was originally published in 1941.

2. Barr, *The Bible in the Modern World* (New York: Harper & Row, 1973).

3. See Ernst Bloch's comments in *Atheism in Christianity*, trans. J. Swann (New York: Herder and Herder, 1972): "To think is to step over, to over step" (p. 9).

4. Pannenberg, *Jesus—God and Man*, trans. L. L. Wilkins and D. A. Priebe (Philadelphia: Westminster Press, 1968), p. 48. Of course, Pannenberg intends to say much more in this statement than is suggested in my use of it here. He speaks, I think wrongly, of "revelation as history," and not simply the latter as the foundation of the former. Consequently he insists upon Jesus' resurrection as a historical event. See also his *Revelation as History*, trans. David Granskou (New York: Macmillan Co., 1969); *Theology and the Kingdom of God* (Philadelphia: Westminster Press, 1969); see also James M. Robinson and John B. Cobb, Jr. (eds.), *Theology as History* (New York: Harper & Row, 1967).

5. While insisting on the necessity of the historical Jesus for christological reflections, I am aware of the historical difficulties associated with the four Gospels, the primary source for knowledge of Jesus. See my discussion in Chap. IV, note 4. See also *A Black Theology of Liberation*, Chap. VI. My point here and elsewhere is clear enough: The truth of Jesus Christ stands or falls on the historical validity of the biblical claim that Jesus identified with the poor and the outcasts. That historical fact alone does not provide the evidence that Jesus is the Christ, for the same could be said of other people in history; but without this historical fact, the claim that God has come to liberate the weak in Jesus is sheer illusion.

Of course I do not intend to make the Christian faith dependent upon scholarly investigations, for scholars are not immune to social and political interests. But the truth of the faith is not threatened by critical scholarship. Furthermore, the risks involved in academic pursuits are related to the risk of faith itself, from which no one is excluded. Indeed the honest acceptance of risk and its implications for faith provides an openness in faith and thus the willingness to listen to other viewpoints. The result of scholarship is merely one viewpoint which must be weighed in the context of human experience. For an excellent analysis of the historical Jesus' relation to the Christian faith, see Leander E. Keck, *A Future for the Historical Jesus* (Nashville: Abingdon Press, 1971).

6. Harnack, *History of Dogma*, Vol. IV, trans. Neil Buchanan (New York: Dover Publications, 1961), p. 139.

7. Athanasius, "On the Incarnation," in *The Library of Christian Classics*, Vol. III, Edward R. Hardy in collaboration with Cyril Richardson (Philadelphia: Westminster Press, 1954),

p. 107. For a more recent interpretation of the function of deification in the development of the early Church doctrines, see Jaroslav Pelikan, *The Christian Tradition*, Vol. I (Chicago: The University of Chicago Press, 1971).

8. See Albert Schweitzer, *The Quest of the Historical Jesus* (original German title, *Von Reimarus zu Wrede* [1906], trans. W. Montgomery (New York: Macmillan Co., 1961).

9. Kierkegaard, *Training in Christianity*, trans. W. Lowrie (Princeton: Princeton University Press, 1941), p. 28. In his *Philosophical Fragments*, trans. D. Swenson (Princeton: Princeton University Press, 1962), he says: "If the contemporary generation had left nothing behind them but these words: 'We have believed that in such and such a year that God appeared among us in the humble figure of a servant, that he lived and taught in our community, and finally died,' it would be more than enough" (p. 130). See the comparison of Kierkegaard and Bultmann in Herbert C. Wolf, *Kierkegaard and Bultmann: The Quest of the Historical Jesus* (Minneapolis: Augsburg Publishing House, 1965).

10. Brunner, *The Mediator*, trans. Olive Wyon (London: Lutterworth Press, 1934).

11. Barth, *The Epistle to the Romans*, trans. E. C. Hoskyns (London: Oxford University Press, 1933).

12. Barth, *The Humanity of God*, trans. T. Wieser and J. Thomas, (Richmond: John Knox Press, 1960).

13. Pannenberg, *Jesus—God and Man*, p. 189. For another contemporary perspective on Christology that emphasizes the humanity of Christ, see W. Norman Pittenger, *The Word Incarnate* (New York: Harper & Row, 1959); by the same author, *Christology Reconsidered* (London: SCM Press, 1970). An excellent treatise on the importance of Jesus' humanity is John Knox, *The Humanity and Divinity of Christ* (Cambridge, Eng.: Cambridge University Press, 1967). On the issue of humanity and divinity in Jesus Christ, he writes: "If we should find ourselves in the position of having to decide between the pre-existence and a fully authentic human life, there is no doubt what our choice should be. Although it would be a grievous error to suppose that the humanity of Jesus is surer or more important than his divinity—the two are equally sure and more important than the pre-existence" (pp. 73–74). Another example of the importance of Jesus' humanity, and thus history for Christology is Peter C. Hodgson, *Jesus—Word and Presence* (Philadelphia: Fortress Press, 1971).

14. J. Mason Brewer, *Worser Days and Better Times* (Chicago: Quadrangle Books, 1965), p. 103.

15. Pannenberg, *Jesus—God and Man,* p. 28.

16. Knox, *The Humanity and Divinity of Christ,* p. 3. Italics added.

17. See note 8, above.

18. Käseman, "The Beginnings of Christian Theology," in Robert W. Funk (ed.), *Apocalypticism: Journal for Theology and the Church* (New York: Herder and Herder, 1969), p. 40. The phrase "hope theology" derives its name primarily from Jürgen Moltmann's *Theology of Hope,* translated by James Leitch (New York: Harper & Row, 1967). This volume was originally published in Germany under the title *Theologie der Hoffnung* (1965). Others associated with the theology of hope are Johannes B. Metz, *Theology of the World,* trans. William Glen-Doepel (New York: Herder and Herder, 1969) and Wolfhart Pannenberg. The latter is less political than Moltmann and Metz. I have already referred to Pannenberg's *Jesus—God and Man* (see note 6 in this chapter). For a discussion of hope, see a symposium edited by Walter H. Capps with articles by Ernst Bloch, Pannenberg, Moltmann, and Metz in *Cross Currents,* Vol. XVIII, No. 3 (Summer 1968). When I speak of "hope theology" in this chapter, I am primarily referring to the work of Jürgen Moltmann. See especially his *Religion, Revolution and the Future,* trans. Douglas Meeks (New York: Charles Scribner's Sons, 1969). For additional discussions of the theology of hope, see W. Capps, *Time Invades the Cathedral: Tensions in the School of Hope,* (Philadelphia: Fortress, 1972).

19. Moltmann, *Theology of Hope,* p. 16.

20. See Thomas Ogletree (ed.), *Opening for Marxist-Christian Dialogue* (Nashville: Abingdon Press, 1968).

21. See the papers on the "Conference on Hope" in Ewert H. Cousins, *Hope and the Future of Man* (Philadelphia: Fortress Press, 1972). The participants included Philip Hefner, Carl Braaten, Jürgen Moltmann, John B. Cobb, Jr., Wolfhart Pannenberg, and Johannes B. Metz. The conference was held in New York City on October 8–10, 1971, and was "sponsored by the American Teilhard de Chardin Association, the Cardinal Bea Institute of Woodstock College, Goethe House New York (a branch of Goethe Institute Munich), Trinity Institute, and Union Theological Seminary in cooperation with Riverside Church" (*ibid.,* pp. vii-viii).

22. Moltmann, "Response to the Opening Presentations" in *ibid.*, p. 59.

23. For a comment on Moltmann's Christology, see Peter Hodgson, *Jesus—Word and Presence*, pp. 60ff. See also Moltmann's *The Crucified God*, trans. R. Wilson and J. Bowden (New York: Harper & Row, 1974).

24. Karl Marx and Friedrich Engels, *On Religion* (New York: Schocken Books, 1964), p. 42.

Chapter VII

1. A letter of "Anthony Burns to the Baptist Church at Union, Fauquier Co., Virginia," in Carter Woodson (ed.), *The Mind of the Negro as Reflected in Letters Written During the Crisis, 1800–1860* (New York: Russell and Russell, 1969), p. 660.

2. David Walker and Henry H. Garnet, *Walker's Appeal/ Garnet's Address* (New York: Arno Press, 1969), pp. 81–82. Walker's *Appeal* was originally published in 1829 and Garnet's address was delivered in 1843.

3. Moltmann, *Religion, Revolution and the Future*, trans. Douglas Meeks (New York: Charles Scribner's Sons, 1969) p. 66.

4. *Ibid.*, p. 203.

5. Clifton H. Johnson (ed.), *God Struck Me Dead* (Boston: Pilgrim Press, 1969), p. 149.

6. Henry D. Spalding (ed.), *Encyclopedia of Black Folklore and Humor* (Middle Village, N.Y.: Jonathan David Publishers 1972), p. XV.

7. Cited by C. Vann Woodward, "History from Slave Sources," in *The American Historical Review*, Vol. 79, 2 (April 1974), p. 477.

8. Casalis, *Portrait of Karl Barth*, introduced and trans. Robert McAfee Brown (Garden City, N.Y.: Doubleday, 1963), pp. 66–67.

9. Moltmann, *Religion, Revolution, and the Future*, p. 66.

10. I am indebted to an unpublished paper "Theology in the Context of Conflict" by Archie Le Mone of the World Council of Churches for this quotation.

11. J. H. Cone, *A Black Theology of Liberation* (Philadelphia: Lippincott, 1970), p. 160.

12. See Bonhoeffer's discussion in *The Cost of Discipleship*, trans. R. H. Fuller (New York: Macmillan Co., 1959).

13. This quotation is taken from Archie Le Mone's unpublished paper "Theology in the Context of Conflict."

14. Franz Fanon, *The Wretched of the Earth* (New York: Grove Press, 66), p. 255.

15. Moltmann, *Religion, Revolution and the Future*, p. 79.

16. Erich Fromm, *Marx's Concept of Man* (New York: Frederick Ungar 1971), p. 65.

17. Herbert Marcuse, *Reason and Revolution* (Boston: Beacon Press, 1960), p. 189.

18. Cited in H. Richard Niebuhr, *The Social Sources of Denominationalism* (Cleveland: Meridian Books, 1969), p. 249.

19. Garnet, *An Address to the Slaves of the United States of America* (New York: Arno Press, 1969 reprint), p. 93.

20. Mari Evans, *I Am a Black Woman* (New York: William Morrow, 1970), p. 75.

21. Freire, *Pedagogy of the Oppressed*, trans. M. A. Ramos (New York: Herder and Herder, 1970), p. 34.

22. Mari Evans, *I Am a Black Woman*, p. 12.

23. *Ibid.*, p. 93.

24. Moltmann, *Religion, Revolution and the Future*, p. 79.

25. Langston Hughes and Arna Bontemps (eds.) *Book of Negro Folklore* (New York; Dodd, Mead, 1958), pp. 252–253 (paraphrased).

26. *Ibid.*, p. 71.

Chapter VIII

1. See William Jones, *Is God a White Racist?* (Garden City, N.Y.: Doubleday, 1973).

2. John Bowker, *Problems of Suffering in Religions of the World* (London: Cambridge University Press, 1970), p. 9.

3. James A. Sanders identifies eight solutions to the problem of

suffering the Old Testament. See his "Suffering as Divine Discipline in the Old Testament and Post-Biblical Judaism," in *Colgate Rochester Divinity School Bulletin*, Vol. XXVIII, (November 1955), Special Issue, Rochester, N.Y., pp. 1f. See also H. Wheeler Robinson *Suffering Human and Divine* (New York, Macmillan, 1939); John Bowker, *Problems of Suffering in Religions of the World*, Chap. 1–2.

4. Fleming James, *Personalities of the Old Testament* (New York: Charles Scribner's Sons, 1939), pp. 533–534.

5. For a survey of the vast literature, see Christopher R. North, *The Suffering Servant in Deutero-Isaiah* (London: Oxford University Press, 1948). For an excellent discussion of the theology of Second Isaiah, see James Muilenburg, "Introduction and Exegesis to Isaiah, Chs. 40–66," in G. A. Buttrick, ed., *The Interpreter's Bible*, Vol. V (Nashville: Abingdon Press, 1956), pp. 381–773. Regarding the identity of the servant, Muilenburg says: "The servant is certainly Israel. . . . Israel, and Israel alone, is able to bear all that is said about the servant of the Lord. For the fundamental fact outweighing all others is the repeated equation of the two in the poems" (pp. 408, 411).

6. For an analysis of the significance of the baptismal saying in relation to Isaiah 42:1, see Chap. IV.

7. See Mark 8:31f., Matt. 16:21f., Luke 9:22; Mark 9:30–32, Matt. 17:22f., Luke 9:44f.; Mark 10:32–34, Matt. 20:17f., Luke 18:31–33.

8. See especially Acts 8:26–29; 3:13, 26; 4:27, 30; Rev. 5:6, 9, 12; Heb. 9:28; I Peter 1:19; 2:22–25.

9. Burrows, *An Outline of Biblical Theology* (Philadelphia: Westminster Press, 1946), p. 88.

10. An important exception is Jürgen Moltmann. See his recent publication *The Crucified God*, trans. A. Wilson and J. Bowden (New York: Harper & Row, 1974). See also his "God and Resurrection," in *Hope and Planning*, trans. Margaret Clarkson (New York: Harper & Row, 1971). It is to Moltmann's credit that he has endeavored to do theology in the light of the struggle for political justice. Although I have not read discussions about the problem of theodicy among the recent theologians of liberation in Latin America, it is assumed that they would seek to develop new starting points of this issue that would reflect the need of poor peoples to fight for justice.

11. Cited in Lactantius (*c.* A.D. 260–*c.* 340) "On the Anger of God," Chap. 13, trans. William Fletscher, in *The Writings of the Ante-Nicene Fathers* (Grand Rapids, Mich.: W. B. Eerdmans, 1951), Vol. VII, p. 271.

12. Hick, *Evil and the God of Love* (New York: Harper & Row, 1966), p. 5.

13. *Ibid.*, pp. 220–221.

14. See Hick's discussion of Gabriel Marcel's perspective on suffering in *ibid.*, pp. 9f.

15. Gabriel Marcel, *The Philosophy of Existence*, trans. Manya Harari (New York: Philosophical Library, 1949), p. 9.

16. Emil Brunner, *Christian Doctrine of Creation and Redemption*, trans. Olive Wyon (Philadelphia: Westminster Press, 1952), pp. 182–183.

17. Käsemann, *Jesus Means Freedom*, p. 13 (see Chap. IV, note 6, above).

18. Negro Folk Expression: Spirituals, Seculars, Ballads and Work Songs," in A. Meier and E. Rudwick, *The Making of Black America*, Vol. II (New York: Atheneum, 1969), pp. 215, 216.

19. W. E. B. DuBois, "A Litany at Atlanta," in *Black Voices*, ed. Abraham Chapman (New York: New American Library, 1968), pp. 372–373.

20. From "A new song" by Langston Hughes, cited in Jean Wagner, *Black Poets of the United States*, trans. Kenneth Douglass (Urbana, Ill.: University of Illinois Press, 1973), p. 438.

21. See Richard Wright, *Native Son* (New York: Harper & Row, 1940).

22. See Baldwin's novel, *Go Tell It on the Mountain* (New York: Dell, 1952) and his essay, *The Fire Next Time* (New York: Dial Press, 1963).

23. I am thoroughly sympathetic with William Jones's attempt to make the problem of black suffering central in Black Theology. But he is absolutely wrong in his assessment of my perspecitive when viewed from the methodolgy of "internal critique." Anyone who reads my works can see that any theological problem (and especially suffering!) can and must be dealt with from the perspective of Jesus Christ. This may

not be true so much for the other black theologians he treated; but for me, Jesus Christ is the essence of the meaning of liberation. Thus he is the decisive historical event beyond which no one needs to appeal. Of course Jones and others may not agree to the high place given to Jesus Christ in black religon generally and my theology in particular, but for Jones to ask about the "definitive event of black liberation" (p. 116, *Is God a White Racist?*) from the method of an *internal* critique, as if Jesus Christ is not a proper answer in my own perspective, is to misunderstand totally what he claims to be doing and thus to distort my perspective. Of course, from the perspective of an *external* critique, Jones analysis is to the point, and Black Theology will have to contend with his persuasive arguments. I do not intend to debate with Jones about the validity of his claim of doing internal criticism. His critique of my position in Chap. VII of his *Is God a White Racist?* is so decidedly externally oriented, especially in his only slight reference to the function of Jesus Christ in my perspective (118–119), that I find it hard to believe that Jones believes what he claims. To do internal criticism is to think as another thinks and to criticize on the basis of another's presuppositions. In this case, Jones claimed to be thinking my thoughts on the basis of my frame of reference, and he concludes that my perspective on divine liberation of blacks from bondage demands that I produce the decisive liberating event. Apparently he has completely overlooked the *christological* orientation of my theology. "Christianity begins and ends with the man Jesus—his life, death, and resurrection. He is the Revelation, the special disclosure of God to man, revealing who God is and what his purpose for man is. In short, Christ is the essence of Christianity" (J. Cone, *Black Theology and Black Power*, p. 34). And again in *A Black Theology of Liberation*, I said: "Christian theology begins and ends with Jesus Christ. He is the point of departure for everything to be said about God, man, and the world" (p. 197). These statements are not isolated comments but are part of the organic structure of my theological perspective. Any casual reader of my theology can see that fact. Thus why is it that William Jones, an astute scholar, fails to point out the importance of Jesus Christ in my theology? I think it is because he was so involved in doing what he called "internal" critique, when in fact it was *external*. I am not demanding that he accept the Christian faith or my theological analysis of it. I am contending for *fairness*. See especially *Is God a White Racist?* Part I, and Part II, Chap. VII.

24. Cited in Benjamin E. Mays, *The Negro's God* (Boston: Chapman and Grimes, 1938), p. 49.

25. Nathaniel Paul, "An Address Delivered on the Celebration of the Abolition of Slavery in the State of New York, July 5, 1827," in Carter G. Woodson, *Negro Orators and Their Orations* (New York: Russell and Russell, 1969), p. 69.

26. Gayraud Wilmore, *Black Religion and Black Radicalism* (Garden City, N.Y.: Doubleday, 1972), p. 160.

27. Edward Blyden, *Liberia's Offering* (New York: John Gray, Printer, 1862), pp. 71–72.

28. Cited in Mays, p. 49.

29. Cited in Woodson, p. 69.

30. "Bishop Daniel Alexander Payne's Protestation of American Slavery," *Journal of Negro History*, Vol. LII (1967), p. 60.

Chapter IX

1. Vitaly Baroxoj, "Why the Gospels Are Revolutionary: The Foundation of a Theology in the Service of Social Revolutions," in IDO—C (ed.), *Where All Else Fails* (Philadelphia: Pilgrim Press, 1970), p. 65.

2. Augustine, *The City of God*, trans. Marcus Dods (New York: Modern Library, 1950), p. 694.

3. Cited in Roger Garaudy, *From Anathema to Dialogue* (New York: Vintage Books, 1968), p. 98.

4. Cited in Roland Bainton, *Here I Stand* (Nashville: Abingdon Press, 1950), p. 280.

5. See Edward L. Long, *A Survey of Christian Ethics* (New York: Oxford University Press, 1967), for an excellent discussion of these issues in Protestant and Catholic Christianity. A noticeable absence in the discussion is the black religious tradition, except for a brief discussion of nonviolence in Martin Luther King, Jr. This is particularly unfortunate, since the book was published during the black revolution of the 1960s, and since Professor Long teaches at Oberlin College, a school with a history of involvement in the black struggle for freedom.

6. Edwards, "Racism and Christian Ethics in America," *Kagallete*, Winter 1971.

7. Cited in *ibid.*, p. 19.

8. Ramsey, *Christian Ethics and the Sit-in* (New York: Association Press, 1961), pp. 48–49. Also cited in Edwards, *op. cit.*, p. 20. One significant exception is Robert McAfee Brown, *Religion and Violence* (Philadelphia: Westminster Press, 1973).

9. Lehmann, *Ethics in a Christian Context* (New York: Harper & Row, 1963), p. 104.

10. In *The Harvard Theological Review*, Vol. 65, No. 4 (October 1972), pp. 485, 488. Italics added.

11. Hughes and Bontemps (eds), *Book of Negro Folklore* (New York: Dodd, Mead, 1958), p. 13.

12. Williams, "James Cone and the Problem of the Black Ethic," *Harvard Theo. Review* p. 485.

13. Hughes and Bontemps, *Negro Folklore*, p. 12.

14. Another misguided attempt at ethics in the black context is Major Jones', *Christian Ethics For Black Theology* (Nashville: Abingdon Press, 1974). As with Preston Williams, Jones' ethical principles, which he defines as necessary for Christian behavior, are derived exclusively from white academicians—none of whom are really concerned about the liberation of the black community. Practically every reference that Jones makes to my writings is quoted out of context. In two places I am so badly misquoted that it cannot be allowed to stand without protest. In the first, Jones writes: "To contend that God would identify with a struggle which aims at the 'complete emancipation of Black people from white oppression by whatever means Black people, not God, deem necessary' seems to commit God to man's way, rather than to commit man to God's way" (p. 72). According to Jones, the quote is supposed to be found in my *A Black Theology of Liberation*, pp. 33–34. But it is not there. Indeed the quotation is not found anywhere in my writings! Furthermore, for me to express the perspective that Jones attributes to me would be a radical negation of everything I have written.

A statement partly similar to the one Jones attributes to me is found in my *Black Theology and Black Power*. Defining Black Power, I said that "it means *complete emancipation of black people from white oppression by whatever means black people deem necessary*" (p. 6.). When Jones *adds* "not God" in the above sentence, it is not only a misquotation that is hard to explain but a gross misrepresentation of my thought. I was defining Black Power over against *white people* by refusing to allow *oppressors* to set the limits of our fight for freedom. In later chapters of the same book as well as in everything I have written, I identified the black liberation struggle with God's struggle. By adding "not God," Jones has *substantively* distorted my perspective. In Jones' analysis, the *overagainstness* in my thought is God and not white people.

In the second instance Jones quotes me as saying "Indeed, it is hard to read objectively the history of the post-Civil War black church and not come to an absolute conclusion that the 'real sin of the black church and its leaders is that they even convinced themselves that they were doing the right thing by advocating the obedience to white oppression as a means of entering at death the future age of heavenly bliss' " (p. 91). This statement is not only out of context, but Jones' addition of the phrase, "Indeed, it is hard to read objectively the history of the post-Civil War black church and not come to the absolute conclusion," attributes to me something I did not say.

15. See Lehmann, *Ethics in a Christian Context*.

16. Cited in Julius Lester, *To Be a Slave* (New York: Dell, 1970), pp. 100–101.

17. Cited in *ibid.*, p. 100.

18. Richard M. Dorson, *Negro Folktales in Michgan* (Cambridge, Mass.: Harvard University Press, 1956), pp. 57–58.

19. Cited in Gilbert Osofsky (ed.), *Puttin' on Ole Massa* (New York: Harper Torchbooks, 1969), p. 9.

20. Cited in William L. Katz (ed.), *Five Slave Narratives* (New York: Arno Press, 1969), p. 31.

21. Cited in Kenneth Stampp, *The Peculiar Institution* (New York: Vintage Books, 1956), pp. 86–87.

22. Cited in *ibid.*, p. 87.

23. For an account of this debate, see the excellent book by Gayraud S. Wilmore, *Black Religion and Black Radicalism* (Garden City, N.Y.: Doubleday, 1972). Gayraud S. Wilmore and Charles H. Long, in conversations and writings, have done much to bring to my attention the importance of our African heritage in the doing of Black Theology. Since I am

272 : GOD OF THE OPPRESSED

sure that my theological perspective is still too strongly influenced by *Christian* terminology for their taste, the debate
must continue. See also Charles H. Long, "Perspectives for
a Study of Afro-American Religion in the United States,"
History of Religions, Vol. 11, No. 1 (August 1971), pp.
54–66. See also Leonard Barrett, *Soul-Force* (Garden City,
N.Y.: Doubleday, 1974).

24. Cited in John Blassingame, *The Slave Community* (New
York: Oxford University Press, 1972), p. 66.

25. *Malcolm X Speaks* (New York: Grove Press, an Evergreen
Black Cat Book, 1966), p. 4.

26. Thomas Merton, *Faith and Violence* (Notre Dame: Notre
Dame University Press, 1968), p. 3.

27. Jürgen Moltmann, *Religion, Revolution and the Future,*
trans. Douglas Meeks (New York: Charles Scribner's Sons,
1969), p. 143.

28. Jacques Ellul, *Violence,* trans. C. G. King (New York: Seabury Press, 1969), p. 3. In this quotation, Ellul is not defending this viewpoint; he is explicating it.

29. Martin Luther King, Jr., *Stride Toward Freedom* (New York:
Harper Perennial Library, 1958), p. 88.

30. See especially Alan Richardson, *The Political Christ*
(Philadelphia: Westminster Press, 1973). He writes: "The
Christian faith did not come into the ancient world as a new
ideology expressing the social consciousness of either an
upper or a lower class but as the restoration of true human
relationship as such, the relationships which the class structure of ancient society (like societies in other ages) had im-
peded or destroyed. It did not preach the solidarity of the
working class (slaves for the most part) or recommend mili-
tancy; instead it created a society in which right relationships
amongst human beings, whatever their social position, could
be restored. It supplied a motive and a power which could
effect this restoration, the love of Christ" (p. 71). It is hard to
believe that such an astute scholar as Richardson could write
this in 1973! Then again, he has been saying this a long time
(see his article on the "Poor" in his edited work entitled
Theological Word Book of the Bible [New York, Macmillan
Co., 1960], especially pp. 168–169) as have countless other
establishment scholars. What is so amazing are the blatant
contradictions. How can human relationships be restored
without changing the structures in which people relate to

each other? On Jesus and violence, see also Oscar Cullmann, *Jesus and the Revolutionaries*, trans. Gareth Putnam (New York: Harper & Row, 1970). For a completely different interpretation which views Jesus as closely identified with the Zealots' cause, see S. G. F. Brandon, *Jesus and the Zealots* (New York: Charles Scribner's Sons, 1967). Most European and American scholars reject this view.

Another typical statement of New Testament scholarship on Jesus and politics is found in Rudolf Schnackenburg, *The Moral Teachings of the New Testament*, trans. J. Holland-Smith and W. J. O'Hara (New York: Herder and Herder, 1971): "Jesus brought a religious message and it was from that message that his moral demands originated. Any attempt to interpret his preaching in any other way (as a criticism, perhaps, of the civilization, or as a programme of social revolution) is wrong from the outset" (p.13). For a contrary point of view that insists on the *political* thrust of Jesus' message but rejects Brandon's suggestion that Jesus might have been violent, see John H. Yoder, *The Politics of Jesus* (Grand Rapids, Michigan: Wm. B. Eerdmans 1972). While insisting on Jesus' nonviolence, he contends that Jesus was politically involved with the weak and helpless. Another important statement that takes seriously the sociopolitical thrust of Jesus' message is Ernst Käsemann, *Jesus Means Freedom*. He writes: "The power of Christ's resurrection becomes a reality, here and now, in the form of Christian freedom, and only in that. That reality is opposed on earth by anything that stands in the way of Christ's freedom, and only by that. . . . Christ's resurrection means Jesus' sovereignty, and such sovereignty becomes an earthly reality only in the realm of Christian freedom. The earth has no scarcity of lords, and they all demand obedience. . . . Christ differs from the other lords in that he effects freedom. He does not just call to it; that would be the law of which there are innumerable characteristic forms. *Jesus gives freedom.* That is what makes him unmistakably Lord and inseparably unites the earthly with the exalted Lord" (pp. 154–155, italics added). See also Peter C. Hodgson, *Children of Freedom*, pp. 36–62, for a similar analysis of Jesus.

Of course J. Moltmann, J. Metz, P. Lehmann, F. Herzog, and other "political" theologians have been placing a great deal of emphasis on the political thrust of Jesus' words and deeds. What is needed is more biblical theologians whose consciousness is defined by the oppressed of the land so that the task and goal of biblical hermeneutics might be rescued from the hands of scholars whose consciousness is obviously limited by the ruling class. The Alan Richardsons and the Rudolf Schnackenburgs must be exposed for what they represent—the status quo! Whatever else the ministry of Jesus might have been, and whatever may be the difficulties in arriving at his true history, we do know, without the slightest doubt, that Jesus stood in opposition to the dehumanization of humankind in *all* forms, and especially social , political, and economic oppression. I am not prepared to defend the status of Jesus' ministry in the community of the Zealots on historical grounds, but that historical uncertainty does not lead to a conclusion that he was indifferent to the political and economic plight of the poor. This point is the crux of my difference with the majority of white biblical scholars on Jesus; and I contend that it is a difference that is traceable to their ideological reading of the Scripture generally and the New Testament in particular.

Chapter X

1. Tolson, "Dark Symphony," in Abraham Chapman (ed.), *Black Voices* (New York: New American Library, 1968), p. 390.

2. Williston Walker, *A History of the Christian Church,* revised by C. Richardson, W. Pauck, and R. Handy (New York: Charles Scribner's Sons, 1959), pp. 239–240.

3. Aulén, *Christus Victor* (London: S.P.C.K., 1953).

4. Karl Barth, *Church Dogmatics,* Vol. IV, Part 2, trans. G. W. Bromily and T. F. Torrance (Edinburgh: T. & T. Clark, 1958), p. 501.

5. *Ibid.,* p. 499.

6. Dietrich Bonhoeffer, *The Cost of Discipleship,* trans. R. H. Fuller (New York: Macmillan Co., 1959), pp. 35–36.

7. *Ibid.,* p. 79.

8. J. Deotis Roberts, *Liberation and Reconciliation: A Black Theology* (Philadelphia: Westminster Press, 1971), p. 72.

9. *Ibid.,* p. 117.

10. *Ibid.,* p. 72.

11. See Chap. 6 entitled "Revolution, Violence, and Reconciliation," in my *Black Theology and Black Power* (New York: Seabury Press, 1969).

12. Roberts, p. 23.

13. *Ibid.*, p. 126.

14. Cited in Carter G. Woodson, *The Mind of the Negro as Reflected in Letters Written during the Crisis, 1800–1860* (New York: Russell and Russell, 1969), p. 194.

15. Alan Richardson, "Repent," in his *A Theological Word Book of the Bible* (New York: Macmillan Co., 1960), p. 191.

16. Bornkamm, *Jesus of Nazareth*, trans. Irene and Fraser McLuskey with James Robinson (New York: Harper & Row, 1960), p. 82.

17. Although Roberts revisits reconcilation in a recent publication entitled *A Black Political Theology* (Philadelphia: Westminster Press, 1974), there are few signs that he recognized the depth of the problem. See the chapter on "Liberation and Reconciliation Revisited".

18. Cited in Sterling Brown, *Negro Poetry and Drama/The Negro in American Fiction* (New York: Atheneum, 1937), p. 64.

Index

$4.95

GOD OF THE OPPRESSED

James H. Cone

"Cone's work is excellent in its understanding and appreciation of the black struggle. . . . Cone has opened the door to a universal theology." —*The Christian Century*

"James Cone has brilliantly joined the themes of *story* and *suffering* to liberation and the result is genuinely new directions for theology everywhere." —*Jurgen Moltmann*

"This is James Cone's most important book. It is clearer, deeper and wider than his previous volume." —*Robert McAffee Brown*

A CROSSROAD BOOK · THE SEABURY PRESS · NEW YORK

ISBN: 0-8164-2607-4